JOHN BULL'S OTHER ISLAND
AND MAJOR BARBARA

JOHN BULL'S OTHER ISLAND AND MAJOR BARBARA · BY BERNARD SHAW

BRENTANO'S · NEW YORK
MCMXV

PRESSWORK BY
THE UNIVERSITY PRESS, CAMBRIDGE, U. S. A.

PREFACE FOR POLITICIANS

JOHN BULL'S OTHER ISLAND was written in 1904 at the request of Mr. William Butler Yeats, as a patriotic contribution to the repertory of the Irish Literary Theatre. Like most people who have asked me to write plays, Mr. Yeats got rather more than he bargained for. The play was at that time beyond the resources of the new Abbey Theatre, which the Irish enterprise owed to the public spirit of Miss A. E. F. Horniman (an Englishwoman, of course), who, twelve years ago, played an important part in the history of the modern English stage as well as in my own personal destiny by providing the necessary capital for that memorable season at the Avenue Theatre which forced my Arms and The Man and Mr. Yeats's Land of Heart's Desire on the recalcitrant London playgoer, and gave a third Irish playwright, Dr. John Todhunter, an opportunity which the commercial theatres could not have afforded him.

There was another reason for changing the destination of John Bull's Other Island. It was uncongenial to the whole spirit of the neo-Gaelic movement, which is bent on creating a new Ireland after its own ideal, whereas my play is a very uncompromising presentment of the real old Ireland. The next thing that happened was the production of the play in London at the Court Theatre by Messrs. Vedrenne and Barker, and its immediate and enormous popularity with delighted and flattered English audiences. This constituted it a successful commercial play, and made it unnecessary to resort to the special machinery or tax the special resources of the Irish Literary Theatre for its production.

v

How Tom Broadbent Took It.

Now I have a good deal more to say about the relations between the Irish and the English than will be found in my play. Writing the play for an Irish audience, I thought it would be good for them to be shewn very clearly that the loudest laugh they could raise at the expense of the absurdest Englishman was not really a laugh on their side; that he would succeed where they would fail; that he could inspire strong affection and loyalty in an Irishman who knew the world and was moved only to dislike, mistrust, impatience and even exasperation by his own countrymen; that his power of taking himself seriously, and his insensibility to anything funny in danger and destruction, was the first condition of economy and concentration of force, sustained purpose, and rational conduct. But the need for this lesson in Ireland is the measure of its demoralizing superfluousness in England. English audiences very naturally swallowed it eagerly and smacked their lips over it, laughing all the more heartily because they felt that they were taking a caricature of themselves with the most tolerant and largeminded goodhumor. They were perfectly willing to allow me to represent Tom Broadbent as infatuated in politics, hypnotized by his newspaper-leader-writers and parliamentary orators into an utter paralysis of his common sense, without moral delicacy or social tact, provided I made him cheerful, robust, goodnatured, free from envy, and above all, a successful muddler-through in business and love. Not only did no English critic allow that the success in business of Messrs. English Broadbent and Irish Doyle might possibly have been due to some extent to Doyle, but one writer actually dwelt with much feeling on the pathos of Doyle's failure as an engineer (a circumstance not mentioned nor suggested in my play) in contrast with Broadbent's solid success. No doubt, when the play is performed in Ireland, the Dublin critics will regard it as self-evident that without Doyle Broadbent would have become bankrupt in six months. I should say, myself, that the combination was probably much more effective than either of the partners would have been alone. I am persuaded further—without pretending to know more about it than anyone else—that Broadbent's special contribution was simply the strength, self-satisfaction, social confidence and cheerful bumptiousness that money, comfort, and good feeding bring to all healthy people; and that Doyle's special contribution was the freedom from illusion, the power of facing facts, the nervous industry, the sharpened wits, the sensitive pride of the imaginative man who has fought his way up through social persecution and poverty. I do not say that the confidence of the Englishman in Broadbent is not for the moment justified. The virtues of the English soil are not less real because they consist of coal and iron, not of metaphysical sources of character. The virtues of Broadbent are not less real because they are the virtues of the money that coal and iron has produced. But as the mineral virtues are being discovered and developed in other soils, their derivative virtues are appearing so rapidly in other nations that Broadbent's relative advantage is vanishing. In truth I am afraid (the misgiving is natural to a by-this-time slightly elderly playwright) that Broadbent is out of date. The successful Englishman of today, when he is not a transplanted Scotchman or Irishman, often turns out on investigation to be, if not an American, an Italian, or a Jew, at least to be depending on the brains, the nervous energy, and the freedom from romantic illusions (often called cynicism) of such foreigners for the management of his sources of income. At all events I am persuaded that a modern nation that is satisfied with Broadbent is in a dream. Much as I like him, I object

to be governed by him, or entangled in his political
destiny. I therefore propose to give him a piece of my
mind here, as an Irishman, full of an instinctive pity
for those of my fellow-creatures who are only English.

WHAT IS AN IRISHMAN?

When I say that I am an Irishman I mean that I was
born in Ireland, and that my native language is the
English of Swift and not the unspeakable jargon of the
mid-XIX. century London newspapers. My extraction
is the extraction of most Englishmen: that is, I have no
trace in me of the commercially imported North Spanish
strain which passes for aboriginal Irish: I am a genuine
typical Irishman of the Danish, Norman, Cromwellian,
and (of course) Scotch invasions. I am violently and
arrogantly Protestant by family tradition; but let no
English Government therefore count on my allegiance:
I am English enough to be an inveterate Republican and
Home Ruler. It is true that one of my grandfathers
was an Orangeman; but then his sister was an abbess;
and his uncle, I am proud to say, was hanged as a rebel.
When I look round me on the hybrid cosmopolitans,
slum poisoned or square pampered, who call themselves
Englishmen today, and see them bullied by the Irish
Protestant garrison as no Bengalee now lets himself be
bullied by an Englishman; when I see the Irishman
everywhere standing clearheaded, sane, hardily callous
to the boyish sentimentalities, susceptibilities, and credu-
lities that make the Englishman the dupe of every charlatan and the idolater of every numskull, I perceive that
Ireland is the only spot on earth which still produces
the ideal Englishman of history. Blackguard, bully,
drunkard, liar, foul-mouth, flatterer, beggar, backbiter,
venal functionary, corrupt judge, envious friend, vindictive opponent, unparalleled political traitor: all these
your Irishman may easily be, just as he may be a gen-

tleman (a species extinct in England, and nobody a
penny the worse); but he is never quite the hysterical,
nonsense-crammed, fact-proof, truth-terrified, unbal-
lasted sport of all the bogey panics and all the silly
enthusiasms that now calls itself " God's Englishman."
England cannot do without its Irish and its Scots today,
because it cannot do without at least a little sanity.

THE PROTESTANT GARRISON.

The more Protestant an Irishman is—the more English he is, if it flatters you to have it put that way, the
more intolerable he finds it to be ruled by English instead of Irish folly. A "loyal" Irishman is an abhorrent phenomenon, because it is an unnatural one. No
doubt English rule is vigorously exploited in the interests of the property, power, and promotion of the Irish
classes as against the Irish masses. Our delicacy is
part of a keen sense of reality which makes us a very
practical, and even, on occasion, a very coarse people.
The Irish soldier takes the King's shilling and drinks
the King's health; and the Irish squire takes the title
deeds of the English settlement and rises uncovered
to the strains of the English national anthem. But do
not mistake this cupboard loyalty for anything deeper.
It gains a broad base from the normal attachment of
every reasonable man to the established government as
long as it is bearable; for we all, after a certain age,
prefer peace to revolution and order to chaos, other
things being equal. Such considerations produce loyal
Irishmen as they produce loyal Poles and Fins, loyal
Hindoos, loyal Filipinos, and faithful slaves. But there
is nothing more in it than that. If there is an entire
lack of gall in the feeling of the Irish gentry towards
the English, it is because the Englishman is always
gaping admiringly at the Irishman as at some clever
child prodigy. He overrates him with a generosity born

of a traditional conviction of his own superiority in the deeper aspects of human character. As the Irish gentleman, tracing his pedigree to the conquest or one of the invasions, is equally convinced that if this superiority really exists, he is the genuine true blue heir to it, and as he is easily able to hold his own in all the superficial social accomplishments, he finds English society agreeable, and English houses very comfortable, Irish establishments being generally straitened by an attempt to keep a park and a stable on an income which would not justify an Englishman in venturing upon a wholly detached villa.

Our Temperaments Contrasted.

But however pleasant the relations between the Protestant garrison and the English gentry may be, they are always essentially of the nature of an *entente cordiale* between foreigners. Personally I like Englishmen much better than Irishmen (no doubt because they make more of me) just as many Englishmen like Frenchmen better than Englishmen, and never go on board a Peninsular and Oriental steamer when one of the ships of the Messageries Maritimes is available. But I never think of an Englishman as my countryman. I should as soon think of applying that term to a German. And the Englishman has the same feeling. When a Frenchman fails to make the distinction, we both feel a certain disparagement involved in the misapprehension. Macaulay, seeing that the Irish had in Swift an author worth stealing, tried to annex him by contending that he must be classed as an Englishman because he was not an aboriginal Celt. He might as well have refused the name of Briton to Addison because he did not stain himself blue and attach scythes to the poles of his sedan chair. In spite of all such trifling with facts, the actual distinction between the idolatrous Englishman and the

fact-facing Irishman, of the same extraction though they
be, remains to explode those two hollowest of fictions,
the Irish and English " races." There is no Irish race
any more than there is an English race or a Yankee race.
There *is* an Irish climate, which will stamp an immigrant
more deeply and durably in two years, apparently, than
the English climate will in two hundred. It is rein-
forced by an artificial economic climate which does some
of the work attributed to the natural geographic one;
but the geographic climate is eternal and irresistible,
making a mankind and a womankind that Kent, Middlesex, and East Anglia cannot produce and do not want to
imitate.

How can I sketch the broad lines of the contrast as
they strike me? Roughly I should say that the Englishman is wholly at the mercy of his imagination, having
no sense of reality to check it. The Irishman, with a
far subtler and more fastidious imagination, has one eye
always on things as they are. If you compare Moore's
visionary Minstrel Boy with Mr. Rudyard Kipling's
quasi-realistic Soldiers Three, you may yawn over Moore
or gush over him, but you will not suspect him of having
had any illusions about the contemporary British private; whilst as to Mr. Kipling, you will see that he has
not, and unless he settles in Ireland for a few years
will always remain constitutionally and congenitally incapable of having, the faintest inkling of the reality
which he idolizes as Tommy Atkins. Perhaps you have
never thought of illustrating the contrast between English and Irish by Moore and Mr. Kipling, or even by
Parnell and Gladstone. Sir Boyle Roche and Shakespear
may seem more to your point. Let me find you a more
dramatic instance. Think of the famous meeting between the Duke of Wellington, that intensely Irish
Irishman, and Nelson, that intensely English Englishman. Wellington's contemptuous disgust at Nelson's
theatricality as a professed hero, patriot, and rhapsode,

a theatricality which in an Irishman would have been an insufferably vulgar affectation, was quite natural and inevitable. Wellington's formula for that kind of thing was a well known Irish one: " Sir: dont be a damned fool." It is the formula of all Irishmen for all Englishmen to this day. It is the formula of Larry Doyle for Tom Broadbent in my play, in spite of Doyle's affection for Tom. Nelson's genius, instead of producing intellectual keenness and scrupulousness, produced mere delirium. He was drunk with glory, exalted by his fervent faith in the sound British patriotism of the Almighty, nerved by the vulgarest anti-foreign prejudice, and apparently unchastened by any reflections on the fact that he had never had to fight a technically capable and properly equipped enemy except on land, where he had never been successful. Compare Wellington, who had to fight Napoleon's armies, Napoleon's marshals, and finally Napoleon himself, without one moment of illusion as to the human material he had to command, without one gush of the " Kiss me, Hardy " emotion which enabled Nelson to idolize his crews and his staff, without forgetting even in his dreams that the normal British officer of that time was an incapable amateur (as he still is) and the normal British soldier a never-do-well (he is now a depressed and respectable young man). No wonder Wellington became an accomplished comedian in the art of anti-climax, scandalizing the unfortunate Croker, responding to the demand for glorious sentiments by the most disenchanting touches of realism, and, generally, pricking the English windbag at its most explosive crises of distention. Nelson, intensely nervous and theatrical, made an enormous fuss about victories so cheap that he would have deserved shooting if he had lost them, and, not content with lavishing splendid fighting on helpless adversaries like the heroic De Brueys or Villeneuve (who had not even the illusion of heroism when he went like a lamb to the slaughter), got himself killed by his passion for exposing himself to death in that sublime defiance of it which was perhaps the supreme tribute of the exquisite coward to the King of Terrors (for, believe me, you cannot be a hero without being a coward: supersense cuts both ways), the result being a tremendous effect on the gallery. Wellington, most capable of captains, was neither a hero nor a patriot: perhaps not even a coward; and had it not been for the Nelsonic anecdotes invented for him — " Up guards, and at em " and so forth—and the fact that the antagonist with whom he finally closed was such a master of theatrical effect that Wellington could not fight him without getting into his limelight, nor overthrow him (most unfortunately for us all) without drawing the eyes of the whole world to the catastrophe, the Iron Duke would have been almost forgotten by this time. Now that contrast is English against Irish all over, and is the more delicious because the real Irishman in it is the Englishman of tradition, whilst the real Englishman is the traditional theatrical foreigner.

The value of the illustration lies in the fact that both Nelson and Wellington were both in the highest degree efficient, and both in the highest degree incompatible with one another on any other footing than one of independence. The government of Nelson by Wellington or of Wellington by Nelson is felt at once to be a dishonorable outrage to the governed and a finally impossible task for the governor.

I daresay some Englishmen will now try to steal Wellington as Macaulay tried to steal Swift. And he may plead with some truth that though it seems impossible that any other country than England could produce a hero so utterly devoid of common sense, intellectual delicacy, and international chivalry as Nelson, it may be contended that Wellington was rather an eighteenth century aristocratic type, than a specifically Irish type. George IV. and Byron, contrasted with Gladstone, seem

Irish in respect of a certain humorous blackguardism, and a power of appreciating art and sentiment without being duped by them into mistaking romantic figments for realities. But faithlessness and the need for carrying off the worthlessness and impotence that accompany it, produce in all nations a gay, sceptical, amusing, blaspheming, witty fashion which suits the flexibility of the Irish mind very well; and the contrast between this fashion and the energetic infatuations that have enabled intellectually ridiculous men, without wit or humor, to go on crusades and make successful revolutions, must not be confused with the contrast between the English and Irish idiosyncrasies. The Irishman makes a distinction which the Englishman is too lazy intellectually (the intellectual laziness and slovenliness of the English is almost beyond belief) to make. The Englishman, impressed with the dissoluteness of the faithless wits of the Restoration and the Regency, and with the victories of the wilful zealots of the patriotic, religious, and revolutionary wars, jumps to the conclusion that wilfulness is the main thing. In this he is right. But he overdoes his jump so far as to conclude also that stupidity and wrong-headedness are better guarantees of efficiency and trustworthiness than intellectual vivacity, which he mistrusts as a common symptom of worthlessness, vice and instability. Now in this he is most dangerously wrong. Whether the Irishman grasps the truth as firmly as the Englishman may be open to question; but he is certainly comparatively free from the error. That affectionate and admiring love of sentimental stupidity for its own sake, both in men and women, which shines so steadily through the novels of Thackeray, would hardly be possible in the works of an Irish novelist. Even Dickens, though too vital a genius and too severely educated in the school of shabby-genteel poverty to have any doubt of the national danger of fatheadedness in high places, evidently assumes rather too hastily the superiority of

Mr. Meagles to Sir John Chester and Harold Skimpole. On the other hand, it takes an Irishman years of residence in England to learn to respect and like a blockhead. An Englishman will not respect nor like anyone else. Every English statesman has to maintain his popularity by pretending to be ruder, more ignorant, more sentimental, more superstitious, more stupid than any man who has lived behind the scenes of public life for ten minutes can possibly be. Nobody dares to publish really intimate memoirs of him or really private letters of his until his whole generation has passed away, and his party can no longer be compromised by the discovery that the platitudinizing twaddler and hypocritical opportunist was really a man of some perception as well as of strong constitution, peg-away industry, personal ambition, and party keenness.

English Stupidity Excused.

I do not claim it as a natural superiority in the Irish nation that it dislikes and mistrusts fools, and expects its political leaders to be clever and humbug-proof. It may be that if our resources included the armed force and virtually unlimited money which push the political and military figureheads of England through bungled enterprises to a muddled success, and create an illusion of some miraculous and divine innate English quality that enables a general to become a conqueror with abilities that would not suffice to save a cabman from having his license marked, and a member of parliament to become Prime Minister with the outlook on life of a sporting country solicitor educated by a private governess, I have no doubt we should lapse into gross intellectual sottishness, and prefer leaders who encouraged our vulgarities by sharing them, and flattered us by associating them with purchased successes, to our betters. But as it is, we cannot afford that sort of encouragement and flattery

in Ireland. The odds against which our leaders have
to fight would be too heavy for the fourth-rate Englishmen whose leadership consists for the most part in mark-
ing time ostentatiously until they are violently shoved,
and then stumbling blindly forward (or backward)
wherever the shove sends them. We cannot crush England as a Pickford's van might crush a perambulator.
We are the perambulator and England the Pickford.
We must study her and our real weaknesses and real
strength; we must practise upon her slow conscience and
her quick terrors; we must deal in ideas and political
principles since we cannot deal in bayonets; we must
outwit, outwork, outstay her; we must embarrass, bully,
even conspire and assassinate when nothing else will
move her, if we are not all to be driven deeper and
deeper into the shame and misery of our servitude. Our
leaders must be not only determined enough, but clever
enough to do this. We have no illusions as to the existence of any mysterious Irish pluck, Irish honesty, Irish
bias on the part of Providence, or sterling Irish solidity
of character, that will enable an Irish blockhead to hold
his own against England. Blockheads are of no use to
us: we were compelled to follow a supercilious, unpopu-
lar, tongue-tied, aristocratic Protestant Parnell, although
there was no lack among us of fluent imbeciles, with
majestic presences and oceans of dignity and sentiment,
to promote into his place could they have done his work
for us. It is obviously convenient that Mr. Redmond
should be a better speaker and rhetorician than Parnell;
but if he began to use his powers to make himself agreeable instead of making himself reckoned with by the
enemy; if he set to work to manufacture and support
English shams and hypocrisies instead of exposing and
denouncing them; if he constituted himself the permanent apologist of doing nothing, and, when the people
insisted on his doing something, only roused himself to
discover how to pretend to do it without really changing

anything, he would lose his leadership as certainly as an English politician would, by the same course, attain a permanent place on the front bench. In short, our circumstances place a premium on political ability whilst the circumstances of England discount it; and the quality of the supply naturally follows the demand. If you miss in my writings that hero-worship of dotards and duffers which is planting England with statues of disastrous statesmen and absurd generals, the explanation is simply that I am an Irishman and you an Englishman.

Irish Protestantism Really Protestant.

When I repeat that I am an Irish Protestant, I come to a part of the relation between England and Ireland that you will never understand unless I insist on explaining it to you with that Irish insistence on intellectual clarity to which my English critics are so intensely recalcitrant.

First, let me tell you that in Ireland Protestantism is really Protestant. It is true that there is an Irish Protestant Church (disestablished some 35 years ago) in spite of the fact that a Protestant Church is, fundamentally, a contradiction in terms. But this means only that the Protestants use the word Church to denote their secular organization, without troubling themselves about the metaphysical sense of Christ's famous pun, " Upon this rock I will build my church." The Church of England, which is a reformed Anglican Catholic Anti-Protestant Church, is quite another affair. An Anglican is acutely conscious that he is not a Wesleyan; and many Anglican clergymen do not hesitate to teach that all Methodists incur damnation. In Ireland all that the member of the Irish Protestant Church knows is that he is not a Roman Catholic. The decorations of even the " lowest " English Church seem to him to be ex-

travagantly Ritualistic and Popish. I myself entered
the Irish Church by baptism, a ceremony performed by
my uncle in "his own church." But I was sent, with
many boys of my own denomination, to a Wesleyan
school where the Wesleyan catechism was taught without the least protest on the part of the parents, although
there was so little presumption in favor of any boy there
being a Wesleyan that if all the Church boys had been
withdrawn at any moment, the school would have become
bankrupt. And this was by no means analogous to the
case of those working class members of the Church of
England in London, who send their daughters to Roman
Catholic schools rather than to the public elementary
schools. They do so for the definite reason that the
nuns teach girls good manners and sweetness of speech,
which have no place in the County Council curriculum.
But in Ireland the Church parent sends his son to a
Wesleyan school (if it is convenient and socially eligible)
because he is indifferent to the form of Protestantism,
provided it is Protestantism. There is also in Ireland
a characteristically Protestant refusal to take ceremonies
and even sacraments very seriously except by way of
strenuous objection to them when they are conducted
with candles or incense. For example, I was never confirmed, although the ceremony was perhaps specially
needed in my case as the failure of my appointed god-
father to appear at the font led to his responsibilities
being assumed on the spot, at my uncle's order, by the
sexton. And my case was a very common one, even
among people quite untouched by modern scepticisms.
Apart from the weekly churchgoing, which holds its own
as a respectable habit, the initiations are perfunctory, the
omissions regarded as negligible. The distinction between churchman and dissenter, which in England is a
class distinction, a political distinction, and even occasionally a religious distinction, does not exist. Nobody
is surprised in Ireland to find that the squire who is the

local pillar of the formerly established Church is also a Plymouth Brother, and, except on certain special or fashionable occasions, attends the Methodist meeting-house. The parson has no priestly character and no priestly influence: the High Church curate of course exists and has his vogue among religious epicures of the other sex; but the general attitude of his congregation towards him is that of Dr. Clifford. The clause in the Apostles' creed professing belief in a Catholic Church is a standing puzzle to Protestant children; and when they grow up they dismiss it from their minds more often than they solve it, because they really are not Catholics but Protestants to the extremest practicable degree of individualism. It is true that they talk of church and chapel with all the Anglican contempt for chapel; but in Ireland the chapel means the Roman Catholic church, for which the Irish Protestant reserves all the class rancor, the political hostility, the religious bigotry, and the bad blood generally that in England separates the Establishment from the non-conforming Protestant organizations. When a vulgar Irish Protestant speaks of a " Papist " he feels exactly as a vulgar Anglican vicar does when he speaks of a Dissenter. And when the vicar is Anglican enough to call himself a Catholic priest, wear a cassock, and bless his flock with two fingers, he becomes horrifically incomprehensible to the Irish Protestant Churchman, who, on his part, puzzles the Anglican by regarding a Methodist as tolerantly as an Irishman who likes grog regards an Irishman who prefers punch.

A Fundamental Anomaly.

Now nothing can be more anomalous, and at bottom impossible, than a Conservative Protestant party standing for the established order against a revolutionary

Catholic party. The Protestant is theoretically an
anarchist as far as anarchism is practicable in human
society: that is, he is an individualist, a freethinker, a
self-helper, a Whig, a Liberal, a mistruster and vilifier
of the State, a rebel. The Catholic is theoretically a
Collectivist, a self-abnegator, a Tory, a Conservative, a
supporter of Church and State one and undivisible, an
obeyer. This would be a statement of fact as well as
of theory if men were Protestants and Catholics by temperament and adult choice instead of by family tradition. The peasant who supposed that Wordsworth's son
would carry on the business now the old gentleman was
gone was not a whit more foolish than we who laugh
at his ignorance of the nature of poetry whilst we take
it as a matter of course that a son should " carry on "
his father's religion. Hence, owing to our family system, the Catholic Churches are recruited daily at the
font by temperamental Protestants, and the Protestant
organizations by temperamental Catholics, with consequences most disconcerting to those who expect history
to be deducible from the religious professions of the
men who make it.

Still, though the Roman Catholic Church may occasionally catch such Tartars as Luther and Voltaire, or
the Protestant organizations as Newman and Manning,
the general run of mankind takes its impress from the
atmosphere in which it is brought up. In Ireland the
Roman Catholic peasant cannot escape the religious atmosphere of his Church. Except when he breaks out
like a naughty child he is docile; he is reverent; he is
content to regard knowledge as something not his business; he is a child before his Church, and accepts it as
the highest authority in science and philosophy. He
speaks of himself as a son of the Church, calling his
priest father instead of brother or Mister. To rebel
politically, he must break away from parish tutelage and
follow a Protestant leader on national questions. His

Church naturally fosters his submissiveness. The British Government and the Vatican may differ very vehemently as to whose subject the Irishman is to be; but they are quite agreed as to the propriety of his being a subject. Of the two, the British Government allows him more liberty, giving him as complete a democratic control of local government as his means will enable him to use, and a voice in the election of a formidable minority in the House of Commons, besides allowing him to read and learn what he likes—except when it makes a tufthunting onslaught on a seditious newspaper. But if he dared to claim a voice in the selection of his parish priest, or a representative at the Vatican, he would be denounced from the altar as an almost inconceivable blasphemer; and his educational opportunities are so restricted by his Church that he is heavily handicapped in every walk of life that requires any literacy. It is the aim of his priest to make him and keep him a submissive Conservative; and nothing but gross economic oppression and religious persecution could have produced the strange phenomenon of a revolutionary movement not only tolerated by the Clericals, but, up to a certain point, even encouraged by them. If there is such a thing as political science, with natural laws like any other science, it is certain that only the most violent external force could effect and maintain this unnatural combination of political revolution with Papal reaction, and of hardy individualism and independence with despotism and subjugation.

That violent external force is the clumsy thumb of English rule. If you would be good enough, ladies and gentlemen of England, to take your thumb away and leave us free to do something else than bite it, the unnaturally combined elements in Irish politics would fly asunder and recombine according to their proper nature with results entirely satisfactory to real Protestantism.

THE NATURE OF POLITICAL HATRED.

Just reconsider the Home Rule question in the light
of that very English characteristic of the Irish people,
their political hatred of priests. Do not be distracted
by the shriek of indignant denial from the Catholic
papers and from those who have witnessed the charming
relations between the Irish peasantry and their spiritual
fathers. I am perfectly aware that the Irish love their
priests as devotedly as the French loved them before
the Revolution or as the Italians loved them before they
imprisoned the Pope in the Vatican. They love their
landlords too: many an Irish gentleman has found in
his nurse a foster-mother more interested in him than
his actual mother. They love the English, as every
Englishman who travels in Ireland can testify. Please
do not suppose that I speak satirically: the world is
full of authentic examples of the concurrence of human
kindliness with political rancor. Slaves and schoolboys
often love their masters; Napoleon and his soldiers
made desperate efforts to save from drowning the
Russian soldiers under whom they had broken the ice
with their cannon; even the relations between nonconformist peasants and country parsons in England are
not invariably unkindly; in the southern States of
America planters are often traditionally fond of negroes
and kind to them, with substantial returns in humble
affection; soldiers and sailors often admire and cheer
their officers sincerely and heartily; nowhere is actual
personal intercourse found compatible for long with the
intolerable friction of hatred and malice. But people
who persist in pleading these amiabilities as political
factors must be summarily bundled out of the room when
questions of State are to be discussed. Just as an Irishman may have English friends whom he may prefer to
any Irishman of his acquaintance, and be kind, hospitable, and serviceable in his intercourse with English-

men, whilst being perfectly prepared to make the
Shannon run red with English blood if Irish freedom
could be obtained at that price; so an Irish Catholic may
like his priest as a man and revere him as a confessor
and spiritual pastor whilst being implacably determined
to seize the first opportunity of throwing off his yoke.
This is political hatred: the only hatred that civilization
allows to be mortal hatred.

The Revolt Against the Priest.

Realize, then, that the popular party in Ireland is
seething with rebellion against the tyranny of the
Church. Imagine the feelings of an English farmer if
the parson refused to marry him for less than £20, and
if he had virtually no other way of getting married!
Imagine the Church Rates revived in the form of an
unofficial Income Tax scientifically adjusted to your tax-
able capacity by an intimate knowledge of your affairs
verified in the confessional! Imagine being one of a
peasantry reputed the poorest in the world, under the
thumb of a priesthood reputed the richest in the world!
Imagine a Catholic middle class continually defeated in
the struggle of professional, official, and fashionable life
by the superior education of its Protestant competitors,
and yet forbidden by its priests to resort to the only
efficient universities in the country! Imagine trying to
get a modern education in a seminary of priests, where
every modern book worth reading is on the index, and
the earth is still regarded, not perhaps as absolutely flat,
yet as being far from so spherical as Protestants allege!
Imagine being forbidden to read this preface because
it proclaims your own grievance! And imagine being
bound to submit to all this because the popular side must
hold together at all costs in the face of the Protestant
enemy! That is, roughly, the predicament of Roman
Catholic Ireland.

PROTESTANT LOYALTY: A FORECAST.

Now let us have a look at Protestant Ireland. I have already said that a "loyal" Irishman is an abhorrent phenomenon, because he is an unnatural one. In Ireland it is not "loyalty" to drink the English king's health and stand uncovered to the English national anthem: it is simply exploitation of English rule in the interests of the property, power, and promotion of the Irish classes as against the Irish masses. From any other point of view it is cowardice and dishonor. I have known a Protestant go to Dublin Castle to be sworn in as a special constable, quite resolved to take the baton and break the heads of a patriotic faction just then upsetting the peace of the town, yet back out at the last moment because he could not bring himself to swallow the oath of allegiance tendered with the baton. There is no such thing as genuine loyalty in Ireland. There is a separation of the Irish people into two hostile camps: one Protestant, gentlemanly, and oligarchical; the other Roman Catholic, popular, and democratic. The oligarchy governs Ireland as a bureaucracy deriving authority from the king of England. It cannot cast him off without casting off its own ascendancy. Therefore it naturally exploits him sedulously, drinking his health, waving his flag, playing his anthem, and using the foolish word "traitor" freely in its cups. But let the English Government make a step towards the democratic party, and the Protestant garrison revolts at once, not with tears and prayers and anguish of soul and years of trembling reluctance, as the parliamentarians of the XVII century revolted against Charles I, but with acrid promptitude and strident threatenings. When England finally abandons the garrison by yielding to the demand for Home Rule, the Protestants will not go under, nor will they waste much time in sulking over their betrayal, and comparing their fate with that of Gordon left by Gladstone to perish on the spears of heathen fanatics. They cannot afford to retire into an Irish Faubourg St. Germain. They will take an energetic part in the national government, which will be sorely in need of parliamentary and official forces independent of Rome. They will get not only the Protestant votes, but the votes of Catholics in that spirit of toleration which is everywhere extended to heresies that happen to be politically serviceable to the orthodox. They will not relax their determination to hold every inch of the government of Ireland that they can grasp; but as that government will then be a national Irish government instead of as now an English government, their determination will make them the vanguard of Irish Nationalism and Democracy as against Romanism and Sacerdotalism, leaving English Unionists grieved and shocked at their discovery of the true value of an Irish Protestant's loyalty.

But there will be no open break in the tradition of the party. The Protestants will still be the party of Union, which will then mean, not the Repeal of Home Rule, but the maintenance of the Federal Union of English-speaking commonwealths, now theatrically called the Empire. They will pull down the Union Jack without the smallest scruple; but they know the value of the Channel Fleet, and will cling closer than brothers to that and any other Imperial asset that can be exploited for the protection of Ireland against foreign aggression or the sharing of expenses with the British taxpayer. They know that the Irish coast is for the English invasion-scaremonger the heel of Achilles, and that they can use this to make him pay for the boot.

PROTESTANT PUGNACITY.

If any Englishman feels incredulous as to this view of Protestantism as an essentially Nationalist force in Ireland, let him ask himself which leader he, if he were an Irishman, would rather have back from the grave to fight England: the Catholic Daniel O'Connell or the Protestant Parnell. O'Connell organized the Nationalist movement only to draw its teeth, to break its determination, and to declare that Repeal of the Union was not worth the shedding of a drop of blood. He died in the bosom of his Church, not in the bosom of his country. The Protestant leaders, from Lord Edward Fitzgerald to Parnell, have never divided their devotion. If any Englishman thinks that they would have been more sparing of blood than the English themselves are, if only so cheap a fluid could have purchased the honor of Ireland, he greatly mistakes the Irish Protestant temper. The notion that Ireland is the only country in the world not worth shedding a drop of blood for is not a Protestant one, and certainly not countenanced by English practice. It was hardly reasonable to ask Parnell to shed blood *quant. suff.* in Egypt to put an end to the misgovernment of the Khedive and replace him by Lord Cromer for the sake of the English bondholders, and then to expect him to become a Tolstoyan or an O'Connellite in regard to his own country. With a wholly Protestant Ireland at his back he might have bullied England into conceding Home Rule; for the insensibility of the English governing classes to philosophical, moral, social considerations—in short, to any considerations which require a little intellectual exertion and sympathetic alertness—is tempered, as we Irish well know, by an absurd susceptibility to intimidation.

For let me halt a moment here to impress on you, O English reader, that no fact has been more deeply stamped into us than that we can do nothing with an English Government unless we frighten it, any more than you can yourself. When power and riches are thrown haphazard into children's cradles as they are in England, you get a governing class without industry, character, courage, or real experience; and under such circumstances reforms are produced only by catastrophes followed by panics in which " something must be done." Thus it costs a cholera epidemic to achieve a Public Health Act, a Crimean War to reform the Civil Service, and a gunpowder plot to disestablish the Irish Church. It was by the light, not of reason, but of the moon, that the need for paying serious attention to the Irish land question was seen in England. It cost the American War of Independence and the Irish Volunteer movement to obtain the Irish parliament of 1782, the constitution of which far overshot the nationalist mark of today in the matter of independence.

It is vain to plead that this is human nature and not class weakness. The Japanese have proved that it is possible to conduct social and political changes intelligently and providentially instead of drifting along helplessly until public disasters compel a terrified and inconsiderate rearrangement. Innumerable experiments in local government have shewn that when men are neither too poor to be honest nor too rich to understand and share the needs of the people—as in New Zealand, for example—they can govern much more providently than our little circle of aristocrats and plutocrats.

THE JUST ENGLISHMAN.

English Unionists, when asked what they have to say in defence of their rule of subject peoples, often reply that the Englishman is just, leaving us divided between our derision of so monstrously inhuman a pretension, and our impatience with so gross a confusion of the mutually exclusive functions of judge and legislator. For there is only one condition on which a man can do justice between two litigants, and that is that he shall have no interest in common with either of them, whereas it is only by having every interest in common with both of them that he can govern them tolerably. The indispensable preliminary to Democracy is the representation of every interest: the indispensable preliminary to justice is the elimination of every interest. When we want an arbitrator or an umpire, we turn to a stranger: when we want a government, a stranger is the one person we will not endure. The Englishman in India, for example, stands, a very statue of justice, between two natives. He says, in effect, " I am impartial in your religious disputes, because I believe in neither of your religions. I am impartial in your conflicts of custom and sentiment, because your customs and sentiments are different from, and abysmally inferior to, my own. Finally, I am impartial as to your interests, because they are both equally opposed to mine, which is to keep you both equally powerless against me in order that I may extract money from you to pay salaries and pensions to myself and my fellow Englishmen as judges and rulers over you. In return for which you get the inestimable benefit of a government that does absolute justice as between Indian and Indian, being wholly preoccupied with the maintenance of absolute injustice as between India and England.

It will be observed that no Englishman, without making himself ridiculous, could pretend to be perfectly just or disinterested in English affairs, or would tolerate a proposal to establish the Indian or Irish system in Great Britain. Yet if the justice of the Englishman is sufficient to ensure the welfare of India or Ireland, it ought to suffice equally for England. But the English are wise enough to refuse to trust to English justice themselves, preferring democracy. They can hardly blame the Irish for taking the same view.

In short, dear English reader, the Irish Protestant stands outside that English Mutual Admiration Society which you call the Union or the Empire. You may buy a common and not ineffective variety of Irish Protestant by delegating your powers to him and in effect making him the oppressor and you his sorely bullied and bothered catspaw and military maintainer; but if you offer him nothing for his loyalty except the natural superiority of the English character, you will—well, try the experiment, and see what will happen! You would have a ten-times better chance with the Roman Catholic; for he has been saturated from his youth up with the Imperial idea of foreign rule by a spiritually superior international power, and is trained to submission and abnegation of his private judgment. A Roman Catholic garrison would take its orders from England and let her rule Ireland if England were Roman Catholic. The Protestant garrison simply seizes on the English power; uses it for its own purposes; and occasionally orders the English Government to remove an Irish secretary who has dared to apply English ideas to the affairs of the garrison. Whereupon the English Government abjectly removes him, and implores him, as a gentleman and a loyal Englishman, not to reproach it in the face of the Nationalist enemy.

Such incidents naturally do not shake the sturdy conviction of the Irish Protestant that he is more than a match for any English Government in determination and intelligence. Here, no doubt, he flatters himself; for his advantage is not really an advantage of character, but of comparative directness of interest, concentration of force on one narrow issue, simplicity of aim, with freedom from the scruples and responsibilities of world-politics. The business is Irish business, not English; and he is Irish. And his object, which is simply to secure the dominance of his own caste and creed behind the power of England, is simpler and clearer than the confused aims of English Cabinets struggling ineptly with the burdens of empire, and biassed by the pressure of capital anywhere rather than in Ireland. He has no responsibility, no interest, no status outside his own country and his own movement, which means that he has no conscience in dealing with England; whereas England, having a very uneasy conscience, and many hindering and hampering responsibilities and interests in dealing with him, gets bullied and driven by him, and finally learns sympathy with Nationalist aims by her experience of the tyranny of the Orange party.

Irish Catholicism Forecast.

Let us suppose that the establishment of a national government were to annihilate the oligarchic party by absorbing the Protestant garrison and making it a Protestant National Guard. The Roman Catholic laity, now a cipher, would organize itself; and a revolt against Rome and against the priesthood would ensue. The Roman Catholic Church would become the official Irish Church. The Irish parliament would insist on a voice in the promotion of churchmen; fees and contributions would be regulated; blackmail would be resisted; sweating in conventual factories and workshops would be stopped; and the ban would be taken off the universities. In a word, the Roman Catholic Church, against which Dublin Castle is powerless, would meet the one force on earth that can cope with it victoriously. That force is Democracy, a thing far more Catholic than itself. Until that force is let loose against it, the Protestant garrison can do nothing to the priesthood except consolidate it and drive the people to rally round it in defence of their altars against the foreigner and the heretic. When it *is* let loose, the Catholic laity will make as short work of sacerdotal tyranny in Ireland as it has done in France and Italy. And in doing so it will be forced to face the old problem of the relations of Church and State. A Roman Catholic party must submit to Rome: an anti-clerical Catholic party must of necessity become an Irish Catholic party. The Holy Roman Empire, like the other Empires, has no future

except as a Federation of national Catholic Churches;
for Christianity can no more escape Democracy than
Democracy can escape Socialism. It is noteworthy in
this connection that the Anglican Catholics have played
and are playing a notable part in the Socialist movement
in England in opposition to the individualist Secularists
of the urban proletariat; but they are quit of the preliminary dead lift that awaits the Irish Catholic. Their
Church has thrown off the yoke of Rome, and is safely
and permanently Anglicized. But the Catholic Church
in Ireland is still Roman. Home Rule will herald the
day when the Vatican will go the way of Dublin Castle,
and the island of the saints assume the headship of her
own Church. It may seem incredible that long after
the last Orangeman shall lay down his chalk for ever,
the familiar scrawl on every blank wall in the north of
Ireland " To hell with the Pope! " may reappear in the
south, traced by the hands of Catholics who shall have
forgotten the traditional counter legend, " To hell with
King William! " (of glorious, pious and immortal memory); but it may happen so. " The island of the saints "
is no idle phrase. Religious genius is one of our national
products; and Ireland is no bad rock to build a Church
on. Holy and beautiful is the soul of Catholic Ireland:
her prayers are lovelier than the teeth and claws of
Protestantism, but not so effective in dealing with the
English.

English Voltaireanism.

Let me familiarize the situation by shewing how
closely it reproduces the English situation in its essen-
tials. In England, as in France, the struggle between
the priesthood and the laity has produced a vast body of
Voltaireans. But the essential identity of the French
and English movements has been obscured by the ignorance of the ordinary Englishman, who, instead of

knowing the distinctive tenets of his church or sect, vaguely believes them to be the eternal truth as opposed to the damnable error of all the other denominations. He thinks of Voltaire as a French " infidel," instead of as the champion of the laity against the official theocracy of the State Church. The Nonconformist leaders of our Free Churches are all Voltaireans. The warcry of the Passive Resisters is Voltaire's warcry, " Ecrasez l'infâme." No account need be taken of the technical difference between Voltaire's " infâme " and Dr. Clifford's. One was the unreformed Roman Church of France: the other is the reformed Anglican Church; but in both cases the attack has been on a priestly tyranny and a professional monopoly. Voltaire convinced the Genevan ministers that he was the philosophic champion of their Protestant, Individualistic, Democratic Deism against the State Church of Roman Catholic France; and his heroic energy and beneficence as a philanthropist, which now only makes the list of achievements on his monument at Ferney the most impressive epitaph in Europe, then made the most earnest of the Lutheran ministers glad to claim a common inspiration with him. Unfortunately Voltaire had an irrepressible sense of humor. He joked about Habakkuk; and jokes about Habakkuk smelt too strongly of brimstone to be tolerated by Protestants to whom the Bible was not a literature but a fetish and a talisman. And so Voltaire, in spite of the church he " erected to God," became in England the bogey-atheist of three generations of English ignoramuses, instead of the legitimate successor of Martin Luther and John Knox.

Nowadays, however, Voltaire's jokes are either forgotten or else fall flat on a world which no longer venerates Habakkuk; and his true position is becoming apparent. The fact that Voltaire was a Roman Catholic layman, educated at a Jesuit college, is the conclusive reply to the shallow people who imagine that Ireland delivered up to the Irish democracy—that is, to the Catholic laity—would be delivered up to the tyranny of the priesthood.

SUPPOSE!

Suppose, now, that the conquest of France by Henry V of England had endured, and that France in the XVIII century had been governed by an English viceroy through a Hugenot bureaucracy and a judicial bench appointed on the understanding that loyalty for them meant loyalty to England, and patriotism a willingness to die in defence of the English conquest and of the English Church, would not Voltaire in that case have been the meanest of traitors and self-seekers if he had played the game of England by joining in its campaign against his own and his country's Church? The energy he threw into the defence of Calais and Sirven would have been thrown into the defence of the Frenchmen whom the English would have called " rebels "; and he would have been forced to identify the cause of freedom and democracy with the cause of " l'infâme." The French revolution would have been a revolution against England and English rule instead of against aristocracy and ecclesiasticism; and all the intellectual and spiritual forces in France, from Turgot to De Tocqueville, would have been burnt up in mere anti-Anglicism and nationalist dithyrambs instead of contributing to political science and broadening the thought of the world.

What would have happened in France is what has happened in Ireland; and that is why it is only the smallminded Irish, incapable of conceiving what religious freedom means to a country, who do not loathe English rule. For in Ireland England is nothing but the Pope's policeman. She imagines she is holding the Vatican cardinals at bay when she is really strangling the Voltaires, the Foxes and Penns, the Cliffords, Hortons,

Campbells, Walters, and Silvester Hornes, who are to
be found among the Roman Catholic laity as plentifully
as among the Anglican Catholic laity in England. She
gets nothing out of Ireland but infinite trouble, infinite
confusion and hindrance in her own legislation, a hatred
that circulates through the whole world and poisons it
against her, a reproach that makes her professions of
sympathy with Finland and Macedonia ridiculous and
hypocritical, whilst the priest takes all the spoils, in
money, in power, in pride, and in popularity.

Ireland's Real Grievance.

But it is not the spoils that matter. It is the waste,
the sterilization, the perversion of fruitful brain power
into flatulent protest against unnecessary evil, the use of
our very entrails to tie our own hands and seal our own
lips in the name of our honor and patriotism. As far as
money or comfort is concerned, the average Irishman
has a more tolerable life—especially now that the population is so scanty—than the average Englishman. It is
true that in Ireland the poor man is robbed and starved
and oppressed under judicial forms which confer the
imposing title of justice on a crude system of bludgeon-
ing and perjury. But so is the Englishman. The Englishman, more docile, less dangerous, too lazy intellectually to use such political and legal power as lies within
his reach, suffers more and makes less fuss about it
than the Irishman. But at least he has nobody to blame
but himself and his fellow countrymen. He does not
doubt that if an effective majority of the English people
made up their minds to alter the Constitution, as the
majority of the Irish people have made up their minds
to obtain Home Rule, they could alter it without having
to fight an overwhelmingly powerful and rich neighbor-
ing nation, and fight, too, with ropes round their necks.
He can attack any institution in his country without

betraying it to foreign vengeance and foreign oppression. True, his landlord may turn him out of his cottage if he goes to a Methodist chapel instead of to the parish church. His customers may stop their orders if he votes Liberal instead of Conservative. English ladies and gentlemen who would perish sooner than shoot a fox do these things without the smallest sense of indecency and dishonor. But they cannot muzzle his intellectual leaders. The English philosopher, the English author, the English orator can attack every abuse and expose every superstition without strengthening the hands of any common enemy. In Ireland every such attack, every such exposure, is a service to England and a stab to Ireland. If you expose the tyranny and rapacity of the Church, it is an argument in favor of Protestant ascendency. If you denounce the nepotism and jobbery of the new local authorities, you are demonstrating the unfitness of the Irish to govern themselves, and the superiority of the old oligarchical grand juries.

And there is the same pressure on the other side. The Protestant must stand by the garrison at all costs: the Unionist must wink at every bureaucratic abuse, connive at every tyranny, magnify every official blockhead, because their exposure would be a victory for the Nationalist enemy. Every Irishman is in Lancelot's position: his honor rooted in dishonor stands; and faith unfaithful keeps him falsely true.

THE CURSE OF NATIONALISM.

It is hardly possible for an Englishman to understand all that this implies. A conquered nation is like a man with cancer: he can think of nothing else, and is forced to place himself, to the exclusion of all better company, in the hands of quacks who profess to treat or cure cancer. The windbags of the two rival platforms are the most insufferable of all windbags. It requires neither

knowledge, character, conscience, diligence in public
affairs, nor any virtue, private or communal, to thump
the Nationalist or Orange tub: nay, it puts a premium
on the rancor or callousness that has given rise to the
proverb that if you put an Irishman on a spit you can
always get another Irishman to baste him. Jingo oratory
in England is sickening enough to serious people: indeed
one evening's mafficking in London produced a determined call for the police. Well, in Ireland all political
oratory is Jingo oratory; and all political demonstrations
are maffickings. English rule is such an intolerable
abomination that no other subject can reach the people.
Nationalism stands between Ireland and the light of the
world. Nobody in Ireland of any intelligence likes
Nationalism any more than a man with a broken arm
likes having it set. A healthy nation is as unconscious
of its nationality as a healthy man of his bones. But if
you break a nation's nationality it will think of nothing
else but getting it set again. It will listen to no re-
former, to no philosopher, to no preacher, until the demand of the Nationalist is granted. It will attend to
no business, however vital, except the business of unifica-
tion and liberation.

That is why everything is in abeyance in Ireland
pending the achievement of Home Rule. The great
movements of the human spirit which sweep in waves
over Europe are stopped on the Irish coast by the English guns of the Pigeon House Fort. Only a quaint
little offshoot of English pre-Raphaelitism called the
Gaelic movement has got a footing by using Nationalism
as a stalking-horse, and popularizing itself as an attack
on the native language of the Irish people, which is
most fortunately also the native language of half the
world, including England. Every election is fought on
nationalist grounds; every appointment is made on nationalist grounds; every judge is a partisan in the nationalist conflict; every speech is a dreary recapitulation of

nationalist twaddle; every lecture is a corruption of
history to flatter nationalism or defame it; every school
is a recruiting station; every church is a barrack; and
every Irishman is unspeakably tired of the whole miserable business, which nevertheless is, and perforce must
remain his first business until Home Rule makes an end
of it, and sweeps the nationalist and the garrison hack
together into the dustbin.

There is indeed no greater curse to a nation than a
nationalist movement, which is only the agonizing symptom of a suppressed natural function.   Conquered
nations lose their place in the world's march because
they can do nothing but strive to get rid of their
nationalist movements by recovering their national liberty.   All demonstrations of the virtues of a foreign
government, though often conclusive, are as useless as
demonstrations of the superiority of artificial teeth, glass
eyes, silver windpipes, and patent wooden legs to the
natural products.   Like Democracy, national self-government is not for the good of the people: it is for the
satisfaction of the people.   One Antonine emperor, one
St. Louis, one Richelieu, may be worth ten democracies
in point of what is called good government; but there
is no satisfaction for the people in them.   To deprive
a dyspeptic of his dinner and hand it over to a man who
can digest it better is a highly logical proceeding; but it
is not a sensible one.   To take the government of Ireland
away from the Irish and hand it over to the English
on the ground that they can govern better would be a
precisely parallel case if the English had managed their
own affairs so well as to place their superior faculty
for governing beyond question.   But as the English are
avowed muddlers—rather proud of it, in fact—even the
logic of that case against Home Rule is not complete.
Read Mr. Charles Booth's account of London, Mr.
Rowntree's account of York, and the latest official report
on Dundee; and then pretend, if you can, that English-

men and Scotchmen have not more cause to hand over
their affairs to an Irish parliament than to clamor for
another nation's cities to devastate and another people's
business to mismanage.

A Natural Right.

The question is not one of logic at all, but of natural
right. English universities have for some time past encouraged an extremely foolish academic exercise which
consists in disproving the existence of natural rights on
the ground that they cannot be deduced from the principles of any known political system. If they could, they
would not be natural rights but acquired ones. Acquired
rights are deduced from political constitutions; but political constitutions are deduced from natural rights.
When a man insists on certain liberties without the
slightest regard to demonstrations that they are not for
his own good, nor for the public good, nor moral, nor
reasonable, nor decent, nor compatible with the existing
constitution of society, then he is said to claim a natural
right to that liberty. When, for instance, he insists, in
spite of the irrefutable demonstrations of many able
pessimists, from the author of the book of Ecclesiastes
to Schopenhauer, that life is an evil, on living, he is
asserting a natural right to live. When he insists on a
vote in order that his country may be governed according
to his ignorance instead of the wisdom of the Privy
Council, he is asserting a natural right to self-government. When he insists on guiding himself at 21 by his
own inexperience and folly and immaturity instead of
by the experience and sagacity of his father, or the well
stored mind of his grandmother, he is asserting a natural
right to independence. Even if Home Rule were as
unhealthy as an Englishman's eating, as intemperate as
his drinking, as filthy as his smoking, as licentious as
his domesticity, as corrupt as his elections, as murder-

ously greedy as his commerce, as cruel as his prisons, and as merciless as his streets, Ireland's claim to self-government would still be as good as England's. King James the First proved so cleverly and conclusively that the satisfaction of natural rights was incompatible with good government that his courtiers called him Solomon. We, more enlightened, call him Fool, solely because we have learnt that nations insist on being governed by their own consent—or, as they put it, by themselves and for themselves — and that they will finally upset a good government which denies them this even if the alternative be a bad government which at least creates and maintains an illusion of democracy. America, as far as one can ascertain, is much worse governed, and has a much more disgraceful political history than England under Charles I; but the American Republic is the stabler government because it starts from a formal concession of natural rights, and keeps up an illusion of safeguarding them by an elaborate machinery of democratic election. And the final reason why Ireland must have Home Rule is that she has a natural right to it.

A WARNING.

Finally, some words of warning to both nations. Ireland has been deliberately ruined again and again by England. Unable to compete with us industrially, she has destroyed our industries by the brute force of prohibitive taxation. She was perfectly right. That brute force was a more honorable weapon than the poverty which we used to undersell her. We lived with and as our pigs, and let loose our wares in the Englishman's market at prices which he could compete with only by living like a pig himself. Having the alternative of stopping our industry altogether, he very naturally and properly availed himself of it. We should have done the same in his place. To bear malice against him on that score is to poison our blood and weaken our constitutions with unintelligent rancor. In wrecking all the industries that were based on the poverty of our people England did us an enormous service. In omitting to do the same on her own soil, she did herself a wrong that has rotted her almost to the marrow. I hope that when Home Rule is at last achieved, one of our first legislative acts will be to fortify the subsistence of our people behind the bulwark of a standard wage, and impose crushing import duties on every English trade that flourishes in the slum and fattens on the starvation of our unfortunate neighbors.

DOWN WITH THE SOLDIER!

Now for England's share of warning. Let her look to her Empire; for unless she makes it such a Federation for civil strength and defence that all free peoples will cling to it voluntarily, it will inevitably become a military tyranny to prevent them from abandoning it; and such a tyranny will drain the English taxpayer of his money more effectually than its worst cruelties can ever drain its victims of their liberty. A political scheme that cannot be carried out except by soldiers will not be a permanent one. The soldier is an anachronism of which we must get rid. Among people who are proof against the suggestions of romantic fiction there can no longer be any question of the fact that military service produces moral imbecility, ferocity, and cowardice, and that the defence of nations must be undertaken by the civil enterprise of men enjoying all the rights and liberties of citizenship, and trained by the exacting discipline of democratic freedom and responsibility. For permanent work the soldier is worse than useless: such efficiency as he has is the result of dehumanization and disablement. His whole training tends to make him a weakling. He has the easiest of lives: he has no freedom and no responsibility. He is politically and socially a child, with rations instead of rights, treated like a child, punished like a child, dressed prettily and washed and combed like a child, excused for outbreaks of naughtiness like a child, forbidden to marry like a child, and called Tommy like a child. He has no real work to keep him from going mad except housemaid's work: all the rest is forced exercise, in the form of endless rehearsals for a destructive and terrifying performance which may never come off, and which, when it does come off, is not like the rehearsals. His officer has not even housekeeper's work to keep him sane. The work of organizing and commanding bodies of men, which builds up the character and resource of the large class of civilians who live by it, only demoralizes the military officer, because his orders, however disastrous or offensive, must be obeyed without regard to consequences: for instance, if he calls his men dogs, and perverts a musketry drill order to make them kneel to him as an act of personal humiliation, and thereby provokes a mutiny among men not yet thoroughly broken in to the abjectness of the military condition, he is not, as might be expected, shot, but, at worst, reprimanded, whilst the leader of the mutiny, instead of getting the Victoria Cross and a public testimonial, is condemned to five years' penal servitude by Lynch Law (technically called martial law) administered by a trade union of officers. Compare with this the position of, for instance, our railway managers or our heads of explosive factories. They have to handle large bodies of men whose carelessness or insubordination may cause wholesale destruction of life and property; yet any of these men may insult them, defy them, or assault them without special penalties of any sort. The military commander dares not face these conditions: he lives in perpetual terror of his men, and will undertake their command only when they are stripped of all their civil rights, gagged, and bound hand and foot by a barbarous slave code. Thus the officer learns to punish, but never to rule; and when an emergency like the Indian Mutiny comes, he breaks down; and the situation has to be saved by a few untypical officers with character enough to have retained their civilian qualities in spite of the messroom. This, unfortunately, is learnt by the public, not on the spot, but from Lord Roberts fifty years later.

Since the Mutiny we have had the Crimean and South African wars, the Dreyfus affair in France, the incidents of the anti-militarist campaign by the Social-Democrats in Germany, and now the Denshawai affair in the Nile delta, all heaping on us sensational demonstrations of the fact that soldiers pay the penalty of their slavery and outlawry by becoming, relatively to free civilians, destructive, cruel, dishonest, tyrannical, hysterical, mendacious, alarmists at home and terrorists abroad, politically reactionary, and professionally incapable. If it were humanly possible to militarize all the humanity out of a man, there would be absolutely no defence to this indictment. But the military system is so idiotically academic and impossible, and renders its victims so incapable of carrying it out with any thoroughness except when, in an occasional hysterical outburst of terror and violence, that hackneyed comedy of civil life, the weak man putting his foot down, becomes the military tragedy of the armed man burning, flogging and murdering in a panic, that a body of soldiers and officers is in the main, and under normal circumstances, much like any other body of laborers and gentlemen. Many of us count among our personal friends and relatives officers whose amiable and honorable character seems to contradict everything I have just said about the military character. You have only to describe Lynch courts and acts of terrorism to them as the work of Ribbonmen, Dacoits, Moonlighters, Boxers, or—to use the general term most familiar to them—" natives," and their honest and generous indignation knows no bounds: they feel about them like men, not like soldiers. But the moment you bring the professional side of them uppermost by describing precisely the same proceedings to them as the work of regular armies, they defend them, applaud them, and are ready to take part in them as if their humanity had been blown out like a candle. You find that there is a blind spot on their moral retina, and that this blind spot is the military spot.

The excuse, when any excuse is made, is that discipline is supremely important in war. Now most soldiers have no experience of war; and to assume that those who have are therefore qualified to legislate for it, is as absurd as to assume that a man who has been run over by an omnibus is thereby qualified to draw up wise regulations for the traffic of London. Neither our military novices nor our veterans are clever enough to see that in the field, discipline either keeps itself or goes to pieces; for humanity under fire is a quite different thing from humanity in barracks: when there is danger the difficulty is never to find men who will obey, but men who can command. It is in time of peace, when an army is either a police force (in which case its work can be better done by a civilian constabulary) or an absurdity, that discipline is difficult, because the wasted life of the soldier is unnatural, except to a lazy man, and his servitude galling and senseless, except to a docile one. Still, the soldier is a man, and the officer sometimes a gentleman in the literal sense of the word; and so, what with humanity, laziness, and docility combined, they manage to rub along with only occasional outbursts of mutiny on the one side and class rancor and class cowardice on the other.

They are not even discontented; for the military and naval codes simplify life for them just as it is simplified for children. No soldier is asked to think for himself, to judge for himself, to consult his own honor and man-

hood, to dread any consequence except the consequence
of punishment to his own person. The rules are plain
and simple; the ceremonies of respect and submission
are as easy and mechanical as a prayer wheel; the orders
are always to be obeyed thoughtlessly, however inept or
dishonorable they may be. As the late Laureate said
in the two stinging lines in which he branded the British
soldier with the dishonor of Esau, " theirs not to reason
why: theirs but to do and die." To the moral imbecile
and political sluggard these conditions are as congenial
and attractive as they are abhorrent and intolerable to
the William Tell temperament. Just as the most incorrigible criminal is always, we are told, the best behaved
convict, so the man with least conscience and initiative
makes the best behaved soldier, and that not wholly
through mere fear of punishment, but through a genuine
fitness for and consequent happiness in the childlike
military life. Such men dread freedom and responsibility as a weak man dreads a risk or a heavy burden;
and the objection to the military system is that it tends
to produce such men by a weakening disuse of the moral
muscles. No doubt this weakness is just what the military system aims at, its ideal soldier being, not a complete
man, but a docile unit of cannonfodder which can be
trusted to respond promptly and certainly to the external
stimulus of a shouted order, and is intimidated to the
pitch of being afraid to run away from a battle. It
may be doubted whether even in the Prussian heyday
of the system, when floggings of hundreds and even
thousands of lashes were matters of ordinary routine,
this detestable ideal was ever realized; but your courts-
martial are not practical enough to take that into account: it is characteristic of the military mind continually to ignore human nature and cry for the moon
instead of facing modern social facts and accepting
modern democratic conditions. And when I say the
military mind, I repeat that I am not forgetting the

patent fact that the military mind and the humane mind can exist in the same person; so that an officer who will take all the civilian risks, from city traffic to foxhunting, without uneasiness, and who will manage all the civil employees on his estate and in his house and stables without the aid of a Mutiny Act, will also, in his military capacity, frantically declare that he dare not walk about in a foreign country unless every crime of violence against an Englishman in uniform is punished by the bombardment and destruction of a whole village, or the wholesale flogging and execution of every native in the neighborhood, and also that unless he and his fellow officers have power, without the intervention of a jury, to punish the slightest self-assertion or hesitation to obey orders, however grossly insulting or disastrous those orders may be, with sentences which are reserved in civil life for the worst crimes, he cannot secure the obedience and respect of his men, and the country will accordingly lose all its colonies and dependencies, and be helplessly conquered in the German invasion which he confidently expects to occur in the course of a fortnight or so. That is to say, in so far as he is an ordinary gentleman he behaves sensibly and courageously; and in so far as he is a military man he gives way without shame to the grossest folly, cruelty and poltroonery. If any other profession in the world had been stained by these vices, and by false witness, forgery, swindling, torture, compulsion of men's families to attend their executions, digging up and mutilation of dead enemies, all wantonly added to the devastation proper to its own business, as the military profession has been within recent memory in England, France, and the United States of America (to mention no other countries), it would be very difficult to induce men of capacity and character to enter it. And in England it is, in fact, largely dependent for its recruits on the refuse of industrial life, and for its officers on the aristocratic and plutocratic

refuse of political and diplomatic life, who join the
army and pay for their positions in the more or less
fashionable clubs which the regimental messes provide
them with—clubs which, by the way, occasionally figure
in ragging scandals as circles of extremely coarse moral
character.

Now in countries which are denied Home Rule: that
is, in which the government does not rest on the consent
of the people, it must rest on military coercion; and the
bureaucracy, however civil and legal it may be in form
and even in the character of its best officials, must connive at all the atrocities of military rule, and become
infected in the end with the chronic panic characteristic
of militarism. In recent witness whereof, let me shift
the scene from Ireland to Egypt, and tell the story of
the Denshawai affair of June 1906 by way of object
lesson.

THE DENSHAWAI HORROR.

Denshawai is a little Egyptian village in the Nile
delta. Besides the dilapidated huts among the reeds by
the roadside, and the palm trees, there are towers of
unbaked brick, as unaccountable to an English villager
as a Kentish oast-house to an Egyptian. These towers
are pigeon houses; for the villagers keep pigeons just
as an English farmer keeps poultry.

Try to imagine the feelings of an English village if a
party of Chinese officers suddenly appeared and began
shooting the ducks, the geese, the hens and the turkeys,
and carried them off, asserting that they were wild birds,
as everybody in China knew, and that the pretended
indignation of the farmers was a cloak for hatred of
the Chinese, and perhaps for a plot to overthrow the
religion of Confucius and establish the Church of England in its place! Well, that is the British equivalent
of what happened at Denshawai when a party of Eng-

lish officers went pigeon-shooting there the year before
last. The inhabitants complained and memorialized; but
they obtained no redress: the law failed them in their
hour of need. So one leading family of pigeon farmers,
Mahfouz by name, despaired of the law; and its head,
Hassan Mahfouz, aged 60, made up his mind not to
submit tamely to a repetition of the outrage. Also, British officers were ordered not to shoot pigeons in the
villages without the consent of the Omdeh, or head man,
though nothing was settled as to what might happen to
the Omdeh if he ventured to refuse.

Fancy the feelings of Denshawai when on the 13th
of June last there drove to the village four khaki-clad
British officers with guns, one of them being a shooter
of the year before, accompanied by one other officer on
horseback, and also by a dragoman and an Ombashi, or
police official! The oriental blood of Hassan Mahfouz
boiled; and he warned them that they would not be
allowed to shoot pigeons; but as they did not understand
his language, the warning had no effect. They sent
their dragoman to ask the Omdeh's permission to shoot;
but the Omdeh was away; and all the interpreter could
get from the Omdeh's deputy, who knew better than to
dare an absolute refusal, was the pretty obvious reply
that they might shoot if they went far enough away
from the village. On the strength of this welcome, they
went from 100 to 300 yards away from the houses
(these distances were afterwards officially averaged at
500 yards), and began shooting the villagers' pigeons.
The villagers remonstrated and finally seized the gun
of the youngest officer. It went off in the struggle, and
wounded three men and the wife of one Abd-el-Nebi,
a young man of 25. Now the lady, though, as it turned
out, only temporarily disabled by a charge of pigeon
shot in the softest part of her person, gave herself up
for dead; and the feeling in the village was much as if
our imaginary Chinese officers, on being interfered with

in their slaughter of turkeys, had killed an English farmer's wife. Abd-el-Nebi, her husband, took the matter to heart, not altogether without reason, we may admit. His threshing floor also caught fire somehow (the official English theory is that he set it on fire as a signal for revolt to the entire Moslem world); and all the lads and loafers in the place were presently on the spot. The other officers, seeing their friend in trouble, joined him. Abd-el-Nebi hit the supposed murderer of his wife with a stick; Hassan Mahfouz used a stick also; and the lads and loafers began to throw stones and bricks. Five London policemen would have seen that there was nothing to be done but fight their way out, as there is no use arguing with an irritated mob, especially if you do not know its language. Had the shooting party been in the charge of a capable non-commissioned officer, he would perhaps have got it safely off. As it was, the officers tried propitiation, making their overtures in pantomime. They gave up their guns; they offered watches and money to the crowd, crying Baksheesh; and the senior officer actually collared the junior and pretended to arrest him for the murder of the woman. Naturally they were mobbed worse than before; and what they did not give to the crowd was taken from them, whether as payment for the pigeons, blood money, or simple plunder was not gone into. The officers, two Irishmen and three Englishmen, having made a hopeless mess of it, and being now in serious danger, made for their carriages, but were dragged out of them again, one of the coachmen being knocked senseless. They then " agreed to run," the arrangement being that the Englishmen, being the juniors, should run away to camp and bring help to the Irishmen. They bolted accordingly; but the third, the youngest, seeing the two Irishmen hard put to it, went back and stood by them. Of the two fugitives, one, after a long race in the Egyptian afternoon sun, got to the next village and there dropped, smitten by sunstroke, of which he died. The other ran on and met a patrol, which started to the rescue.

Meanwhile, the other three officers had been taken out of the hands of the lads and the loafers, of Abd-el-Nebi and Hassan Mahfouz, by the elders and watchmen, and saved from further injury, but not before they had been severely knocked about, one of them having one of the bones of his left arm broken near the wrist—simple fracture of the thin end of the ulna. They were also brought to the threshing floor; shewn the wounded woman; informed by gestures that they deserved to have their throats cut for murdering her; and kicked (with naked feet, fortunately); but at this point the elders and constables stopped the mobbing. Finally the three were sent off to camp in their carriages; and the incident ended for that day.

No English mob, under similar provocation, would have behaved any better; and few would have done as little mischief. It is not many months since an old man —not a foreigner and not an unbeliever—was kicked to death in the streets of London because the action of a park constable in turning him out of a public park exposed him to suspicion of misconduct. At Denshawai, the officers were not on duty. In their private capacity as sportsmen, they committed a serious depredation on a very poor village by slaughtering its stock. In an English village they would have been tolerated because the farmers would have expected compensation for damage, and the villagers coals and blankets and employment in country house, garden and stable, or as beaters, huntsmen and the like, from them. But Denshawai had no such inducements to submit to their thoughtless and selfish aggression. One of them had apparently killed a woman and wounded three men with his gun: in fact his own comrade virtually convicted him of it before the crowd by collaring him as a prisoner. In short, the officers had given outrageous provocation; and they had shown an amiable but disastrous want of determination and judgment in dealing with the riot they provoked. They should have been severely reprimanded and informed that they had themselves to thank for what happened to them; and the villagers who assaulted them should have been treated with leniency, and assured that pigeon-shooting would not be allowed in future.

That is what should have ensued. Now for what actually did ensue.

Abd-el-Nebi, in consideration of the injury to his wife, was only sentenced to penal servitude for life. And our clemency did not stop there. His wife was not punished at all—not even charged with stealing the shot which was found in her person. And lest Abd-el-Nebi should feel lonely at 25 in beginning penal servitude for the rest of his days, another young man, of 20, was sent to penal servitude for life with him.

No such sentimentality was shewn to Hassan Mahfouz. An Egyptian pigeon farmer who objects to British sport; threatens British officers and gentlemen when they shoot his pigeons; and actually hits those officers with a substantial stick, is clearly a ruffian to be made an example of. Penal servitude was not enough for a man of 60 who looked 70, and might not have lived to suffer five years of it. So Hassan was hanged; but as a special mark of consideration for his family, he was hanged in full view of his own house, with his wives and children and grandchildren enjoying the spectacle from the roof. And lest this privilege should excite jealousy in other households, three other Denshavians were hanged with him. They went through the ceremony with dignity, professing their faith ("Mahometan, I regret to say," Mr. Pecksniff would have said). Hassan, however, "in a loud voice invoked ruin upon the houses of those who had given evidence against him"; and Darweesh was impatient and presumed to tell the hangman to be quick. But then Darweesh was a bit of a brigand: he had been imprisoned for bearing false witness; and his resistance to the British invasion is the only officially recorded incident of his life which is entirely to his credit. He and Abd-el-Nebi (who had been imprisoned for theft) were the only disreputable characters among the punished. Ages of the four hanged men respectively, 60, 50, 22 and 20.

Hanging, however, is the least sensational form of public execution: it lacks those elements of blood and torture for which the military and bureaucratic imagination lusts. So, as they had room for only one man on the gallows, and had to leave him hanging half an hour to make sure work and give his family plenty of time to watch him swinging ("slowly turning round and round on himself," as the local papers described it), thus having two hours to kill as well as four men, they kept the entertainment going by flogging eight men with fifty lashes each: eleven more than the utmost permitted by the law of Moses in times which our Army of Occupation no doubt considers barbarous. But then Moses conceived his law as being what he called the law of God, and not simply an instrument for the gratification of his own cruelty and terror. It is unspeakably reassuring to learn from the British official reports laid before parliament that "due dignity was observed in carrying out the executions," that "all possible humanity was shown in carrying them out," and that "the arrangements were admirable, and reflect great credit on all concerned." As this last testimonial apparently does not refer to the victims, they are evidently officially considered not to have been concerned in the proceedings at all. Finally, Lord Cromer certifies that the Englishman in charge of the proceedings is "a singularly humane man, and is very popular amongst the natives of Egypt by reason of the great sympathy he has always shown for them." It will be seen that Parliamentary Papers, Nos. 3 and 4, Egypt, 1906, are not lacking in unconscious humor. The official walrus pledges himself in every case for the kindliness of the official carpenter.

One man was actually let off, to the great danger of the British Empire perhaps. Still, as he was an epileptic, and had already had several fits in the court of Judge Lynch, the doctor said Better not; and he escaped. This was very inconvenient; for the number of floggees had been made up solely to fill the time occupied by the hangings at the rate of two floggings per hanging; and the breakdown of the arrangement through Said Suleiman Kheirallah's inconsiderate indisposition made the execution of Darweesh tedious, as he was hanging for fully quarter of an hour without any flogging to amuse his fellow villagers and the officers and men of the Inniskilling Dragoons, the military mounted police, and the mounted infantry. A few spare sentences of flogging should have been kept in hand to provide against accidents.

In any case there was not time to flog everybody, nor to flog three of the floggees enough; so these three had a year's hard labor apiece in addition to their floggings. Six others were not flogged at all, but were sent to penal servitude for seven years each. One man got fifteen years. Total for the morning's work: four hanged, two to penal servitude for life, one to fifteen years penal servitude, six to seven years penal servitude, three to imprisonment for a year with hard labor and fifty lashes, and five to fifty lashes.

Lord Cromer certifies that these proceedings were "just and necessary." He also gives his reasons. It appears that the boasted justice introduced into Egypt by the English in 1882 was imaginary, and that the real work of coping with Egyptian disorder was done by Brigandage Commissions, composed of Egyptians. These Commissions, when an offence was reported, descended on the inculpated village; seized everybody concerned; and plied them with tortures, mentionable and unmentionable, until they accused everybody they were expected to accuse. The accused were in turn tortured until they confessed anything and everything they were accused of. They were then killed, flogged, or sent to penal servitude. This was the reality behind the illusion that soothed us after bombarding Alexandria. The bloodless, white-gloved native courts set up to flatter our sense of imperial justice had, apparently, about as much to do with the actual government of the fellaheen as the annual court which awards the Dunmow flitch of bacon has to do with our divorce court. Eventually a Belgian judge, who was appointed Procureur-Général, exposed the true state of affairs.

Then the situation had to be faced. Order had to be maintained somehow; but the regular native courts which saved the face of the British Occupation were useless for the purpose; and the Brigandage Commissions were so abominable and demoralizing that they made more mischief than they prevented. Besides, there was Mr. Wilfrid Scawen Blunt on the warpath against tyranny and torture, threatening to get questions asked in parliament. A new sort of tribunal in the nature of a court-martial had therefore to be invented to replace the Brigandage Commissions; but simple British military courts-martial, though probably the best available form of official Lynch Law, were made impossible by the jealousy of the " loyal " (to England) Egyptians, who, it seems, rule the Occupation and bully England exactly as the " loyal " Irish rule the Garrison and bully the Unionists nearer home. That kind of loyalty, not being a natural product, has to be purchased; and the price is an official job of some sort with a position and a salary attached. Hence we got, in 1895, a tribunal constituted in which three English officials sat with two Egyptian officials, exercising practically unlimited powers of punishment without a jury and without appeal. They represent the best of our judicial and mili-

tary officialism. And what that best is may be judged
by the sentences on the Denshawai villagers.

Lord Cromer's justification of the tribunal is practically that, bad as it is, the Brigandage Commissions
were worse. Also (lest we should propose to carry our
moral superiority any further), that the Egyptians are
so accustomed to associate law and order with floggings,
executions, torture and Lynch Law, that they will not
respect any tribunal which does not continue these prac-
tices. This is a far-reaching argument: for instance, it
suggests that Church of England missionaries might do
well to adopt the rite of human sacrifice when evangeliz-
ing tribes in whose imagination that practice is insep-
arably bound up with religion. It suggests that the
sole reason why the Denshawai tribunal did not resort
to torture for the purpose of extorting confessions and
evidence was that parliament might not stand it—though
really a parliament which stood the executions would,
one would think, stand anything. The tribunal had certainly no intention of allowing witnesses to testify
against British officers; for, as it happened, the Ombashi
who accompanied them on the two shooting expeditions,
one Ahmed Hassan Zakzouk, aged 26, was rash enough
to insist that after the shot that struck the woman, the
officers fired on the mob twice. This appears in the
parliamentary paper; but the French newspaper
L'Egypte is quoted by Mr. Wilfrid Scawen Blunt as
reporting that Zakzouk, on being asked by one of the
English judges whether he was not afraid to say such
a thing, replied " Nobody in the world is able to frighten
me: the truth is the truth," and was promptly told to
stand down. Mr. Blunt adds that Zakzouk was then
tried for his conduct in connection with the affair before
a Court of Discipline, which awarded him two years
imprisonment and fifty lashes. Without rudely calling
this a use of torture to intimidate anti-British witnesses,
I may count on the assent of most reasonable people

when I say that Zakzouk probably regards himself as having received a rather strong hint to make his evidence agreeable to the Occupation in future.

Not only was there of course no jury at the trial, but considerably less than no defence. Barristers of sufficient standing to make it very undesirable for them to offend the Occupation were instructed to " defend " the prisoners. Far from defending them, they paid high compliments to the Occupation as one of the choicest benefits rained by Heaven on their country, and appealed for mercy for their miserable clients, whose conduct had " caused the unanimous indignation of all Egyptians." " Clemency," they said, " was above equity." The tribunal in delivering judgment remarked that " the counsel for the defence had a full hearing: nevertheless the defence broke down completely, and all that their counsel could say on behalf of the prisoners practically amounted to an appeal to the mercy of the Court."

Now the proper defence, if put forward, would probably have convinced Lord Cromer that nothing but the burning of the village and the crucifixion of all its inhabitants could preserve the British Empire. That defence was obvious enough: the village was invaded by five armed foreigners who attempted for the second time to slaughter the villagers' farming stock and carry it off; in resisting an attempt to disarm them four villagers had been wounded; the villagers had lost their tempers and knocked the invaders about; and the older men and watchmen had finally rescued the aggressors and sent them back with no worse handling than they would have got anywhere for the like misconduct.

One can imagine what would have happened to the man, prisoner or advocate, who should have dared to tell the truth in this fashion. The prisoners knew better than to attempt it. On the scaffold, Darweesh turned to his house as he stood on the trap, and exclaimed " May God compensate us well for this world of meanness, for

this world of injustice, for this world of cruelty." If
he had dared in court thus to compare God with the
tribunal to the disadvantage of the latter, he would no
doubt have had fifty lashes before his hanging, to teach
him the greatness of the Empire. As it was, he kept
his views to himself until it was too late to do anything
worse to him than hang him. In court, he did as all
the rest did. They lied; they denied; they set up desperate alibis; they protested they had been in the next
village, or tending cattle a mile off, or threshing, or
what not. One of them, when identified, said " All men
are alike." He had only one eye. Darweesh, who had
secured one of the officers' guns, declared that his enemies had come in the night and buried it in his house,
where his mother sat on it, like Rachel on Laban's stolen
teraphim, until she was dragged off. A pitiable business,
yet not so pitiable as the virtuous indignation with which
Judge Lynch, himself provable by his own reports to
be a prevaricator, hypocrite, tyrant and coward of the
first water, preened himself at its expense. When Lord
Cromer says that " the prisoners had a perfectly fair
trial "—not, observe, a trial as little unfair as human
frailty could make it, which is the most that can be said
for any trial on earth, but " a *perfectly* fair trial "—he
no doubt believes what he says; but his opinion is interesting mainly as an example of the state of his mind,
and of the extent to which, after thirty years of official
life in Egypt, one loses the plain sense of English words.

Lord Cromer recalls how, in the eighties, a man threatened with the courbash by a Moudir in the presence of
Sir Claude MacDonald, said " You dare not flog me
now that the British are here." " So bold an answer,"
says Lord Cromer, " was probably due to the presence
of a British officer." What would that man say now?
What does Lord Cromer say now? He deprecates
" premature endeavors to thrust Western ideas on an
Eastern people," by which he means that when you are

in Egypt you must do as the Egyptians do: terrorize by the lash and the scaffold. Thus does the East conquer its conquerors. In 1883 Lord Dufferin was abolishing the bastinado as " a horrible and infamous punishment." In 1906 Lord Cromer guarantees ferocious sentences of flogging as " just and necessary," and can see " nothing reprehensible in the manner in which they were carried out." " I have," he adds, " passed nearly thirty years of my life in an earnest endeavour to raise the moral and material condition of the people of Egypt. I have been assisted by a number of very capable officials, all of whom, I may say, have been animated by the same spirit as myself." Egypt may well shudder as she reads those words. If the first thirty years have been crowned by the Denshawai incident, what will Egypt be like at the end of another thirty years of moral elevation " animated by the same spirit "?

It is pleasanter to return to Lord Cromer's first letter on Denshawai, written to Sir Edward Grey the day after the shooting party. It says that " orders will shortly be issued by the General prohibiting officers in the army from shooting pigeons in the future under any circumstances whatever." But pray why this prohibition, if, as the tribunal declared, the officers were " guests (actually *guests!*) who had done nothing to deserve blame "?

Mr. Findlay is another interesting official correspondent of Sir Edward. Even after the trial, at which it had been impossible to push the medical evidence further than to say that the officer who died of sunstroke had been predisposed to it by the knocking about he had suffered and by his flight under the Egyptian sun, whilst the officers who had remained defenceless in the hands of the villagers were in court, alive and well, Mr. Findlay writes that the four hanged men were " convicted of a brutal and premeditated murder," and complains that " the native press disregards the fact" and " is being conducted with such an absolute disregard for truth as to make it evident that large sums of money have been expended." Mr. Findlay is also a bit of a philosopher. " The Egyptian, being a fatalist," he says, " does not greatly fear death, and there is therefore much to be said for flogging as a judicial punishment in Egypt." Logically, then, the four hanged men ought to have been flogged instead. But Mr. Findlay does not draw that conclusion. Logic is not his strong point: he is a man of feeling, and a very nervous one at that. " I do not believe that this brutal attack on British officers had anything directly to do with political animosity. It is, however, due to the insubordinate spirit which has been sedulously fostered during the last year by unscrupulous and interested agitators." Again, " it is my duty to warn you of the deplorable effect which is being produced in Egypt by the fact that Members of Parliament have seriously called in question the unanimous sentence passed by a legally constituted Court, of which the best English and the best native Judge were members. This fact will, moreover, supply the lever which has, up to the present, been lacking to the venal agitators who are at the head of the so-called patriotic party." I find Mr. Findlay irresistible, so exquisitely does he give us the measure and flavor of officialism. " A few days after the Denshawai affray some natives stoned and severely injured an irrigation inspector. Two days ago three natives knocked a soldier off his donkey and kicked him in the stomach: his injuries are serious. In the latter case theft appears to have been the motive. My object in mentioning these instances is to shew the results to be expected if once respect for the law is shaken. Should the present state of things continue, and, still more, should the agitation in this country find support at home, the date is not far distant when the necessity will arise for bringing in a press law and for considerably increasing the army of occupation." Just think of it! In a population of nearly ten millions, one irrigation inspector is stoned. The Denshawai executions are then carried out to make the law respected. The result is that three natives knock a soldier off his donkey and rob him. Thereupon Mr. Findlay, appalled at the bankruptcy of civilization, sees nothing for it now but suppression of the native newspapers and a considerable increase in the army of occupation! And Lord Cromer writes " All I need say is that I concur generally in Mr. Findlay's remarks, and that, had I remained in Egypt, I should in every respect have adopted the same course as that which he pursued."

But I must resolutely shut this rich parliamentary paper. I have extracted enough to paint the picture, and enforce my warning to England that if her Empire means ruling the world as Denshawai has been ruled in 1906—and that, I am afraid, is what the Empire does mean to the main body of our aristocratic-military caste and to our Jingo plutocrats—then there can be no more sacred and urgent political duty on earth than the disruption, defeat, and suppression of the Empire, and, incidentally, the humanization of its supporters by the sternest lessons of that adversity which comes finally to institutions which make themselves abhorred by the aspiring will of humanity towards divinity. As for the Egyptians, any man cradled by the Nile who, after the Denshawai incident, will ever voluntarily submit to British rule, or accept any bond with us except the bond of a Federation of free and equal states, will deserve the worst that Lord Cromer can consider " just and necessary " for him. That is what you get by attempting to prove your supremacy by the excesses of frightened soldiers and denaturalized officials instead of by courageous helpfulness and moral superiority.

In any case let no Englishman who is content to leave Abd-el-Nebi and his twenty-year-old neighbor in penal servitude for life, and to plume himself on the power to do it, pretend to be fit to govern either my country or his own. The responsibility cannot be confined to the tribunal and to the demoralized officials of the Occupation. The House of Commons had twenty-four hours clear notice, with the telegraph under the hand of Sir Edward Grey, to enable it to declare that England was a civilized Power and would not stand these barbarous lashings and vindictive hangings. Yet Mr. Dillon, representing the Irish party, which well knows what British Occupations and Findlay "loyalism" mean, protested in vain. Sir Edward, on behalf of the new Liberal Government (still simmering with virtuous indignation at the flogging of Chinamen and the military executions in South Africa in the forced presence of the victims' families under the late Imperialist Government) not only permitted and defended the Denshawai executions, but appealed to the House almost passionately not to criticize or repudiate them, on the ground—how incredible it now appears!—that Abd-el-Nebi and Hassan Mahfouz and Darweesh and the rest were the fuglemen of a gigantic Moslem plot to rise against Christendom in the name of the Prophet and sweep Christendom out of Africa and Asia by a colossal second edition of the Indian Mutiny. That this idiotic romance, gross and ridiculous as the lies of Falstaff, should have imposed on any intelligent and politically experienced human being, is strange enough—though the secret shame of revolted humanity will make cabinet ministers snatch at fantastic excuses—but what humanity will not forgive our foreign secretary for is his failure to see that even if such a conspiracy really existed, England should have faced it and fought it bravely by honorable means, instead of wildly lashing and strangling a handful of poor peasants to scare Islam into terrified submission. Were I abject enough to grant to Sir Edward Grey as valid that main asset of "thinking Imperially," the conviction that we are all going to be murdered, I should still suggest to him that we can at least die like gentlemen?

Might I even be so personal as to say that the reason for giving him a social position and political opportunities that are denied to his tradesmen is that he is supposed to understand better than they that honor is worth its danger and its cost, and that life is worthless without honor? It is true that Sir John Falstaff did not think so; but Sir John is hardly a model for Sir Edward. Yet even Sir John would have had enough gumption to see that the Denshawai panic was more dangerous to the Empire than the loss of ten pitched battles.

As cowardice is highly infectious, would it not be desirable to supersede officials who, after years of oriental service, have lost the familiar art of concealing their terrors? I am myself a sedentary literary civilian, constitutionally timid; but I find it possible to keep up appearances, and can even face the risk of being run over, or garotted, or burnt out in London without shrieking for martial law, suppression of the newspapers, exemplary flogging and hanging of motor-bus drivers, and compulsory police service. Why are soldiers and officials on foreign service so much more cowardly than citizens? Is it not clearly because the whole Imperial military system of coercion and terrorism is unnatural, and that the truth formulated by William Morris, that "no man is good enough to be another man's master" is true also of nations, and very specially true of those plutocrat-ridden Powers which have of late stumbled into an enormous increase of material wealth without having made any intelligent provision for its proper distribution and administration?

However, the economic reform of the Empire is a long business, whereas the release of Abd-el-Nebi and his neighbors is a matter of the stroke of a pen, once public opinion is shamed into activity. I fear I have stated their case very unfairly and inadequately, because I am hampered, as an Irishman, by my implacable hostility to English domination. Mistrusting my own prejudices, I have taken the story from the two parliamentary papers in which our officials have done their utmost to whitewash the tribunals and the pigeon-shooting party, and to blackwash the villagers. Those who wish to have it told to them by an Englishman of unquestionable personal and social credentials, and an intimate knowledge of Egypt and the Egyptians, can find it in Mr. Wilfrid Scawen Blunt's pamphlet entitled "Atrocities of British Rule in Egypt." When they have read it they will appreciate my forbearance; and when I add that English rule in Ireland has been "animated by the same spirit" (I thank Lord Cromer for the phrase) as English rule in Egypt, and that this is the inevitable spirit of all coercive military rule, they will perhaps begin to understand why Home Rule is a necessity not only for Ireland, but for all constituents of those Federations of Commonwealths which are now the only permanently practicable form of Empire.

JOHN BULL'S OTHER ISLAND

JOHN BULL'S OTHER ISLAND

ACT I

Great George Street, Westminster, is the address of Doyle and Broadbent, civil engineers. On the threshold one reads that the firm consists of Mr. Laurence Doyle and Mr. Thomas Broadbent, and that their rooms are on the first floor. Most of these rooms are private; for the partners, being bachelors and bosom friends, live there; and the door marked Private, next the clerks' office, is their domestic sitting room as well as their reception room for clients. Let me describe it briefly from the point of view of a sparrow on the window sill. The outer door is in the opposite wall, close to the right hand corner. Between this door and the left hand corner is a hatstand and a table consisting of large drawing boards on trestles, with plans, rolls of tracing paper, mathematical instruments and other draughtsman's accessories on it. In the left hand wall is the fireplace, and the door of an inner room between the fireplace and our observant sparrow. Against the right hand wall is a filing cabinet, with a cupboard on it, and, nearer, a tall office desk and stool for one person. In the middle of the room a large double writing table is set across, with a chair at each end for the two partners. It is a room which no woman would tolerate, smelling of tobacco, and much in need of repapering, repainting, and recarpeting; but this is the effect of bachelor untidiness and indifference, not want of means; for nothing that Doyle and Broadbent themselves have purchased is

3

*cheap; nor is anything they want lacking.   On the walls
hang a large map of South America, a pictorial advertisement of a steamship company, an impressive portrait
of Gladstone, and several caricatures of Mr. Balfour as
a rabbit and Mr. Chamberlain as a fox by Francis Car-
ruthers Gould.*

*At twenty minutes to five o'clock on a summer after-
noon in 1904, the room is empty.   Presently the outer
door is opened, and a valet comes in laden with a large
Gladstone bag, and a strap of rugs.   He carries them
into the inner room.   He is a respectable valet, old
enough to have lost all alacrity, and acquired an air of
putting up patiently with a great deal of trouble and
indifferent health.   The luggage belongs to Broadbent,
who enters after the valet.   He pulls off his overcoat
and hangs it with his hat on the stand.   Then he comes
to the writing table and looks through the letters which
are waiting for him.   He is a robust, full-blooded, energetic man in the prime of life, sometimes eager and
credulous, sometimes shrewd and roguish, sometimes
portentously solemn, sometimes jolly and impetuous, always buoyant and irresistible, mostly likeable, and enormously absurd in his most earnest moments.   He bursts
open his letters with his thumb, and glances through
them, flinging the envelopes about the floor with reckless untidiness whilst he talks to the valet.*

BROADBENT (*calling*).   Hodson.

HODSON (*in the bedroom*).   Yes sir.

BROADBENT.   Dont unpack.   Just take out the things
Ive worn; and put in clean things.

HODSON (appearing at the bedroom door).   Yes sir.
(*He turns to go back into the bedroom.*)

BROADBENT.   And look here!   (*Hodson turns again.*)
Do you remember where I put my revolver?

HODSON.   Revolver, sir?   Yes sir.   Mr. Doyle uses
it as a paper-weight, sir, when he's drawing.

BROADBENT. Well, I want it packed. Theres a packet of cartridges somewhere, I think. Find it and pack it as well.

HODSON. Yes sir.

BROADBENT. By the way, pack your own traps too. I shall take you with me this time.

HODSON (*hesitant*). Is it a dangerous part youre going to, sir? Should I be expected to carry a revolver, sir?

BROADBENT. Perhaps it might be as well. I'm going to Ireland.

HODSON (*reassured*). Yes sir.

BROADBENT. You dont feel nervous about it, I suppose?

HODSON. Not at all, sir. I'll risk it, sir.

BROADBENT. Have you ever been in Ireland?

HODSON. No sir. I understand it's a very wet climate, sir. I'd better pack your india-rubber overalls.

BROADBENT. Do. Wheres Mr. Doyle?

HODSON. I'm expecting him at five, sir. He went out after lunch.

BROADBENT. Anybody been looking for me?

HODSON. A person giving the name of Haffigan has called twice to-day, sir.

BROADBENT. Oh, I'm sorry. Why didnt he wait? I told him to wait if I wasnt in.

HODSON. Well sir, I didnt know you expected him; so I thought it best to—to—not to encourage him, sir.

BROADBENT. Oh, hes all right. Hes an Irishman, and not very particular about his appearance.

HODSON. Yes sir, I noticed that he was rather Irish.

BROADBENT. If he calls again let him come up.

HODSON. I think I saw him waiting about, sir, when you drove up. Shall I fetch him, sir?

BROADBENT. Do, Hodson.

HODSON. Yes sir. (*He makes for the outer door.*)

BROADBENT. He'll want tea. Let us have some.

HODSON (*stopping*). I shouldn't think he drank tea, sir.

BROADBENT. Well, bring whatever you think he'd like.

HODSON. Yes sir. (*An electric bell rings.*) Here he is, sir. Saw you arrive, sir.

BROADBENT. Right. Shew him in. (*Hodson goes out. Broadbent gets through the rest of his letters before Hodson returns with the visitor.*)

HODSON. Mr. Affigan.

Haffigan is a stunted, shortnecked, smallheaded, red-haired man of about 30, with reddened nose and furtive eyes. He is dressed in seedy black, almost clerically, and might be a tenth-rate schoolmaster ruined by drink. He hastens to shake Broadbent's hand with a show of reckless geniality and high spirits, helped out by a rollicking stage brogue. This is perhaps a comfort to himself, as he is secretly pursued by the horrors of incipient delirium tremens.

HAFFIGAN. Tim Haffigan, sir, at your service. The top o the mornin to you, Misther Broadbent.

BROADBENT (*delighted with his Irish visitor*). Good afternoon, Mr. Haffigan.

TIM. An is it the afthernoon it is already? Begorra, what I call the mornin is all the time a man fasts afther breakfast.

BROADBENT. Havnt you lunched?

TIM. Divil a lunch!

BROADBENT. I'm sorry I couldnt get back from Brighton in time to offer you some; but—

TIM. Not a word, sir, not a word. Sure itll do tomorrow. Besides, I'm Irish, sir: a poor ather, but a powerful dhrinker.

BROADBENT. I was just about to ring for tea when you came. Sit down, Mr. Haffigan.

TIM. Tay is a good dhrink if your nerves can stand it. Mine cant.

Haffigan sits down at the writing table, with his back to the filing cabinet. Broadbent sits opposite him. Hodson enters emptyhanded; takes two glasses, a siphon, and a tantalus from the cupboard; places them before Broadbent on the writing table; looks ruthlessly at Haffigan, who cannot meet his eye; and retires.

BROADBENT. Try a whisky and soda.

TIM (*sobered*). There you touch the national wakeness, sir. (*Piously.*) Not that I share it meself. Ive seen too much of the mischief of it.

BROADBENT (*pouring the whisky*). Say when.

TIM. Not too sthrong. (*Broadbent stops and looks enquiringly at him.*) Say half-an-half. (*Broadbent, somewhat startled by this demand, pours a little more, and again stops and looks.*) Just a dhrain more: the lower half o the tumbler doesnt hold a fair half. Thankya.

BROADBENT (*laughing*). You Irishmen certainly do know how to drink. (*Pouring some whisky for himself.*) Now thats my poor English idea of a whisky and soda.

TIM. An a very good idea it is too. Dhrink is the curse o me unhappy counthry. I take it meself because Ive a wake heart and a poor digestion; but in principle I'm a teetoatler.

BROADBENT (*suddenly solemn and strenuous*). So am I, of course. I'm a Local Optionist to the backbone. You have no idea, Mr. Haffigan, of the ruin that is wrought in this country by the unholy alliance of the publicans, the bishops, the Tories, and The Times. We must close the public-houses at all costs (*he drinks*).

TIM. Sure I know. Its awful (*he drinks*). I see youre a good Liberal like meself, sir.

BROADBENT. I am a lover of liberty, like every true Englishman, Mr. Haffigan. My name is Broadbent. If my name were Breitstein, and I had a hooked nose and a house in Park Lane, I should carry a Union Jack handkerchief and a penny trumpet, and tax the food of the people to support the Navy League, and clamor for the destruction of the last remnants of national liberty—

TIM. Not another word. Shake hands.

BROADBENT. But I should like to explain—

TIM. Sure I know every word youre goin to say before yev said it. *I* know the sort o man yar. An so youre thinkin o comin to Ireland for a bit?

BROADBENT. Where else can I go? I am an Englishman and a Liberal; and now that South Africa has been enslaved and destroyed, there is no country left to me to take an interest in but Ireland. Mind: I dont say that an Englishman has not other duties. He has a duty to Finland and a duty to Macedonia. But what sane man can deny that an Englishman's first duty is his duty to Ireland? Unfortunately, we have politicians here more unscrupulous than Bobrikoff, more bloodthirsty than Abdul the Damned; and it is under their heel that Ireland is now writhing.

TIM. Faith, theyve reckoned up with poor oul Bobrikoff anyhow.

BROADBENT. Not that I defend assassination: God forbid! However strongly we may feel that the unfortunate and patriotic young man who avenged the wrongs of Finland on the Russian tyrant was perfectly right from his own point of view, yet every civilized man must regard murder with abhorrence. Not even in defence of Free Trade would I lift my hand against a political opponent, however richly he might deserve it.

TIM. Im sure you wouldnt; and I honor you for it. Youre goin to Ireland, then, out o sympithy: is it?

BROADBENT. I'm going to develop an estate there for the Land Development Syndicate, in which I am interested. I am convinced that all it needs to make it pay is to handle it properly, as estates are handled in England. You know the English plan, Mr. Haffigan, dont you?

Tim. Bedad I do, sir. Take all you can out of Ireland and spend it in England: thats it.

Broadbent (*not quite liking this*). My plan, sir, will be to take a little money out of England and spend it in Ireland.

Tim. More power to your elbow! an may your shadda never be less! for youre the broth of a boy intirely. An how can I help you? Command me to the last dhrop o me blood.

Broadbent. Have you ever heard of Garden City?

Tim (*doubtfully*). D'ye mane Heavn?

Broadbent. Heaven! No: it's near Hitchin. If you can spare half an hour I'll go into it with you.

Tim. I tell you hwat. Gimme a prospectus. Lemme take it home and reflect on it.

Broadbent. Youre quite right: I will. (*He gives him a copy of Mr. Ebenezer Howard's book, and several pamphlets.*) You understand that the map of the city —the circular construction—is only a suggestion.

Tim. I'll make a careful note o that (*looking dazedly at the map*).

Broadbent. What I say is, why not start a Garden City in Ireland?

Tim (*with enthusiasm*). Thats just what was on the tip o me tongue to ask you. Why not? (*Defiantly.*) Tell me why not.

Broadbent. There are difficulties. I shall overcome them; but there are difficulties. When I first arrive in Ireland I shall be hated as an Englishman. As a Protestant, I shall be denounced from every altar. My life may be in danger. Well, I am prepared to face that.

Tim. Never fear, sir. We know how to respict a brave innimy.

Broadbent. What I really dread is misunderstanding. I think you could help me to avoid that. When I heard you speak the other evening in Bermondsey at the meeting of the National League, I saw at once that you were—You wont mind my speaking frankly?

TIM. Tell me all me faults as man to man. I can stand anything but flatthery.

BROADBENT. May I put it in this way?—that I saw at once that you were a thorough Irishman, with all the faults and all the qualities of your race: rash and improvident but brave and goodnatured; not likely to succeed in business on your own account perhaps, but eloquent, humorous, a lover of freedom, and a true follower of that great Englishman Gladstone.

TIM. Spare me blushes. I mustnt sit here to be praised to me face. But I confess to the goodnature: its an Irish wakeness. I'd share me last shillin with a friend.

BROADBENT. I feel sure you would, Mr. Haffigan.

TIM (*impulsively*). Damn it! call me Tim. A man that talks about Ireland as you do may call me anything. Gimme a howlt o that whisky bottle (*he replenishes*).

BROADBENT (*smiling indulgently*). Well, Tim, will you come with me and help to break the ice between me and your warmhearted, impulsive countrymen?

TIM. Will I come to Madagascar or Cochin China wid you? Bedad I'll come to the North Pole wid you if yll pay me fare; for the divil a shillin I have to buy a third class ticket.

BROADBENT. Ive not forgotten that, Tim. We must put that little matter on a solid English footing, though the rest can be as Irish as you please. You must come as my—my—well, I hardly know what to call it. If we call you my agent, theyll shoot you. If we call you a bailiff, theyll duck you in the horsepond. I have a secretary already; and—

TIM. Then we'll call him the Home Secretary and me the Irish Secretary. Eh?

BROADBENT (*laughing industriously*). Capital. Your

Irish wit has settled the first difficulty. Now about your salary—

TIM. A salary, is it? Sure I'd do it for nothin, only me cloes ud disgrace you; and I'd be dhriven to borra money from your friends: a thing thats agin me nacher. But I wont take a penny more than a hundherd a year. (*He looks with restless cunning at Broadbent, trying to guess how far he may go.*)

BROADBENT. If that will satisfy you—

TIM (*more than reassured*). Why shouldnt it satisfy me? A hundherd a year is twelve-pound a month, isnt it?

BROADBENT. No. Eight pound six and eightpence.

TIM. Oh murdher! An I'll have to sind five timme poor oul mother in Ireland. But no matther: I said a hundherd; and what I said I'll stick to, if I have to starve for it.

BROADBENT (*with business caution*). Well, let us say twelve pounds for the first month. Afterwards, we shall see how we get on.

TIM. Youre a gentleman, sir. Whin me mother turns up her toes, you shall take the five pounds off; for your expinses must be kep down wid a sthrong hand; an— (*He is interrupted by the arrival of Broadbent's partner.*)

Mr. Laurence Doyle is a man of 36, with cold grey eyes, strained nose, fine fastidious lips, critical brows, clever head, rather refined and goodlooking on the whole, but with a suggestion of thinskinnedness and dissatisfaction that contrasts strongly with Broadbent's eupeptic jollity.

He comes in as a man at home there, but on seeing the stranger shrinks at once, and is about to withdraw when Broadbent reassures him. He then comes forward to the table, between the two others.

DOYLE (*retreating*). Youre engaged.

BROADBENT. Not at all, not at all. Come in. (*To

Tim.) This gentleman is a friend who lives with me here: my partner, Mr. Doyle. (*To Doyle.*) This is a new Irish friend of mine, Mr. Tim Haffigan.

TIM (*rising with effusion*). Sure its meself thats proud to meet any friend o Misther Broadbent's. The top o the mornin to you, sir! Me heart goes out teeye both. Its not often I meet two such splendid speciments iv the Anglo-Saxon race.

BROADBENT (*chuckling*). Wrong for once, Tim. My friend Mr. Doyle is a countryman of yours.

Tim is noticeably dashed by this announcement. He draws in his horns at once, and scowls suspiciously at Doyle under a vanishing mask of goodfellowship: cringing a little, too, in mere nerveless fear of him.

DOYLE (*with cool disgust*). Good evening. (*He retires to the fireplace, and says to Broadbent in a tone which conveys the strongest possible hint to Haffigan that he is unwelcome*) Will you soon be disengaged?

TIM (*his brogue decaying into a common would-be genteel accent with an unexpected strain of Glasgow in it*). I must be going. Ivnmportnt engeegement in the west end.

BROADBENT (*rising*). It's settled, then, that you come with me.

TIM. Ishll be verra pleased to accompany ye, sir.

BROADBENT. But how soon? Can you start tonight —from Paddington? We go by Milford Haven.

TIM (*hesitating*). Well — I'm afreed — I (*Doyle goes abruptly into the bedroom, slamming the door and shattering the last remnant of Tim's nerve. The poor wretch saves himself from bursting into tears by plunging again into his role of daredevil Irishman. He rushes to Broadbent; plucks at his sleeve with trembling fingers; and pours forth his entreaty with all the brogue he can muster, subduing his voice lest Doyle should hear and return.*) Misther Broadbent: dont humiliate me before a fella counthryman. Look here: me cloes is up the spout. Gimme a fypounnote—I'll pay ya nex Choosda whin me ship comes home—or you can stop it out o me month's sallery. I'll be on the platform at Paddnton punctial an ready. Gimme it quick, before he comes back. You wont mind me axin, will ye?

BROADBENT. Not at all. I was about to offer you an advance for travelling expenses. (*He gives him a bank note.*)

TIM (*pocketing it*). Thank you. I'll be there half an hour before the thrain starts. (*Larry is heard at the bedroom door, returning.*) Whisht: hes comin back. Goodbye an God bless ye. (*He hurries out almost crying, the £5 note and all the drink it means to him being too much for his empty stomach and overstrained nerves.*)

DOYLE (*returning*). Where the devil did you pick up that seedy swindler? What was he doing here? (*He goes up to the table where the plans are, and makes a note on one of them, referring to his pocket book as he does so.*)

BROADBENT. There you go! Why are you so down on every Irishman you meet, especially if hes a bit shabby? poor devil! Surely a fellow-countryman may pass you the top of the morning without offence, even if his coat is a bit shiny at the seams.

DOYLE (*contemptuously*). The top of the morning! Did he call you the broth of a boy? (*He comes to the writing table.*)

BROADBENT (*triumphantly*). Yes.

DOYLE. And wished you more power to your elbow?

BROADBENT. He did.

DOYLE. And that your shadow might never be less?

BROADBENT. Certainly.

DOYLE (*taking up the depleted whisky bottle and shaking his head at it*). And he got about half a pint of whisky out of you.

BROADBENT. It did him no harm. He never turned a hair.

DOYLE. How much money did he borrow?

BROADBENT. It was not borrowing exactly. He shewed a very honorable spirit about money. I believe he would share his last shilling with a friend.

DOYLE. No doubt he would share his friend's last shilling if his friend was fool enough to let him. How much did he touch you for?

BROADBENT. Oh, nothing. An advance on his salary —for travelling expenses.

DOYLE. Salary! In Heaven's name, what for?

BROADBENT. For being my Home Secretary, as he very wittily called it.

DOYLE. I dont see the joke.

BROADBENT. You can spoil any joke by being cold blooded about it. I saw it all right when he said it. It was something—something really very amusing—about the Home Secretary and the Irish Secretary. At all events, hes evidently the very man to take with me to Ireland to break the ice for me. He can gain the confidence of the people there, and make them friendly to me. Eh? (*He seats himself on the office stool, and tilts it back so that the edge of the standing desk supports his back and prevents his toppling over.*)

DOYLE. A nice introduction, by George! Do you suppose the whole population of Ireland consists of drunken begging letter writers, or that even if it did, they would accept one another as references?

BROADBENT. Pooh! nonsense! hes only an Irishman. Besides, you dont seriously suppose that Haffigan can humbug me, do you?

DOYLE. No: hes too lazy to take the trouble. All he has to do is to sit there and drink your whisky while you humbug yourself. However, we neednt argue about Haffigan, for two reasons. First, with your money in his pocket he will never reach Paddington: there are too many public houses on the way. Second, hes not an Irishman at all.

BROADBENT. Not an Irishman! (*He is so amazed by the statement that he straightens himself and brings the stool bolt upright.*)

DOYLE. Born in Glasgow. Never was in Ireland in his life. I know all about him.

BROADBENT. But he spoke—he behaved just like an Irishman.

DOYLE. Like an Irishman!! Is it possible that you dont know that all this top-o-the-morning and broth-of-a-boy and more-power-to-your-elbow business is as peculiar to England as the Albert Hall concerts of Irish music are? No Irishman ever talks like that in Ireland, or ever did, or ever will. But when a thoroughly worthless Irishman comes to England, and finds the whole place full of romantic duffers like you, who will let him loaf and drink and sponge and brag as long as he flatters your sense of moral superiority by playing the fool and degrading himself and his country, he soon learns the antics that take you in. He picks them up at the theatre or the music hall. Haffigan learnt the rudiments from his father, who came from my part of Ireland. I knew his uncles, Matt and Andy Haffigan of Rosscullen.

BROADBENT (*still incredulous*). But his brogue!

DOYLE. His brogue! A fat lot you know about brogues! Ive heard you call a Dublin accent that you could hang your hat on, a brogue. Heaven help you! you dont know the difference between Connemara and Rathmines. (*With violent irritation.*) Oh, damn Tim Haffigan! lets drop the subject: hes not worth wrangling about.

BROADBENT. Whats wrong with you today, Larry? Why are you so bitter?

Doyle looks at him perplexedly; comes slowly to the

writing table; and sits down at the end next the fireplace before replying.

DOYLE.   Well: your letter completely upset me, for one thing.

BROADBENT.   Why?

LARRY.   Your foreclosing this Rosscullen mortgage and turning poor Nick Lestrange out of house and home has rather taken me aback; for I liked the old rascal when I was a boy and had the run of his park to play in. I was brought up on the property.

BROADBENT.   But he wouldnt pay the interest. I had to foreclose on behalf of the Syndicate. So now I'm off to Rosscullen to look after the property myself. (*He sits down at the writing table opposite Larry, and adds, casually, but with an anxious glance at his partner.*) Youre coming with me, of course?

DOYLE (*rising nervously and recommencing his restless movements*). Thats it. Thats what I dread. Thats what has upset me.

BROADBENT.   But dont you want to see your country again after 18 years absence? to see your people? to be in the old home again? to—

DOYLE (*interrupting him very impatiently*). Yes, yes: I know all that as well as you do.

BROADBENT.   Oh well, of course (*with a shrug*) if you take it in that way, I'm sorry.

DOYLE.   Never you mind my temper: its not meant for you, as you ought to know by this time. (*He sits down again, a little ashamed of his petulance; reflects a moment bitterly; then bursts out.*) I have an instinct against going back to Ireland: an instinct so strong that I'd rather go with you to the South Pole than to Rosscullen.

BROADBENT.   What! Here you are, belonging to a nation with the strongest patriotism! the most inveterate homing instinct in the world! and you pretend youd rather go anywhere than back to Ireland.

You dont suppose I believe you, do you? In your heart—

DOYLE. Never mind my heart: an Irishman's heart is nothing but his imagination. How many of all those millions that have left Ireland have ever come back or wanted to come back? But whats the use of talking to you? Three verses of twaddle about the Irish emigrant " sitting on the stile, Mary," or three hours of Irish patriotism in Bermondsey or the Scotland Division of Liverpool, go further with you than all the facts that stare you in the face. Why, man alive, look at me! You know the way I nag, and worry, and carp, and cavil, and disparage, and am never satisfied and never quiet, and try the patience of my best friends.

BROADBENT. Oh, come, Larry! do yourself justice. Youre very amusing and agreeable to strangers.

DOYLE. Yes, to strangers. Perhaps if I was a bit stiffer to strangers, and a bit easier at home, like an Englishman, I'd be better company for you.

BROADBENT. We get on well enough. Of course you have the melancholy of the Keltic race—

DOYLE (*bounding out of his chair*). Good God!!!

BROADBENT (*slyly*)—and also its habit of using strong language when theres nothing the matter.

DOYLE. Nothing the matter! When people talk about the Celtic race, I feel as if I could burn down London. That sort of rot does more harm than ten Coercion Acts. Do you suppose a man need be a Celt to feel melancholy in Rosscullen? Why, man, Ireland was peopled just as England was; and its breed was crossed by just the same invaders.

BROADBENT. True. All the capable people in Ireland are of English extraction. It has often struck me as a most remarkable circumstance that the only party in parliament which shews the genuine old English character and spirit is the Irish party. Look at its independence, its determination, its defiance of bad Governments, its sympathy with oppressed nationalities all the world over! How English!

DOYLE. Not to mention the solemnity with which it talks old-fashioned nonsense which it knows perfectly well to be a century behind the times. Thats English, if you like.

BROADBENT. No, Larry, no. You are thinking of the modern hybrids that now monopolize England. Hypocrites, humbugs, Germans, Jews, Yankees, foreigners, Park Laners, cosmopolitan riffraff. Dont call them English. They dont belong to the dear old island, but to their confounded new empire; and by George! theyre worthy of it; and I wish them joy of it.

DOYLE (*unmoved by this outburst*). There! You feel better now, dont you?

BROADBENT (*defiantly*). I do. Much better.

DOYLE. My dear Tom, you only need a touch of the Irish climate to be as big a fool as I am myself. If all my Irish blood were poured into your veins, you wouldnt turn a hair of your constitution and character. Go and marry the most English Englishwoman you can find, and then bring up your son in Rosscullen; and that son's character will be so like mine and so unlike yours that everybody will accuse me of being his father. (*With sudden anguish.*) Rosscullen! oh, good Lord, Rosscullen! The dullness! the hopelessness! the ignorance! the bigotry!

BROADBENT (*matter-of-factly*). The usual thing in the country, Larry. Just the same here.

DOYLE (*hastily*). No, no: the climate is different. Here, if the life is dull, you can be dull too, and no great harm done. (*Going off into a passionate dream.*) But your wits cant thicken in that soft moist air, on those white springy roads, in those misty rushes and brown bogs, on those hillsides of granite rocks and magenta heather. Youve no such colors in the sky, no such lure in the distances, no such sadness in the even-

ings. Oh, the dreaming! the dreaming! the torturing,
heartscalding, never satisfying dreaming, dreaming,
dreaming, dreaming! (*Savagely.*) No debauchery that
ever coarsened and brutalized an Englishman can take
the worth and usefulness out of him like that dreaming.
An Irishman's imagination never lets him alone, never
convinces him, never satisfies him; but it makes him
that he cant face reality nor deal with it nor handle it
nor conquer it: he can only sneer at them that do, and
(*bitterly, at Broadbent*) be " agreeable to strangers,"
like a good-for-nothing woman on the streets. (*Gab-
bling at Broadbent across the table.*) Its all dreaming,
all imagination. He cant be religious. The inspired
Churchman that teaches him the sanctity of life and
the importance of conduct is sent away empty; while
the poor village priest that gives him a miracle or a
sentimental story of a saint, has cathedrals built for
him out of the pennies of the poor. He cant be intelligently political: he dreams of what the Shan Van
Vocht said in ninetyeight. If you want to interest him
in Ireland youve got to call the unfortunate island Kath-
leen ni Hoolihan and pretend shes a little old woman.
It saves thinking. It saves working. It saves everything except imagination, imagination, imagination; and
imagination's such a torture that you cant bear it without whisky. (*With fierce shivering self-contempt.*) At
last you get that you can bear nothing real at all: youd
rather starve than cook a meal; youd rather go shabby
and dirty than set your mind to take care of your
clothes and wash yourself; you nag and squabble at
home because your wife isnt an angel, and she despises
you because youre not a hero; and you hate the whole
lot round you because theyre only poor slovenly useless
devils like yourself. (*Dropping his voice like a man
making some shameful confidence.*) And all the while
there goes on a horrible, senseless, mischievous laughter.
When youre young, you exchange drinks with other

young men; and you exchange vile stories with them; and as youre too futile to be able to help or cheer them, you chaff and sneer and taunt them for not doing the things you darent do yourself. And all the time you laugh, laugh, laugh! eternal derision, eternal envy, eternal folly, eternal fouling and staining and degrading, until, when you come at last to a country where men take a question seriously and give a serious answer to it, you deride them for having no sense of humor, and plume yourself on your own worthlessness as if it made you better than them.

BROADBENT (*roused to intense earnestness by Doyle's eloquence*). Never despair, Larry. There are great possibilities for Ireland. Home Rule will work wonders under English guidance.

DOYLE (*pulled up short, his face twitching with a reluctant smile*). Tom: why do you select my most tragic moments for your most irresistible strokes of humor?

BROADBENT. Humor! I was perfectly serious. What do you mean? Do you doubt my seriousness about Home Rule?

DOYLE. I am sure you are serious, Tom, about the English guidance.

BROADBENT (*quite reassured*). Of course I am. Our guidance is the important thing. We English must place our capacity for government without stint at the service of nations who are less fortunately endowed in that respect; so as to allow them to develop in perfect freedom to the English level of self-government, you know. You understand me?

DOYLE. Perfectly. And Rosscullen will understand you too.

BROADBENT (*cheerfully*). Of course it will. So thats all right. (*He pulls up his chair and settles himself comfortably to lecture Doyle.*) Now, Larry, Ive listened carefully to all youve said about Ireland; and

I can see nothing whatever to prevent your coming with me. What does it all come to? Simply that you were only a young fellow when you were in Ireland. Youll find all that chaffing and drinking and not knowing what to be at in Peckham just the same as in Donnybrook. You looked at Ireland with a boy's eyes and saw only boyish things. Come back with me and look at it with a man's, and get a better opinion of your country.

DOYLE. I daresay youre partly right in that: at all events I know very well that if I had been the son of a laborer instead of the son of a country landagent, I should have struck more grit than I did. Unfortunately I'm not going back to visit the Irish nation, but to visit my father and Aunt Judy and Nora Reilly and Father Dempsey and the rest of them.

BROADBENT. Well, why not? Theyll be delighted to see you, now that England has made a man of you.

DOYLE (struck by this). Ah! you hit the mark there, Tom, with true British inspiration.

BROADBENT. Common sense, you mean.

DOYLE (quickly). No I dont: youve no more common sense than a gander. No Englishman has any common sense, or ever had, or ever will have. Youre going on a sentimental expedition for perfectly ridiculous reasons, with your head full of political nonsense that would not take in any ordinarily intelligent donkey; but you can hit me in the eye with the simple truth about myself and my father.

BROADBENT (amazed). I never mentioned your father.

DOYLE (not heeding the interruption). There he is in Rosscullen, a landagent who's always been in a small way because hes a Catholic, and the landlords are mostly Protestants. What with land courts reducing rents and Land Acts turning big estates into little holdings, he'd be a beggar this day if he hadnt bought his own little farm under the Land Purchase Act. I doubt if hes been further from home than Athenmullet for the last twenty years. And here am I, made a man of, as you say, by England.

BROADBENT (*apologetically*). I assure you I never meant——

DOYLE. Oh, dont apologize: it's quite true. I daresay Ive learnt something in America and a few other remote and inferior spots; but in the main it is by living with you and working in double harness with you that I have learnt to live in a real world and not in an imaginary one. I owe more to you than to any Irishman.

BROADBENT (*shaking his head with a twinkle in his eye*). Very friendly of you, Larry, old man, but all blarney. I like blarney; but it's rot, all the same.

DOYLE. No it's not. I should never have done anything without you; although I never stop wondering at that blessed old head of yours with all its ideas in watertight compartments, and all the compartments warranted impervious to anything that it doesnt suit you to understand.

BROADBENT (*invincible*). Unmitigated rot, Larry, I assure you.

DOYLE. Well, at any rate you will admit that all my friends are either Englishmen or men of the big world that belongs to the big Powers. All the serious part of my life has been lived in that atmosphere: all the serious part of my work had been done with men of that sort. Just think of me as I am now going back to Rosscullen! to that hell of littleness and monotony! How am I to get on with a little country landagent that ekes out his 5 per cent with a little farming and a scrap of house property in the nearest country town? What am I to say to him? What is he to say to me?

BROADBENT (*scandalized*). But youre father and son, man!

DOYLE. What difference does that make? What would you say if I proposed a visit to y o u r father?

BROADBENT (*with filial rectitude*). I always made a point of going to see my father regularly until his mind gave way.

DOYLE (*concerned*). Has he gone mad? You never told me.

BROADBENT. He has joined the Tariff Reform League. He would never have done that if his mind had not been weakened. (*Beginning to declaim.*) He has fallen a victim to the arts of a political charlatan who——

DOYLE (*interrupting him*). You mean that you keep clear of your father because he differs from you about Free Trade, and you dont want to quarrel with him. Well, think of me and my father! Hes a Nationalist and a Separatist. I'm a metallurgical chemist turned civil engineer. Now whatever else metallurgical chemistry may be, it's not national. It's international. And my business and yours as civil engineers is to join countries, not to separate them. The one real political conviction that our business has rubbed into us is that frontiers are hindrances and flags confounded nuisances.

BROADBENT (*still smarting under Mr. Chamberlain's economic heresy*). Only when there is a protective tariff——

DOYLE (*firmly*). Now look here, Tom: you want to get in a speech on Free Trade; and youre not going to do it: I wont stand it. My father wants to make St. George's Channel a frontier and hoist a green flag on College Green; and I want to bring Galway within 3 hours of Colchester and 24 of New York. I want Ireland to be the brains and imagination of a big Commonwealth, not a Robinson Crusoe island. Then theres the religious difficulty. My Catholicism is the Catholicism of Charlemagne or Dante, qualified by a great deal of modern science and folklore which Father Dempsey

would call the ravings of an Atheist. Well, my father's
Catholicism is the Catholicism of Father Dempsey.

BROADBENT (*shrewdly*). I dont want to interrupt
you, Larry; but you know this is all gammon. These
differences exist in all families; but the members rub
on together all right. (*Suddenly relapsing into por-
tentousness.*) Of course there are some questions which
touch the very foundations of morals; and on these I
grant you even the closest relationships cannot excuse
any compromise or laxity. For instance——

DOYLE (*impatiently springing up and walking about*).
For instance, Home Rule, South Africa, Free Trade,
and the Education Rate. Well, I should differ from
my father on every one of them, probably, just as I
differ from you about them.

BROADBENT. Yes; but you are an Irishman; and
these things are not serious to you as they are to an
Englishman.

DOYLE. What! not even Home Rule!

BROADBENT (*steadfastly*). Not even Home Rule.
We owe Home Rule not to the Irish, but to our English
Gladstone. No, Larry: I cant help thinking that theres
something behind all this.

DOYLE (*hotly*). What is there behind it? Do you
think I'm humbugging you?

BROADBENT. Dont fly out at me, old chap. I only
thought—

DOYLE. What did you think?

BROADBENT. Well, a moment ago I caught a name
which is new to me: a Miss Nora Reilly, I think.
(*Doyle stops dead and stares at him with something
like awe.*) I dont wish to be impertinent, as you know,
Larry; but are you sure she has nothing to do with your
reluctance to come to Ireland with me?

DOYLE (*sitting down again, vanquished*). Thomas
Broadbent: I surrender. The poor silly-clever Irishman takes off his hat to God's Englishman. The man

who could in all seriousness make that recent remark of yours about Home Rule and Gladstone must be simply the champion idiot of all the world. Yet the man who could in the very next sentence sweep away all my special pleading and go straight to the heart of my motives must be a man of genius. But that the idiot and the genius should be the same man! how is that possible? (*Springing to his feet.*) By Jove, I see it all now. I'll write an article about it, and send it to Nature.

BROADBENT (*staring at him*). What on earth—

DOYLE. It's quite simple. You know that a caterpillar—

BROADBENT. A caterpillar!!!

DOYLE. Yes, a caterpillar. Now give your mind to what I am going to say; for it's a new and important scientific theory of the English national character. A caterpillar—

BROADBENT. Look here, Larry: dont be an ass.

DOYLE (*insisting*). I say a caterpillar and I mean a caterpillar. Youll understand presently. A caterpillar (*Broadbent mutters a slight protest, but does not press it*) when it gets into a tree, instinctively makes itself look exactly like a leaf; so that both its enemies and its prey may mistake it for one and think it not worth bothering about.

BROADBENT. Whats that got to do with our English national character?

DOYLE. I'll tell you. The world is as full of fools as a tree is full of leaves. Well, the Englishman does what the caterpillar does. He instinctively makes himself look like a fool, and eats up all the real fools at his ease while his enemies let him alone and laugh at him for being a fool like the rest. Oh, nature is cunning, cunning! (*He sits down, lost in contemplation of his word-picture.*)

BROADBENT (*with hearty admiration*). Now you

know, Larry, that would never have occurred to me.
You Irish people are amazingly clever. Of course it's
all tommy rot; but it's so brilliant, you know! How
the dickens do you think of such things! You really
must write an article about it: theyll pay you something
for it. If Nature wont have it, I can get it into Engineering for you: I know the editor.

DOYLE. Lets get back to business. I'd better tell
you about Nora Reilly.

BROADBENT. No: never mind. I shouldnt have alluded to her.

DOYLE. I'd rather. Nora has a fortune.

BROADBENT (*keenly interested*). Eh? How much?

DOYLE. Forty per annum.

BROADBENT. Forty thousand?

DOYLE. No, forty. Forty pounds.

BROADBENT (*much dashed*). Thats what you call a
fortune in Rosscullen, is it?

DOYLE. A girl with a dowry of f i v e pounds calls it
a fortune in Rosscullen. Whats more, £40 a year i s a
fortune there; and Nora Reilly enjoys a good deal of
social consideration as an heiress on the strength of it.
It has helped my father's household through many a
tight place. My father was her father's agent. She
came on a visit to us when he died, and has lived with
us ever since.

BROADBENT (*attentively, beginning to suspect Larry
of misconduct with Nora, and resolving to get to the
bottom of it*). Since when? I mean how old were you
when she came?

DOYLE. I was seventeen. So was she: if she'd been
older she'd have had more sense than to stay with us.
We were together for 18 months before I went up to
Dublin to study. When I went home for Christmas
and Easter, she was there: I suppose it used to be
something of an event for her, though of course I never
thought of that then.

BROADBENT. Were you at all hard hit?

DOYLE. Not really. I had only two ideas at that time: first, to learn to do something; and then to get out of Ireland and have a chance of doing it. She didnt count. I was romantic about her, just as I was romantic about Byron's heroines or the old Round Tower of Rosscullen; but she didnt count any more than they did. Ive never crossed St. George's Channel since for her sake—never even landed at Queenstown and come back to London through Ireland.

BROADBENT. But did you ever say anything that would justify her in waiting for you?

DOYLE. No, never. But she i s waiting for me.

BROADBENT. How do you know?

DOYLE. She writes to me—on her birthday. She used to write on mine, and send me little things as presents; but I stopped that by pretending that it was no use when I was travelling, as they got lost in the foreign post-offices. (*He pronounces post-offices with the stress on offices, instead of on post.*)

BROADBENT. You answer the letters?

DOYLE. Not very punctually. But they get acknowledged at one time or another.

BROADBENT. How do you feel when you see her handwriting?

DOYLE. Uneasy. I'd give £50 to escape a letter.

BROADBENT (*looking grave, and throwing himself back in his chair to intimate that the cross-examination is over, and the result very damaging to the witness*). Hm!

DOYLE. What d'ye mean by Hm!?

BROADBENT. Of course I know that the moral code is different in Ireland. But in England it's not considered fair to trifle with a woman's affections.

DOYLE. You mean that an Englishman would get engaged to another woman and return Nora her letters

and presents with a letter to say he was unworthy of
her and wished her every happiness?

BROADBENT. Well, even that would set the poor
girl's mind at rest.

DOYLE. Would it? I wonder! One thing I can tell
you; and that is that Nora would wait until she died of
old age sooner than ask my intentions or condescend
to hint at the possibility of my having any. You dont
know what Irish pride is. England may have knocked
a good deal of it out of me; but shes never been in
England; and if I had to choose between wounding that
delicacy in her and hitting her in the face, I'd hit her
in the face without a moment's hesitation.

BROADBENT (*who has been nursing his knee and reflecting, apparently rather agreeably*). You know, all
this sounds rather interesting. Theres the Irish charm
about it. Thats the worst of you: the Irish charm
doesnt exist for you.

DOYLE. Oh yes it does. But it's the charm of a
dream. Live in contact with dreams and you will get
something of their charm: live in contact with facts
and you will get something of their brutality. I wish
I could find a country to live in where the facts were
not brutal and the dreams not unreal.

BROADBENT (*changing his attitude and responding to
Doyle's earnestness with deep conviction: his elbows on
the table and his hands clenched*). Dont despair, Larry,
old boy: things may look black; but there will be a
great change after the next election.

DOYLE (*jumping up*). Oh get out, you idiot!

BROADBENT (*rising also, not a bit snubbed*). Ha!
ha! you may laugh; but we shall see. However, dont
let us argue about that. Come now! you ask my advice
about Miss Reilly?

DOYLE (*reddening*). No I dont. Damn your advice!
(*Softening.*) Lets have it, all the same.

BROADBENT. Well, everything you tell me about her

impresses me favorably. She seems to have the feelings of a lady; and though we must face the fact that in England her income would hardly maintain her in the lower middle class—

DOYLE (*interrupting*). Now look here, Tom. That reminds me. When you go to Ireland, just drop talking about the middle class and bragging of belonging to it. In Ireland youre either a gentleman or youre not. If you want to be particularly offensive to Nora, you can call her a Papist; but if you call her a middle-class woman, Heaven help you!

BROADBENT (*irrepressible*). Never fear. Youre all descended from the ancient kings: I know that. (*Complacently.*) I'm not so tactless as you think, my boy. (*Earnest again.*) I expect to find Miss Reilly a perfect lady; and I strongly advise you to come and have another look at her before you make up your mind about her. By the way, have you a photograph of her?

DOYLE. Her photographs stopped at twenty-five.

BROADBENT (*saddened*). Ah yes, I suppose so. (*With feeling, severely.*) Larry: youve treated that poor girl disgracefully.

DOYLE. By George, if she only knew that two men were talking about her like this—!

BROADBENT. She wouldnt like it, would she? Of course not. We ought to be ashamed of ourselves, Larry. (*More and more carried away by his new fancy.*) You know, I have a sort of presentiment that Miss Reilly is a very superior woman.

DOYLE (*staring hard at him*). Oh! you have, have you?

BROADBENT. Yes I have. There is something very touching about the history of this beautiful girl.

DOYLE. Beau—! Oho! Heres a chance for Nora! and for me! (*Calling.*) Hodson.

HODSON (*appearing at the bedroom door*). Did you call, sir?

DOYLE. Pack for me too. I'm going to Ireland with Mr. Broadbent.

HODSON. Right, sir. (*He retires into the bedroom.*)

BROADBENT (*clapping Doyle on the shoulder*). Thank you, old chap. Thank you.

END OF ACT I.

ACT II

Rosscullen.   Westward a hillside of granite rock and heather slopes upward across the prospect from south to north.   A huge stone stands on it in a naturally impossible place, as if it had been tossed up there by a giant.   Over the brow, in the desolate valley beyond, is a round tower.   A lonely white high road trending away westward past the tower loses itself at the foot of the far mountains.   It is evening; and there are great breadths of silken green in the Irish sky.   The sun is setting.

A man with the face of a young saint, yet with white hair and perhaps 50 years on his back, is standing near the stone in a trance of intense melancholy, looking over the hills as if by mere intensity of gaze he could pierce the glories of the sunset and see into the streets of heaven.   He is dressed in black, and is rather more clerical in appearance than most English curates are nowadays; but he does not wear the collar and waistcoat of a parish priest.   He is roused from his trance by the chirp of an insect from a tuft of grass in a crevice of the stone.   His face relaxes: he turns quietly, and gravely takes off his hat to the tuft, addressing the insect in a brogue which is the jocular assumption of a gentleman and not the natural speech of a peasant.

THE MAN.   An is that yourself, Misther Grasshopper?   I hope I see you well this fine evenin.

THE GRASSHOPPER (*prompt and shrill in answer*). X.X.

31

THE MAN (*encouragingly*). Thats right. I suppose now youve come out to make yourself miserable be admyerin the sunset?

THE GRASSHOPPER (*sadly*). X.X.

THE MAN. Aye, youre a thrue Irish grasshopper.

THE GRASSHOPPER (*loudly*). X.X.X.

THE MAN. Three cheers for ould Ireland, is it? That helps you to face out the misery and the poverty and the torment, doesnt it?

THE GRASSHOPPER (*plaintively*). X.X.

THE MAN. Ah, its no use, me poor little friend. If you could jump as far as a kangaroo you couldnt jump away from your own heart an its punishment. You can only look at Heaven from here: you cant reach it. There! (*pointing with his stick to the sunset*) thats the gate o glory, isnt it?

THE GRASSHOPPER (*assenting*). X.X.

THE MAN. Sure it's the wise grasshopper yar to know that! But tell me this, Misther Unworldly Wiseman: why does the sight of Heaven wring your heart an mine as the sight of holy wather wrings the heart o the divil? What wickedness have you done to bring that curse on you? Here! where are you jumpin to? Wheres your manners to go skyrocketin like that out o the box in the middle o your confession (*he threatens it with his stick*)?

THE GRASSHOPPER (*penitently*). X.

THE MAN (*lowering the stick*). I accept your apology; but dont do it again. And now tell me one thing before I let you go home to bed. Which would you say this counthry was: hell or purgatory?

THE GRASSHOPPER. X.

THE MAN. Hell! Faith I'm afraid youre right. I wondher what you and me did when we were alive to get sent here.

THE GRASSHOPPER (*shrilly*). X.X.

THE MAN (*nodding*). Well, as you say, its a deli-

cate subject; and I wont press it on you. Now off
widja.

THE GRASSHOPPER. X.X. (*It springs away.*)

THE MAN (*waving his stick*). God speed you! (*He
walks away past the stone towards the brow of the hill.
Immediately a young laborer, his face distorted with
terror, slips round from behind the stone.*

THE LABORER (*crossing himself repeatedly*). Oh
glory be to God! glory be to God! Oh Holy Mother
an all the saints! Oh murdher! murdher! (*Beside
himself, calling.*) Fadher Keegan! Fadher Keegan!

THE MAN (*turning*). Who's there? Whats that?
(*He comes back and finds the laborer, who clasps his
knees.*) Patsy Farrell! What are you doing here?

PATSY. O for the love o God dont lave me here wi
dhe grasshopper. I hard it spakin to you. Dont let
it do me any harm, Father darlint.

KEEGAN. Get up, you foolish man, get up. Are you
afraid of a poor insect because I pretended it was talking to me?

PATSY. Oh, it was no pretending, Fadher dear.
Didnt it give three cheers n say it was a divil out o
hell? Oh say youll see me safe home, Fadher; n put
a blessin on me or somethin (*he moans with terror*).

KEEGAN. What were you doin there, Patsy, listnin?
Were you spyin on me?

PATSY. No, Fadher: on me oath an soul I wasnt: I
was waitn to meet Masther Larry n carry his luggage
from the car; n I fell asleep on the grass; n you woke
me talkin to the grasshopper; n I hard its wicked little
voice. Oh, d'ye think I'll die before the year's out,
Fadher?

KEEGAN. For shame, Patsy! Is that your religion,
to be afraid of a little deeshy grasshopper? Suppose
it was a divil, what call have you to fear it? If I
could ketch it, I'd make you take it home widja in your
hat for a penance.

Patsy. Sure, if you wont let it harm me, I'm not afraid, your riverence. (*He gets up, a little reassured. He is a callow, flaxen polled, smoothfaced, downy chinned lad, fully grown but not yet fully filled out, with blue eyes and an instinctively acquired air of helplessness and silliness, indicating, not his real character, but a cunning developed by his constant dread of a hostile dominance, which he habitually tries to disarm and tempt into unmasking by pretending to be a much greater fool than he really is. Englishmen think him half-witted, which is exactly what he intends them to think. He is clad in corduroy trousers, unbuttoned waistcoat, and coarse blue striped shirt.*)

Keegan (*admonitorily*). Patsy: what did I tell you about callin me Father Keegan an your reverence? What did Father Dempsey tell you about it?

Patsy. Yis, Fadher.

Keegan. Father!

Patsy (*desperately*). Arra, hwat am I to call you? Fadher Dempsey sez youre not a priest; n we all know youre not a man; n how do we know what ud happen to us if we shewed any disrespect to you? N sure they say wanse a priest always a priest.

Keegan (*sternly*). Its not for the like of you, Patsy, to go behind the instruction of your parish priest and set yourself up to judge whether your Church is right or wrong.

Patsy. Sure I know that, sir.

Keegan. The Church let me be its priest as long as it thought me fit for its work. When it took away my papers it meant you to know that I was only a poor madman, unfit and unworthy to take charge of the souls of the people.

Patsy. But wasnt it only because you knew more Latn than Father Dempsey that he was jealous of you?

Keegan (*scolding him to keep himself from smiling*). How dar you, Patsy Farrell, put your own wicked little

spites and foolishnesses into the heart of your priest?
For two pins I'd tell him what you just said.

PATSY (*coaxing*). Sure you wouldnt—

KEEGAN. Wouldnt I? God forgive you! youre little
better than a heathen.

PATSY. Deedn I am, Fadher: it's me bruddher the
tinsmith in Dublin youre thinkin of. Sure he had to
be a freethinker when he larnt a thrade and went to
live in the town.

KEEGAN. Well, he'll get to Heaven before you if
youre not careful, Patsy. And now you listen to me,
once and for all. Youll talk to me and pray for me by
the name of Pether Keegan, so you will. And when
youre angry and tempted to lift your hand agen the
donkey or stamp your foot on the little grasshopper,
remember that the donkey's Pether Keegan's brother,
and the grasshopper Pether Keegan's friend. And
when youre tempted to throw a stone at a sinner or a
curse at a beggar, remember that Pether Keegan is a
worse sinner and a worse beggar, and keep the stone
and the curse for him the next time you meet him.
Now say God bless you, Pether, to me before I go, just
to practise you a bit.

PATSY. Sure it wouldnt be right, Fadher. I cant—

KEEGAN. Yes you can. Now out with it; or I'll
put this stick into your hand an make you hit me with it.

PATSY (*throwing himself on his knees in an ecstasy
of adoration*). Sure its your blessin I want, Fadher
Keegan. I'll have no luck widhout it.

KEEGAN (*shocked*). Get up out o that, man. Dont
kneel to me: I'm not a saint.

PATSY (*with intense conviction*). Oh in throth yar,
sir. (*The grasshopper chirps. Patsy, terrified, clutches
at Keegan's hands.*) Dont set it on me, Fadher: I'll
do anythin you bid me.

KEEGAN (*pulling him up*). You bosthoon, you!
Dont you see that it only whistled to tell me Miss

Reilly's comin? There! Look at her and pull yourself together for shame. Off widja to the road: youll be late for the car if you dont make haste (*bustling him down the hill*). I can see the dust of it in the gap already.

PATSY. The Lord save us! (*He goes down the hill towards the road like a haunted man.*)

Nora Reilly comes down the hill. A slight weak woman in a pretty muslin print gown (her best), she is a figure commonplace enough to Irish eyes; but on the inhabitants of fatter-fed, crowded, hustling and bustling modern countries she makes a very different impression. The absence of any symptoms of coarseness or hardness or appetite in her, her comparative delicacy of manner and sensibility of apprehension, her thin hands and slender figure, her novel accent, with the caressing plaintive Irish melody of her speech, give her a charm which is all the more effective because, being untravelled, she is unconscious of it, and never dreams of deliberately dramatizing and exploiting it, as the Irishwoman in England does. For Tom Broadbent therefore, an attractive woman, whom he would even call ethereal. To Larry Doyle, an everyday woman fit only for the eighteenth century, helpless, useless, almost sexless, an invalid without the excuse of disease, an incarnation of everything in Ireland that drove him out of it. These judgments have little value and no finality; but they are the judgments on which her fate hangs just at present. Keegan touches his hat to her: he does not take it off.

NORA. Mr. Keegan: I want to speak to you a minute if you dont mind.

KEEGAN (*dropping the broad Irish vernacular of his speech to Patsy*). An hour if you like, Miss Reilly: youre always welcome. Shall we sit down?

NORA. Thank you. (*They sit on the heather. She is shy and anxious; but she comes to the point promptly because she can think of nothing else.*) They say you did a gradle o travelling at one time.

KEEGAN. Well you see I'm not a Mnooth man (*he means that he was not a student at Maynooth College*). When I was young I admired the older generation of priests that had been educated in Salamanca. So when I felt sure of my vocation I went to Salamanca. Then I walked from Salamanca to Rome, an sted in a monastery there for a year. My pilgrimage to Rome taught me that walking is a better way of travelling than the train; so I walked from Rome to the Sorbonne in Paris; and I wish I could have walked from Paris to Oxford; for I was very sick on the sea. After a year of Oxford I had to walk to Jerusalem to walk the Oxford feeling off me. From Jerusalem I came back to Patmos, and spent six months at the monastery of Mount Athos. From that I came to Ireland and settled down as a parish priest until I went mad.

NORA (*startled*). Oh dont say that.

KEEGAN. Why not? Dont you know the story? how I confessed a black man and gave him absolution; and how he put a spell on me and drove me mad.

NORA. How can you talk such nonsense about yourself? For shame!

KEEGAN. It's not nonsense at all: it's true—in a way. But never mind the black man. Now that you know what a travelled man I am, what can I do for you? (*She hesitates and plucks nervously at the heather. He stays her hand gently.*) Dear Miss Nora: dont pluck the little flower. If it was a pretty baby you wouldnt want to pull its head off and stick it in a vawse o water to look at. (*The grasshopper chirps: Keegan turns his head and addresses it in the vernacular.*) Be aisy, me son: she wont spoil the swing-swong in your little three. (*To Nora, resuming his urbane style.*) You see I'm quite cracked; but never mind: I'm harmless. Now what is it?

Nora (*embarrassed*). Oh, only idle curiosity. I wanted to know whether you found Ireland—I mean the country part of Ireland, of course—very small and backwardlike when you came back to it from Rome and Oxford and all the great cities.

Keegan. When I went to those great cities I saw wonders I had never seen in Ireland. But when I came back to Ireland I found all the wonders there waiting for me. You see they had been there all the time; but my eyes had never been opened to them. I did not know what my own house was like, because I had never been outside it.

Nora. D'ye think thats the same with everybody?

Keegan. With everybody who has eyes in his soul as well as in his head.

Nora. But really and truly now, werent the people rather disappointing? I should think the girls must have seemed rather coarse and dowdy after the foreign princesses and people? But I suppose a priest wouldnt notice that.

Keegan. It's a priest's business to notice everything. I wont tell you all I noticed about women; but I'll tell you this. The more a man knows, and the farther he travels, the more likely he is to marry a country girl afterwards.

Nora (*blushing with delight*). Youre joking, Mr. Keegan: I'm sure yar.

Keegan. My way of joking is to tell the truth. It's the funniest joke in the world.

Nora (*incredulous*). Galong with you!

Keegan (*springing up actively*). Shall we go down to the road and meet the car? (*She gives him her hand and he helps her up.*) Patsy Farrell told me you were expecting young Doyle.

Nora (*tossing her chin up at once*). Oh, I'm not expecting him particularly. It's a wonder hes come back at all. After staying away eighteen years he can

harly expect us to be very anxious to see him, can he
now?

KEEGAN.   Well, not anxious perhaps; but you will
be curious to see how much hes changed in all these
years.

NORA (*with a sudden bitter flush*).   I suppose thats
all that brings him back to look at u s, just to see how
much w e v e changed.   Well, he can wait and see me
be candlelight: I didnt come out to meet him: I'm going
to walk to the Round Tower (*going west across the
hill*).

KEEGAN.   You couldnt do better this fine evening.
(*Gravely.*) I'll tell him where youve gone. (*She turns
as if to forbid him; but the deep understanding in his
eyes makes that impossible; and she only looks at him
earnestly and goes.   He watches her disappear on the
other side of the hill; then says*) Aye, hes come to torment you; and youre driven already to torment him.
(*He shakes his head, and goes slowly away across the
hill in the opposite direction, lost in thought.*)

*By this time the car has arrived, and dropped three
of its passengers on the high road at the foot of the
hill.   It is a monster jaunting car, black and dilapidated,
one of the last survivors of the public vehicles known to
earlier generations as Beeyankiny cars, the Irish having
laid violent tongues on the name of their projector, ono
Bianconi, an enterprising Italian.   The three passengers are the parish priest, Father Dempsey; Cornelius
Doyle, Larry's father; and Broadbent, all in overcoats
and as stiff as only an Irish car could make them.*

*The priest, stout and fatherly, falls far short of that
finest type of countryside pastor which represents the
genius of priesthood; but he is equally far above the
base type in which a strong-minded and unscrupulous
peasant uses the Church to extort money, power, and
privilege.   He is a priest neither by vocation nor ambition, but because the life suits him.   He has boundless*

*authority over his flock, and taxes them stiffly enough
to be a rich man. The old Protestant ascendency is now
too broken to gall him. On the whole, an easygoing,
amiable, even modest man as long as his dues are paid
and his authority and dignity fully admitted.*

*Cornelius Doyle is an elder of the small wiry type,
with a hardskinned, rather worried face, clean shaven
except for sandy whiskers blanching into a lustreless
pale yellow and quite white at the roots. His dress is
that of a country-town man of business: that is, an oldish shooting suit, and elastic sided boots quite uncon-
nected with shooting. Feeling shy with Broadbent, he
is hasty, which is his way of trying to appear genial.*

*Broadbent, for reasons which will appear later, has
no luggage except a field glass and a guide book. The
other two have left theirs to the unfortunate Patsy Farrell, who struggles up the hill after them, loaded with
a sack of potatoes, a hamper, a fat goose, a colossal
salmon, and several paper parcels.*

*Cornelius leads the way up the hill, with Broadbent
at his heels. The priest follows; and Patsy lags labori-
ously behind.*

CORNELIUS. This is a bit of a climb, Mr. Broadbent;
but its shorter than goin round be the road.

BROADBENT (*stopping to examine the great stone*).
Just a moment, Mr. Doyle: I want to look at this stone.
It must be Finian's die-cast.

CORNELIUS (*in blank bewilderment*). Hwat?

BROADBENT. Murray describes it. One of your
great national heroes—I cant pronounce the name—
Finian Somebody, I think.

FATHER DEMPSEY (*also perplexed, and rather scandalized*). Is it Fin McCool you mean?

BROADBENT. I daresay it is. (*Referring to the
guide book.*) Murray says that a huge stone, probably
of Druidic origin, is still pointed out as the die cast by
Fin in his celebrated match with the devil.

CORNELIUS (*dubiously*). Jeuce a word I ever heard of it!

FATHER DEMPSEY (*very seriously indeed, and even a little severely*). Dont believe any such nonsense, sir. There never was any such thing. When people talk to you about Fin McCool and the like, take no notice of them. It's all idle stories and superstition.

BROADBENT (*somewhat indignantly; for to be rebuked by an Irish priest for superstition is more than he can stand*). You dont suppose I believe it, do you?

FATHER DEMPSEY. Oh, I thought you did. D'ye see the top o the Roun Tower there? thats an antiquity worth lookin at.

BROADBENT (*deeply interested*). Have you any theory as to what the Round Towers were for?

FATHER DEMPSEY (*a little offended*). A theory? Me! (*Theories are connected in his mind with the late Professor Tyndall, and with scientific scepticism generally: also perhaps with the view that the Round Towers are phallic symbols.*)

CORNELIUS (*remonstrating*). Father Dempsey is the priest of the parish, Mr. Broadbent. What would he be doing with a theory?

FATHER DEMPSEY (*with gentle emphasis*). I have a k n o w l e d g e of what the Roun Towers were, if thats what you mean. They are the forefingers of the early Church, pointing us all to God.

Patsy, intolerably overburdened, loses his balance, and sits down involuntarily. His burdens are scattered over the hillside. Cornelius and Father Dempsey turn furiously on him, leaving Broadbent beaming at the stone and the tower with fatuous interest.

CORNELIUS. Oh, be the hokey, the sammin's broke in two! You schoopid ass, what d'ye mean?

FATHER DEMPSEY. Are you drunk, Patsy Farrell? Did I tell you to carry that hamper carefully or did I not?

PATSY (*rubbing the back of his head, which has almost dinted a slab of granite*). Sure me fut slipt. Howkn I carry three men's luggage at wanst?

FATHER DEMPSEY. You were told to leave behind what you couldnt carry, an go back for it.

PATSY. An whose things was I to lave behind? Hwat would your reverence think if I left your hamper behind in the wet grass; n hwat would the masther say if I left the sammin and the goose be the side o the road for annywan to pick up?

CORNELIUS. Oh, youve a dale to say for yourself, you butther-fingered omadhaun. Waitll Ant Judy sees the state o that sammin: s h e ' l l talk to you. Here! gimme that birdn that fish there; an take Father Dempsey's hamper to his house for him; n then come back for the rest.

FATHER DEMPSEY. Do, Patsy. And mind you dont fall down again.

PATSY. Sure I—

CORNELIUS (*bustling him up the hill*). Whisht! heres Ant Judy. (*Patsy goes grumbling in disgrace, with Father Dempsey's hamper.*)

Aunt Judy comes down the hill, a woman of 50, in no way remarkable, lively and busy without energy or grip, placid without tranquillity, kindly without concern for others: indeed without much concern for herself: a contented product of a narrow, strainless life. She wears her hair parted in the middle and quite smooth, with a flattened bun at the back. Her dress is a plain brown frock, with a woollen pelerine of black and aniline mauve over her shoulders, all very trim in honor of the occasion. She looks round for Larry; is puzzled; then stares incredulously at Broadbent.

AUNT JUDY. Surely to goodness thats not you, Larry!

CORNELIUS. Arra how could he be Larry, woman alive? Larry's in no hurry home, it seems. I havnt set eyes on him. This is his friend, Mr. Broadbent. Mr. Broadbent: me sister Judy.

AUNT JUDY (*hospitably: going to Broadbent and shaking hands heartily*). Mr. Broadbent! Fancy me takin you for Larry! Sure we havnt seen a sight of him for eighteen years, n he only a lad when he left us.

BROADBENT. Its not Larry's fault: he was to have been here before me. He started in our motor an hour before Mr. Doyle arrived, to meet us at Athenmullet, intending to get here long before me.

AUNT JUDY. Lord save us! do you think hes had n axidnt?

BROADBENT. No: hes wired to say hes had a breakdown and will come on as soon as he can. He expects to be here at about ten.

AUNT JUDY. There now! Fancy him trustn himself in a motor and we all expectn him! Just like him! he'd never do anything like anybody else. Well, what cant be cured must be injoored. Come on in, all of you. You must be dyin for your tea, Mr. Broadbent.

BROADBENT (*with a slight start*). Oh, I'm afraid it's too late for tea (*he looks at his watch*).

AUNT JUDY. Not a bit: we never have it airlier than this. I hope they gave you a good dinner at Athenmullet.

BROADBENT (*trying to conceal his consternation as he realizes that he is not going to get any dinner after his drive*). Oh—er—excellent, excellent. By the way, hadnt I better see about a room at the hotel? (*They stare at him.*)

CORNELIUS. The hotel!

FATHER DEMPSEY. Hwat hotel?

AUNT JUDY. Indeedn youre not goin to a hotel. Youll stay with us. I'd have put you into Larry's room, only the boy's pallyass is too short for you; but we'll make a comfortable bed for you on the sofa in the parlor.

parish, let me know. (*He shakes hands with Broadbent.*)

BROADBENT (*effusively cordial*). Thank you, Father Dempsey. Delighted to have met you, sir.

FATHER DEMPSEY (*passing on to Aunt Judy*). Goodnight, Miss Doyle.

AUNT JUDY. Wont you stay to tea?

FATHER DEMPSEY. Not to-night, thank you kindly: I have business to do at home. (*He turns to go, and meets Patsy Farrell returning unloaded.*) Have you left that hamper for me?

PATSY. Yis, your reverence.

FATHER DEMPSEY. Thats a good lad (*going*).

PATSY (*to Aunt Judy*). Fadher Keegan sez—

FATHER DEMPSEY (*turning sharply on him*). Whats that you say?

PATSY (*frightened*). Fadher Keegan—

FATHER DEMPSEY. How often have you heard me bid you call Mister Keegan in his proper name, the same as I do? Father Keegan indeed! Cant you tell the difference between your priest and any ole madman in a black coat?

PATSY. Sure I'm afraid he might put a spell on me.

FATHER DEMPSEY (*wrathfully*). You mind what I tell you or I'll put a spell on you thatll make you lep. D'ye mind that now? (*He goes home.*)

Patsy goes down the hill to retrieve the fish, the bird, and the sack.

AUNT JUDY. Ah, hwy cant you hold your tongue, Patsy, before Father Dempsey?

PATSY. Well, what was I to do? Father Keegan bid me tell you Miss Nora was gone to the Roun Tower.

AUNT JUDY. An hwy couldnt you wait to tell us until Father Dempsey was gone?

PATSY. I was afeerd o forgetn it; and then may be he'd a sent the grasshopper or the little dark looker into me at night to remind me of it. (*The dark looker*

*is the common grey lizard, which is supposed to walk
down the throats of incautious sleepers and cause them
to perish in a slow decline.*)

CORNELIUS. Yah, you great gaum, you! Widjer
grasshoppers and dark lookers! Here: take up them
things and let me hear no more o your foolish lip.
(*Patsy obeys.*) You can take the sammin under your
oxther. (*He wedges the salmon into Patsy's axilla.*)

PATSY. I can take the goose too, sir. Put it on me
back and gimme the neck of it in me mouth. (*Cornelius
is about to comply thoughtlessly.*)

AUNT JUDY (*feeling that Broadbent's presence demands special punctiliousness*). For shame, Patsy! to
offer to take the goose in your mouth that we have to
eat after you! The masterll bring it in for you. (*Patsy,
abashed, yet irritated by this ridiculous fastidiousness,
takes his load up the hill.*)

CORNELIUS. What the jeuce does Nora want to go
to the Roun Tower for?

AUNT JUDY. Oh, the Lord knows! Romancin, I
suppose. Praps she thinks Larry would go there to
look for her and see her safe home.

BROADBENT. I'm afraid it's all the fault of my motor.
Miss Reilly must not be left to wait and walk home
alone at night. Shall I go for her?

AUNT JUDY (*contemptuously*). Arra hwat ud happen to her? Hurry in now, Corny. Come, Mr. Broadbent. I left the tea on the hob to draw; and itll be
black if we dont go in an drink it.

They go up the hill. It is dusk by this time.

*Broadbent does not fare so badly after all at Aunt
Judy's board. He gets not only tea and bread-and-
butter, but more mutton chops than he has ever conceived it possible to eat at one sitting. There is also
a most filling substance called potato cake. Hardly
have his fears of being starved been replaced by his
first misgiving that he is eating too much and will be*

sorry for it to-morrow, when his appetite is revived by the production of a bottle of illicitly distilled whisky, called potcheen, which he has read and dreamed of (he calls it pottine) and is now at last to taste. His good-humor rises almost to excitement before Cornelius shews signs of sleepiness. The contrast between Aunt Judy's table service and that of the south and east coast hotels at which he spends his Fridays-to-Tuesdays when he is in London, seems to him delightfully Irish. The almost total atrophy of any sense of enjoyment in Cornelius, or even any desire for it or toleration of the possibility of life being something better than a round of sordid worries, relieved by tobacco, punch, fine mornings, and petty successes in buying and selling, passes with his guest as the whimsical affectation of a shrewd Irish humorist and incorrigible spendthrift. Aunt Judy seems to him an incarnate joke. The likelihood that the joke will pall after a month or so, and is probably not apparent at any time to born Rossculleners, or that he himself unconsciously entertains Aunt Judy by his fantastic English personality and English mispronunciations, does not occur to him for a moment. In the end he is so charmed, and so loth to go to bed and perhaps dream of prosaic England, that he insists on going out to smoke a cigar and look for Nora Reilly at the Round Tower. Not that any special insistence is needed; for the English inhibitive instinct does not seem to exist in Rosscullen. Just as Nora's liking to miss a meal and stay out at the Round Tower is accepted as a sufficient reason for her doing it, and for the family going to bed and leaving the door open for her, so Broadbent's whim to go out for a late stroll provokes neither hospitable remonstrance nor surprise. Indeed Aunt Judy wants to get rid of him whilst she makes a bed for him on the sofa. So off he goes, full fed, happy and enthusiastic, to explore the valley by moon-light.

*The Round Tower stands about half an Irish mile
from Rosscullen, some fifty yards south of the road on
a knoll with a circle of wild greensward on it. The
road once ran over this knoll; but modern engineering
has tempered the level to the Beeyankiny car by carrying the road partly round the knoll and partly through a
cutting; so that the way from the road to the tower is a
footpath up the embankment through furze and brambles.*

*On the edge of this slope, at the top of the path,
Nora is straining her eyes in the moonlight, watching
for Larry. At last she gives it up with a sob of impatience, and retreats to the hoary foot of the tower,
where she sits down discouraged and cries a little. Then
she settles herself resignedly to wait, and hums a song
—not an Irish melody, but a hackneyed English draw-
ing-room ballad of the season before last—until some
slight noise suggests a footstep, when she springs up
eagerly and runs to the edge of the slope again. Some
moments of silence and suspense follow, broken by un-
mistakable footsteps. She gives a little gasp as she
sees a man approaching.*

NORA. Is that you, Larry? (*Frightened a little.*)
Who's that?

BROADBENT's *voice from below on the path.* Dont be
alarmed.

NORA. Oh, what an English accent youve got!

BROADBENT (*rising into view*). I must introduce myself—

NORA (*violently startled, retreating*). Its not you!
Who are you? What do you want?

BROADBENT (*advancing*). I'm really s o sorry to have
alarmed you, Miss Reilly. My name is Broadbent.
Larry's friend, you know.

NORA (*chilled*). And has Mr. Doyle not come with
you?

BROADBENT. No. Ive come instead. I hope I am
not unwelcome.

NORA (*deeply mortified*). I'm sorry Mr. Doyle should have given you the trouble, I'm sure.

BROADBENT. You see, as a stranger and an Englishman, I thought it would be interesting to see the Round Tower by moonlight.

NORA. Oh, you came to see the tower. I thought— (*confused, trying to recover her manners*). Oh, of course. I was so startled— It's a beautiful night, isnt it?

BROADBENT. Lovely. I must explain why Larry has not come himself.

NORA. Why should he come? Hes seen the tower often enough: it's no attraction to h i m. (*Genteelly.*) An what do you think of Ireland, Mr. Broadbent? Have you ever been here before?

BROADBENT. Never.

NORA. An how do you like it?

BROADBENT (*suddenly betraying a condition of extreme sentimentality*). I can hardly trust myself to say how much I like it. The magic of this Irish scene, and—I really dont want to be personal, Miss Reilly; but the charm of your Irish voice—

NORA (*quite accustomed to gallantry, and attaching no seriousness whatever to it*). Oh, get along with you, Mr. Broadbent! Youre breaking your heart about me already, I daresay, after seeing me for two minutes in the dark.

BROADBENT. The voice is just as beautiful in the dark, you know. Besides, Ive heard a great deal about you from Larry.

NORA (*with bitter indifference*). Have you now? Well, thats a great honor, I'm sure.

BROADBENT. I have looked forward to meeting you more than to anything else in Ireland.

NORA (*ironically*). Dear me! did you now?

BROADBENT. I did really. I wish you had taken half as much interest in me.

NORA. Oh, I was dying to see you, of course. I daresay you can imagine the sensation an Englishman like you would make among us poor Irish people.

BROADBENT. Ah, now youre chaffing me, Miss Reilly: you know you are. You mustnt chaff me. I'm very much in earnest about Ireland and everything Irish. I'm very much in earnest about you and about Larry.

NORA. Larry has nothing to do with me, Mr. Broadbent.

BROADBENT. If I really thought that, Miss Reilly, I should—well, I should let myself feel that charm of which I spoke just now more deeply than I—than I—

NORA. Is it making love to me you are?

BROADBENT (*scared and much upset*). On my word I believe I am, Miss Reilly. If you say that to me again I shant answer for myself: all the harps of Ireland are in your voice. (*She laughs at him. He suddenly loses his head and seizes her arms, to her great indignation.*) Stop laughing: do you hear? I am in earnest—in English earnest. When I say a thing like that to a woman, I mean it. (*Releasing her and trying to recover his ordinary manner in spite of his bewildering emotion.*) I beg your pardon.

NORA. How dare you touch me?

BROADBENT. There are not many things I would not dare for you. That does not sound right perhaps; but I really— (*he stops and passes his hand over his forehead, rather lost*).

NORA. I think you ought to be ashamed. I think if you were a gentleman, and me alone with you in this place at night, you would die rather than do such a thing.

BROADBENT. You mean that it's an act of treachery to Larry?

NORA. Deed I dont. What has Larry to do with it? It's an act of disrespect and rudeness to me: it shews what you take me for. You can go your way now; and I'll go mine. Goodnight, Mr. Broadbent.

BROADBENT. No, please, Miss Reilly. One moment. Listen to me. I'm serious: I'm desperately serious. Tell me that I'm interfering with Larry; and I'll go straight from this spot back to London and never see you again. Thats on my honor: I will. Am I interfering with him?

NORA (*answering in spite of herself in a sudden spring of bitterness*). I should think you ought to know better than me whether youre interfering with him. Youve seen him oftener than I have. You know him better than I do, by this time. Youve come to me quicker than he has, havnt you?

BROADBENT. I'm bound to tell you, Miss Reilly, that Larry has not arrived in Rosscullen yet. He meant to get here before me; but his car broke down; and he may not arrive until to-morrow.

NORA (*her face lighting up*). Is that the truth?

BROADBENT. Yes: thats the truth. (*She gives a sigh of relief.*) Youre glad of that?

NORA (*up in arms at once*). Glad indeed! Why should I be glad? As weve waited eighteen years for him we can afford to wait a day longer, I should think.

BROADBENT. If you really feel like that about him, there may be a chance for another man yet. Eh?

NORA (*deeply offended*). I suppose people are different in England, Mr. Broadbent; so perhaps you dont mean any harm. In Ireland nobody'd mind what a man'd say in fun, nor take advantage of what a woman might say in answer to it. If a woman couldnt talk to a man for two minutes at their first meeting without being treated the way youre treating me, no decent woman would ever talk to a man at all.

BROADBENT. I dont understand that. I dont admit that. I am sincere; and my intentions are perfectly honorable. I think you will accept the fact that I'm

a Englishman as a guarantee that I am not a man to act
hastily or romantically, though I confess that your voice
had such an extraordinary effect on me just now when
you asked me so quaintly whether I was making love
to you—

NORA (*flushing*). I never thought—

BROADBENT (*quickly*). Of course you didnt. I'm
not so stupid as that. But I couldnt bear your laughing
at the feeling it gave me. You— (*again struggling with
a surge of emotion*) you dont know what I— (*he chokes
for a moment and then blurts out with unnatural steadiness*) Will you be my wife?

NORA (*promptly*). Deed I wont. The idea! (*Looking at him more carefully.*) Arra, come home, Mr.
Broadbent; and get your senses back again. I think
youre not accustomed to potcheen punch in the evening
after your tea.

BROADBENT (*horrified*). Do you mean to say that I
—I—I—my God! that I appear d r u n k to you, Miss
Reilly?

NORA (*compassionately*). How many tumblers had
you?

BROADBENT (*helplessly*). Two.

NORA. The flavor of the turf prevented you noticing
the strength of it. Youd better come home to bed.

BROADBENT (*fearfully agitated*). But this is such a
horrible doubt to put into my mind—to—to— For
Heaven's sake, Miss Reilly, am I really drunk?

NORA (*soothingly*). Youll be able to judge better in
the morning. Come on now back with me, an think no
more about it. (*She takes his arm with motherly solici-
tude and urges him gently towards the path.*)

BROADBENT (*yielding in despair*). I must be drunk
—frightfully drunk; for your voice drove me out of my
senses— (*he stumbles over a stone*). No: on my word,
on my most sacred word of honor, Miss Reilly, I tripped
over that stone. It was an accident; it was indeed.

NORA. Yes, of course it was. Just take my arm, Mr. Broadbent, while we're goin down the path to the road. Youll be all right then.

BROADBENT (*submissively taking it*). I cant sufficiently apologize, Miss Reilly, or express my sense of your kindness when I am in such a disgusting state. How could I be such a bea— (*he trips again*) damn the heather! my foot caught in it.

NORA. Steady now, steady. Come along: come. (*He is led down to the road in the character of a convicted drunkard. To him there is something divine in the sympathetic indulgence she substitutes for the angry disgust with which one of his own countrywomen would resent his supposed condition. And he has no suspicion of the fact, or of her ignorance of it, that when an Englishman is sentimental he behaves very much as an Irishman does when he is drunk.*)

END OF ACT II.

ACT III

Next morning Broadbent and Larry are sitting at the ends of a breakfast table in the middle of a small grass plot before Cornelius Doyle's house. They have finished their meal, and are buried in newspapers. Most of the crockery is crowded upon a large square black tray of japanned metal. The teapot is of brown delft ware. There is no silver; and the butter, on a dinner plate, is e n b l o c. The background to this breakfast is the house, a small white slated building, accessible by a half-glazed door. A person coming out into the garden by this door would find the table straight in front of him, and a gate leading to the road half way down the garden on his right; or, if he turned sharp to his left, he could pass round the end of the house through an unkempt shrubbery. The mutilated remnant of a huge plaster statue, nearly dissolved by the rains of a century, and vaguely resembling a majestic female in Roman draperies, with a wreath in her hand, stands neglected amid the laurels. Such statues, though apparently works of art, grow naturally in Irish gardens. Their germination is a mystery to the oldest inhabitants, to whose means and tastes they are totally foreign.

There is a rustic bench, much soiled by the birds, and decorticated and split by the weather, near the little gate. At the opposite side, a basket lies unmolested because it might as well be there as anywhere else. An empty chair at the table was lately occupied by Cornelius, who has finished his breakfast and gone in to the room in which he receives rents and keeps his books and cash, known in the household as "the office." This chair, like the two occupied by Larry and Broadbent, has a mahogany frame and is upholstered in black horsehair.

Larry rises and goes off through the shrubbery with his newspaper. Hodson comes in through the garden gate, disconsolate. Broadbent, who sits facing the gate, augurs the worst from his expression.

BROADBENT. Have you been to the village?

HODSON. No use, sir. We'll have to get everything from London by parcel post.

BROADBENT. I hope they made you comfortable last night.

HODSON. I was no worse than you were on that sofa, sir. One expects to rough it here, sir.

BROADBENT. We shall have to look out for some other arrangement. (*Cheering up irrepressibly.*) Still, it's no end of a joke. How do you like the Irish, Hodson?

HODSON. Well, sir, theyre all right anywhere but in their own country. Ive known lots of em in England, and generally liked em. But here, sir, I seem simply to hate em. The feeling come over me the moment we landed at Cork, sir. It's no use my pretendin, sir: I cant bear em. My mind rises up agin their ways, somehow: they rub me the wrong way all over.

BROADBENT. Oh, their faults are on the surface: at heart they arc one of the finest races on earth. (*Hodson turns away, without affecting to respond to his enthusiasm.*) By the way, Hodson—

HODSON (*turning*). Yes, sir.

BROADBENT. Did you notice anything about me last night when I came in with that lady?

HODSON (*surprised*). No, sir.

BROADBENT. Not any — er — ? You may speak frankly.

HODSON. I didnt notice nothing, sir. What sort of thing did you mean, sir?

BROADBENT. Well—er—er—well, to put it plainly, was I drunk?

HODSON (*amazed*). No, sir.

BROADBENT. Quite sure?

HODSON. Well, I should a said rather the opposite, sir. Usually when youve been enjoying yourself, youre a bit hearty like. Last night you seemed rather low, if anything.

BROADBENT. I certainly have no headache. Did you try the pottine, Hodson?

HODSON. I just took a mouthful, sir. It tasted of peat: oh! something horrid, sir. The people here call peat turf. Potcheen and strong porter is what they like, sir. I'm sure I dont know how they can stand it. Give me beer, I say.

BROADBENT. By the way, you told me I couldnt have porridge for breakfast; but Mr. Doyle had some.

HODSON. Yes, sir. Very sorry, sir. They call it stirabout, sir: thats how it was. They know no better, sir.

BROADBENT. All right: I'll have some tomorrow.

Hodson goes to the house. When he opens the door he finds Nora and Aunt Judy on the threshold. He stands aside to let them pass, with the air of a well trained servant oppressed by heavy trials. Then he goes in. Broadbent rises. Aunt Judy goes to the table and collects the plates and cups on the tray. Nora goes to the back of the rustic seat and looks out at the gate with the air of a woman accustomed to have nothing to do. Larry returns from the shrubbery.

BROADBENT. Good morning, Miss Doyle.

AUNT JUDY (*thinking it absurdly late in the day for such a salutation*). Oh, good morning. (*Before moving his plate.*) Have you done?

BROADBENT. Quite, thank you. You must excuse us for not waiting for you. The country air tempted us to get up early.

AUNT JUDY.   N d'ye call this airly, God help you?

LARRY.   Aunt Judy probably breakfasted about half past six.

AUNT JUDY.   Whisht, you!—draggin the parlor chairs out into the gardn n givin Mr. Broadbent his death over his meals out here in the cold air. (*To Broadbent.*)   Why d'ye put up with his foolishness, Mr. Broadbent?

BROADBENT.   I assure you I like the open air.

AUNT JUDY.   Ah galong! How can you like whats not natural? I hope you slept well.

NORA.   Did anything wake yup with a thump at three o'clock? I thought the house was falling. But then I'm a very light sleeper.

LARRY.   I seem to recollect that one of the legs of the sofa in the parlor had a way of coming out unexpectedly eighteen years ago. Was that it, Tom?

BROADBENT (*hastily*).   Oh, it doesnt matter: I was not hurt—at least—er—

AUNT JUDY.   Oh now what a shame! An I told Patsy Farrll to put a nail in it.

BROADBENT.   He did, Miss Doyle. There was a nail, certainly.

AUNT JUDY.   Dear oh dear!

An oldish peasant farmer, small, leathery, peat-faced, with a deep voice and a surliness that is meant to be aggressive, and is in effect pathetic—the voice of a man of hard life and many sorrows—comes in at the gate. He is old enough to have perhaps worn a long tailed frieze coat and knee breeches in his time; but now he is dressed respectably in a black frock coat, tall hat, and pollard colored trousers; and his face is as clean as washing can make it, though that is not saying much, as the habit is recently acquired and not yet congenial.

THE NEW-COMER (*at the gate*).   God save all here! (*He comes a little way into the garden.*)

LARRY (*patronizingly, speaking across the garden to*

him). Is that yourself, Matt Haffigan? Do you remember me?

MATTHEW (*intentionally rude and blunt*). No. Who are you?

NORA. Oh, I'm sure you remember him, Mr. Haffigan.

MATTHEW (*grudgingly admitting it*). I suppose he'll be young Larry Doyle that was.

LARRY. Yes.

MATTHEW (*to Larry*). I hear you done well in America.

LARRY. Fairly well.

MATTHEW. I suppose you saw me brother Andy out dhere.

LARRY. No. It's such a big place that looking for a man there is like looking for a needle in a bundle of hay. They tell me hes a great man out there.

MATTHEW. So he is, God be praised. Wheres your father?

AUNT JUDY. He's inside, in the office, Mr. Haffigan, with Barney Doarn n Father Dempsey.

Matthew, without wasting further words on the company, goes curtly into the house.

LARRY (*staring after him*). Is anything wrong with old Matt?

NORA. No. Hes the same as ever. Why?

LARRY. Hes not the same to me. He used to be very civil to Master Larry: a deal too civil, I used to think. Now hes as surly and stand-off as a bear.

AUNT JUDY. Oh sure hes bought his farm in the Land Purchase. Hes independent now.

NORA. It's made a great change, Larry. Youd harly know the old tenants now. Youd think it was a liberty to speak t'dhem—some o dhem. (*She goes to the table, and helps to take off the cloth, which she and Aunt Judy fold up between them.*)

AUNT JUDY. I wonder what he wants to see Corny for. He hasnt been here since he paid the last of his old rent; and then he as good as threw it in Corny's face, I thought.

LARRY. No wonder! Of course they all hated us like the devil. Ugh! (*Moodily.*) Ive seen them in that office, telling my father what a fine boy I was, and plastering him with compliments, with your honor here and your honor there, when all the time their fingers were itching to be at his throat.

AUNT JUDY. Deedn why should they want to hurt poor Corny? It was he that got Matt the lease of his farm, and stood up for him as an industrious decent man.

BROADBENT. Was he industrious? Thats remarkable, you know, in an Irishman.

LARRY. Industrious! That man's industry used to make me sick, even as a boy. I tell you, an Irish peasant's industry is not human: it's worse than the industry of a coral insect. An Englishman has some sense about working: he never does more than he can help—and hard enough to get him to do that without scamping it; but an Irishman will work as if he'd die the moment he stopped. That man Matthew Haffigan and his brother Andy made a farm out of a patch of stones on the hillside—cleared it and dug it with their own naked hands and bought their first spade out of their first crop of potatoes. Talk of making two blades of wheat grow where one grew before! those two men made a whole field of wheat grow where not even a furze bush had ever got its head up between the stones.

BROADBENT. That was magnificent, you know. Only a great race is capable of producing such men.

LARRY. Such fools, you mean! What good was it to them? The moment theyd done it, the landlord put a rent of £5 a year on them, and turned them out because they couldnt pay it.

AUNT JUDY. Why couldnt they pay as well as Billy Byrne that took it after them?

LARRY (*angrily*). You know very well that Billy Byrne never paid it. He only offered it to get possession. He never paid it.

AUNT JUDY. That was because Andy Haffigan hurt him with a brick so that he was never the same again. Andy had to run away to America for it.

BROADBENT (*glowing with indignation*). Who can blame him, Miss Doyle? Who can blame him?

LARRY (*impatiently*). Oh, rubbish! whats the good of the man thats starved out of a farm murdering the man thats starved into it? Would you have done such a thing?

BROADBENT. Yes. I—I—I—I— (*stammering with fury*) I should have shot the confounded landlord, and wrung the neck of the damned agent, and blown the farm up with dynamite, and Dublin Castle along with it.

LARRY. Oh yes: youd have done great things; and a fat lot of good youd have got out of it, too! Thats an Englishman all over! make bad laws and give away all the land, and then, when your economic incompetence produces its natural and inevitable results, get virtuously indignant and kill the people that carry out your laws.

AUNT JUDY. Sure never mind him, Mr. Broadbent. It doesnt matter, anyhow, because theres harly any landlords left! and therll soon be none at all.

LARRY. On the contrary, therll soon be nothing else; and the Lord help Ireland then!

AUNT JUDY. Ah, youre never satisfied, Larry. (*To Nora.*) Come on, alanna, an make the paste for the pie. We can leave them to their talk. They dont want us (*she takes up the tray and goes into the house*).

BROADBENT (*rising and gallantly protesting*). Oh, Miss Doyle! Really, really—

Nora, following Aunt Judy with the rolled-up cloth in her hands, looks at him and strikes him dumb. He

*watches her until she disappears; then comes to Larry
and addresses him with sudden intensity.*

BROADBENT.   Larry.

LARRY.   What is it?

BROADBENT.   I got drunk last night, and proposed to
Miss Reilly.

LARRY.   You h w a t??? (*He screams with laughter
in the falsetto Irish register unused for that purpose in
England.*)

BROADBENT.   What are you laughing at?

LARRY (*stopping dead*).   I dont know.   Thats the
sort of thing an Irishman laughs at.   Has she accepted
you?

BROADBENT.   I shall never forget that with the chivalry of her nation, though I was utterly at her mercy,
she refused me.

LARRY.   That was extremely improvident of her.
(*Beginning to reflect.*)   But look here: when were you
drunk?   You were sober enough when you came back
from the Round Tower with her.

BROADBENT.   No, Larry, I was drunk, I am sorry to
say.   I had two tumblers of punch.   She had to lead
me home.   You must have noticed it.

LARRY.   I did not.

BROADBENT.   She did.

LARRY.   May I ask how long it took you to come to
business?   You can hardly have known her for more
than a couple of hours.

BROADBENT.   I am afraid it was hardly a couple of
minutes.   She was not here when I arrived; and I saw
her for the first time at the tower.

LARRY.   Well, you a r e a nice infant to be let loose
in this country!   Fancy the potcheen going to your head
like that!

BROADBENT.   Not to my head, I think.   I have no
headache; and I could speak distinctly.   No: potcheen
goes to the heart, not to the head.   What ought I to do?

Lᴀʀʀʏ. Nothing. What need you do?

Bʀᴏᴀᴅʙᴇɴᴛ. There is rather a delicate moral question involved. The point is, was I drunk enough not to be morally responsible for my proposal? Or was I sober enough to be bound to repeat it now that I am undoubtedly sober?

Lᴀʀʀʏ. I should see a little more of her before deciding.

Bʀᴏᴀᴅʙᴇɴᴛ. No, no. That would not be right. That would not be fair. I am either under a moral obligation or I am not. I wish I knew how drunk I was.

Lᴀʀʀʏ. Well, you were evidently in a state of blithering sentimentality, anyhow.

Bʀᴏᴀᴅʙᴇɴᴛ. That is true, Larry: I admit it. Her voice has a most extraordinary effect on me. That Irish voice!

Lᴀʀʀʏ (*sympathetically*). Yes, I know. When I first went to London I very nearly proposed to walk out with a waitress in an Aerated Bread shop because her Whitechapel accent was so distinguished, so quaintly touching, so pretty—

Bʀᴏᴀᴅʙᴇɴᴛ (*angrily*). Miss Reilly is not a waitress, is she?

Lᴀʀʀʏ. Oh, come! The waitress was a very nice girl.

Bʀᴏᴀᴅʙᴇɴᴛ. You think every Englishwoman an angel. You really have coarse tastes in that way, Larry. Miss Reilly is one of the finer types: a type rare in England, except perhaps in the best of the aristocracy.

Lᴀʀʀʏ. Aristocracy be blowed! Do you know what Nora eats?

Bʀᴏᴀᴅʙᴇɴᴛ. Eats! what do you mean?

Lᴀʀʀʏ. Breakfast: tea and bread-and-butter, with an occasional rasher, and an egg on special occasions: say on her birthday. Dinner in the middle of the day, one course and nothing else. In the evening, tea and bread-and-butter again. You compare her with your English-

women who wolf down from three to five meat meals a
day; and naturally you find her a sylph. The difference
is not a difference of type: its the difference between
the woman who eats not wisely but too well, and the
woman who eats not wisely but too little.

BROADBENT (*furious*). Larry: you—you—you disgust me. You are a damned fool. (*He sits down
angrily on the rustic seat, which sustains the shock with
difficulty.*)

LARRY. Steady! stead-eee! (*He laughs and seats
himself on the table.*)

*Cornelius Doyle, Father Dempsey, Barney Doran,
and Matthew Haffigan come from the house. Doran is
a stout bodied, short armed, roundheaded, red haired
man on the verge of middle age, of sanguine temperament, with an enormous capacity for derisive, obscene,
blasphemous, or merely cruel and senseless fun, and a
violent and impetuous intolerance of other temperaments
and other opinions, all this representing energy and
capacity wasted and demoralized by want of sufficient
training and social pressure to force it into beneficent
activity and build a character with it; for Barney is by
no means either stupid or weak. He is recklessly untidy
as to his person; but the worst effects of his neglect are
mitigated by a powdering of flour and mill dust; and
his unbrushed clothes, made of a fashionable tailor's
sackcloth, were evidently chosen regardless of expense
for the sake of their appearance.*

*Matthew Haffigan, ill at ease, coasts the garden shyly
on the shrubbery side until he anchors near the basket,
where he feels least in the way. The priest comes to
the table and slaps Larry on the shoulder. Larry, turning quickly, and recognizing Father Dempsey, alights
from the table and shakes the priest's hand warmly.
Doran comes down the garden between Father Dempsey
and Matt; and Cornelius, on the other side of the table,
turns to Broadbent, who rises genially.*

CORNELIUS. I think we all met las night.

DORAN. I hadnt that pleasure.

CORNELIUS. To be sure, Barney: I forgot. (*To Broadbent, introducing Barney.*) Mr. Doran. He owns that fine mill you noticed from the car.

BROADBENT (*delighted with them all*). Most happy, Mr. Doran. Very pleased indeed.

Doran, not quite sure whether he is being courted or patronized, nods independently.

DORAN. Hows yourself, Larry?

LARRY. Finely, thank you. No need to ask y o u. (*Doran grins; and they shake hands.*)

CORNELIUS. Give Father Dempsey a chair, Larry.

Matthew Haffigan runs to the nearest end of the table and takes the chair from it, placing it near the basket; but Larry has already taken the chair from the other end and placed it in front of the table. Father Dempsey accepts that more central position.

CORNELIUS. Sit down, Barney, will you; and you, Mat.

Doran takes the chair Mat is still offering to the priest; and poor Matthew, outfaced by the miller, humbly turns the basket upside down and sits on it. Cornelius brings his own breakfast chair from the table and sits down on Father Dempsey's right. Broadbent resumes his seat on the rustic bench. Larry crosses to the bench and is about to sit down beside him when Broadbent holds him off nervously.

BROADBENT. Do you think it will bear two, Larry?

LARRY. Perhaps not. Dont move. I'll stand. (*He posts himself behind the bench.*)

They are all now seated, except Larry; and the session assumes a portentous air, as if something important were coming.

CORNELIUS. Praps youll explain, Father Dempsey.

FATHER DEMPSEY. No, no: go on, you: the Church has no politics.

BROADBENT. Youre very kind, Miss Doyle; but really I'm ashamed to give you so much trouble unnecessarily. I shant mind the hotel in the least.

FATHER DEMPSEY. Man alive! theres no hotel in Rosscullen.

BROADBENT. No hotel! Why, the driver told me there was the finest hotel in Ireland here. (*They regard him joylessly.*)

AUNT JUDY. Arra would you mind what the like of him world tell you? Sure he'd say hwatever was the least trouble to himself and the pleasantest to you, thinkin you might give him a thruppeny bit for himself or the like.

BROADBENT. Perhaps theres a public house.

FATHER DEMPSEY (*grimly*). Theres seventeen.

AUNT JUDY. Ah then, how could you stay at a public house? theyd have no place to put you even if it was a right place for you to go. Come! is it the sofa youre afraid of? If it is, you can have me own bed. I can sleep with Nora.

BROADBENT. Not at all, not at all: I should be only too delighted. But to upset your arrangements in this way—

CORNELIUS (*anxious to cut short the discussion, which makes him ashamed of his house; for he guesses Broadbent's standard of comfort a little more accurately than his sister does*). Thats all right: itll be no trouble at all. Hweres Nora?

AUNT JUDY. Oh, how do I know? She slipped out a little while ago: I thought she was goin to meet the car.

CORNELIUS (*dissatisfied*). Its a queer thing of her to run out o the way at such a time.

AUNT JUDY. Sure shes a queer girl altogether. Come. Come in, come in.

FATHER DEMPSEY. I'll say good-night, Mr. Broadbent. If theres anything I can do for you in this

CORNELIUS. Were yever thinkin o goin into parliament at all, Larry?

LARRY. Me!

FATHER DEMPSEY (*encouragingly*). Yes, you. Hwy not?

LARRY. I'm afraid my ideas would not be popular enough.

CORNELIUS. I dont know that. Do you, Barney?

DORAN. Theres too much blatherumskite in Irish politics: a dale too much.

LARRY. But what about your present member? Is he going to retire?

CORNELIUS. No: I dont know that he is.

LARRY (*interrogatively*). Well? then?

MATTHEW (*breaking out with surly bitterness*). Weve had enough of his foolish talk agen lanlords. Hwat call has he to talk about the lan, that never was outside of a city office in his life?

CORNELIUS. We're tired of him. He doesnt know hwere to stop. Every man cant own land; and some men must own it to employ them. It was all very well when solid men like Doran and me and Mat were kep from ownin land. But hwat man in his senses ever wanted to give land to Patsy Farrll an dhe like o him?

BROADBENT. But surely Irish landlordism was accountable for what Mr. Haffigan suffered.

MATTHEW. Never mind hwat I suffered. I know what I suffered adhout you tellin me. But did I ever ask for more dhan the farm I made wid me own hans: tell me that, Corny Doyle, and you that knows. Was I fit for the responsibility or was I not? (*Snarling angrily at Cornelius.*) Am I to be compared to Patsy Farrll, that doesnt harly know his right hand from his left? What did he ever suffer, I'd like to know?

CORNELIUS. Thats just what I say. I wasnt comparin you to your disadvantage.

MATTHEW (*implacable*). Then hwat did you mane
be talkin about givin him lan?

DORAN. Aisy, Mat, aisy. Youre like a bear with a
sore back.

MATTHEW (*trembling with rage*). An who are you,
to offer to taitch me manners?

FATHER DEMPSEY (*admonitorily*). Now, now, now,
Mat! none o dhat. How often have I told you youre
too ready to take offence where none is meant? You
dont understand: Corny Doyle is saying just what you
want to have said. (*To Cornelius.*) Go on, Mr. Doyle;
and never mind him.

MATTHEW (*rising*). Well, if me lan is to be given
to Patsy and his like, I'm goin oura dhis. I—

DORAN (*with violent impatience*). Arra who's goin
to give your lan to Patsy, yowl fool ye?

FATHER DEMPSEY. Aisy, Barney, aisy. (*Sternly, to
Mat.*) I told you, Matthew Haffigan, that Corny Doyle
was sayin nothin against you. I'm sorry your priest's
word is not good enough for you. I'll go, sooner than
stay to make you commit a sin against the Church.
Good morning, gentlemen. (*He rises. They all rise,
except Broadbent.*)

DORAN (*to Mat*). There! Sarve you dam well right,
you cantankerous oul noodle.

MATTHEW (*appalled*). Dont say dhat, Fadher Dempsey. I never had a thought agen you or the Holy
Church. I know I'm a bit hasty when I think about
the lan. I ax your pardon for it.

FATHER DEMPSEY (*resuming his seat with dignified
reserve*). Very well: I'll overlook it this time. (*He
sits down. The others sit down, except Matthew. Father
Dempsey, about to ask Corny to proceed, remembers
Matthew and turns to him, giving him just a crumb of
graciousness.*) Sit down, Mat. (*Matthew, crushed, sits
down in disgrace, and is silent, his eyes shifting pite-
ously from one speaker to another in an intensely mis-*

trustful effort to understand them.) Go on, Mr. Doyle.
We can make allowances. Go on.

CORNELIUS. Well, you see how it is, Larry. Round
about here, weve got the land at last; and we want no
more Government meddlin. We want a new class o man
in parliament: one dhat knows dhat the farmer's the real
backbone o the country, n doesnt care a snap of his
fingers for the shoutn o the riff-raff in the towns, or
for the foolishness of the laborers.

DORAN. Aye; an dhat can afford to live in London
and pay his own way until Home Rule comes, instead
o wantin subscriptions and the like.

FATHER DEMPSEY. Yes: thats a good point, Barney.
When too much money goes to politics, it's the Church
that has to starve for it. A member of parliament ought
to be a help to the Church instead of a burden on it.

LARRY. Heres a chance for you, Tom. What do you
say?

BROADBENT (*deprecatory, but important and smiling*).
Oh, I have no claim whatever to the seat. Besides, I'm
a Saxon.

DORAN. A hwat?

BROADBENT. A Saxon. An Englishman.

DORAN. An Englishman. Bedad I never heard it
called dhat before.

MATTHEW (*cunningly*). If I might make so bould,
Fadher, I wouldnt say but an English Prodestn
mightnt have a more indepindent mind about the lan,
an be less afeerd to spake out about it, dhan an Irish
Catholic.

CORNELIUS. But sure Larry's as good as English:
arnt you, Larry?

LARRY. You may put me out of your head, father,
once for all.

CORNELIUS. Arra why?

LARRY. I have strong opinions which wouldnt suit
you.

DORAN (*rallying him blatantly*). Is it still Larry the bould Fenian?

LARRY. No: the bold Fenian is now an older and possibly foolisher man.

CORNELIUS. Hwat does it matter to us hwat your opinions are? You know that your father's bought his farm, just the same as Mat here n Barney's mill. All we ask now is to be let alone. Youve nothin against that, have you?

LARRY. Certainly I have. I dont believe in letting anybody or anything alone.

CORNELIUS (*losing his temper*). Arra what d'ye mean, you young fool? Here Ive got you the offer of a good seat in parliament; n you think yourself mighty smart to stand there and talk foolishness to me. Will you take it or leave it?

LARRY. Very well: I'll take it with pleasure if youll give it to me.

CORNELIUS (*subsiding sulkily*). Well, why couldnt you say so at once? It's a good job youve made up your mind at last.

DORAN (*suspiciously*). Stop a bit, stop a bit.

MATTHEW (*writhing between his dissatisfaction and his fear of the priest*). Its not because hes your son that hes to get the sate. Fadher Dempsey: wouldnt you think well to ask him what he manes about the lan?

LARRY (*coming down on Mat promptly*). I'll tell you, Mat. I always thought it was a stupid, lazy, good-for-nothing sort of thing to leave the land in the hands of the old landlords without calling them to a strict account for the use they made of it, and the condition of the people on it. I could see for myself that they thought of nothing but what they could get out of it to spend in England; and that they mortgaged and mort-gaged until hardly one of them owned his own property or could have afforded to keep it up decently if he'd wanted to. But I tell you plump and plain, Mat, that

if anybody thinks things will be any better now that
the land is handed over to a lot of little men like you,
without calling you to account either, theyre mistaken.

MATTHEW (*sullenly*). What call have you to look
down on me? I suppose you think youre everybody because your father was a land agent.

LARRY. What call have you to look down on Patsy
Farrell? I suppose you think youre everybody because
you own a few fields.

MATTHEW. Was Patsy Farrll ever ill used as I was
ill used? tell me dhat.

LARRY. He will be, if ever he gets into your power
as you were in the power of your old landlord. Do you
think, because youre poor and ignorant and half-crazy
with toiling and moiling morning noon and night, that
youll be any less greedy and oppressive to them that
have no land at all than old Nick Lestrange, who was
an educated travclled gentleman that would not have
been tempted as hard by a hundred pounds as youd be
by five shillings? Nick was too high above Patsy Farrell to be jealous of him; but you, that are only one
little step above him, would die sooner than let him
come up that step; and well you know it.

MATTHEW (*black with rage, in a low growl*). Lemme
oura this. (*He tries to rise; but Doran catches his coat
and drags him down again.*) I'm goin, I say. (*Raising
his voice.*) Leggo me coat, Barney Doran.

DORAN. Sit down, yowl omadhaun, you. (*Whispering.*) Dont you want to stay an vote against him?

FATHER DEMPSEY (*holding up his finger*). Mat!
(*Mat subsides.*) Now, now, now! come, come! Hwats
all dhis about Patsy Farrll? Hwy need you fall out
about h i m?

LARRY. Because it was by using Patsy's poverty to
undersell England in the markets of the world that we
drove England to ruin Ireland. And she'll ruin us
again the moment we lift our heads from the dust if

we trade in cheap labor; and serve us right too! If I
get into parliament, I'll try to get an Act to prevent any
of you from giving Patsy less than a pound a week
(*they all start, hardly able to believe their ears*) or
working him harder than youd work a horse that cost
you fifty guineas.

DORAN. Hwat!!!

CORNELIUS (*aghast*). A pound a—God save us! the
boy's mad.

*Matthew, feeling that here is something quite beyond
his powers, turns openmouthed to the priest, as if looking for nothing less than the summary excommunication
of Larry.*

LARRY. How is the man to marry and live a decent
life on less?

FATHER DEMPSEY. Man alive, hwere have you been
living all these years? and hwat have you been dreaming
of? Why, some o dhese honest men here cant make
that much out o the land for themselves, much less give
it to a laborer.

LARRY (*now thoroughly roused*). Then let them
make room for those who can. Is Ireland never to have
a chance? First she was given to the rich; and now
that they have gorged on her flesh, her bones are to be
flung to the poor, that can do nothing but suck the marrow out of her. If we cant have men of honor own the
land, lets have men of ability. If we cant have men
with ability, let us at least have men with capital. Anybody's better than Mat, who has neither honor, nor
ability, nor capital, nor anything but mere brute labor
and greed in him, Heaven help him!

DORAN. Well, we're not all foostherin' oul doddher-
ers like Mat. (*Pleasantly, to the subject of this descrip-
tion.*) Are we, Mat?

LARRY. For modern industrial purposes you might
just as well be, Barney. Youre all children: the big
world that I belong to has gone past you and left you.

Anyhow, we Irishmen were never made to be farmers;
and we'll never do any good at it. We're like the Jews:
the Almighty gave us brains, and bid us farm t h e m,
and leave the clay and the worms alone.

FATHER DEMPSEY (*with gentle irony*). Oh! is it
Jews you want to make of us? I must catechize you a
bit meself, I think. The next thing youll be proposing
is to repeal the disestablishment of the so-called Irish
Church.

LARRY. Yes: why not? (*Sensation.*)

MATTHEW (*rancorously*). He's a turncoat.

LARRY. St. Peter, the rock on which our Church was
built, was crucified head downwards for being a turncoat.

FATHER DEMPSEY (*with a quiet authoritative dignity
which checks Doran, who is on the point of breaking
out*). Thats true. You hold your tongue as befits your
ignorance, Matthew Haffigan; and trust your priest to
deal with this young man. Now, Larry Doyle, whatever
the blessed St Peter was crucified for, it was not for
being a Prodestan. Are you one?

LARRY. No. I am a Catholic intelligent enough to
see that the Protestants are never more dangerous to us
than when they are free from all alliances with the
State. The so-called Irish Church is stronger today
than ever it was.

MATTHEW. Fadher Dempsey: will you tell him dhat
me mother's ant was shot and kilt dead in the sthreet o
Rosscullen be a soljer in the tithe war? (*Frantically.*)
He wants to put the tithes on us again. He—

LARRY (*interrupting him with overbearing contempt*).
Put the tithes on you again! Did the tithes ever come
off you? Was your land any dearer when you paid
the tithe to the parson than it was when you paid the
same money to Nick Lestrange as rent, and he handed
it over to the Church Sustentation Fund? Will you
always be duped by Acts of Parliament that change

nothing but the necktie of the man that picks your pocket? I'll tell you what I'd do with you, Mat Haffigan: I'd make you pay tithes to your own Church. I want the Catholic Church established in Ireland: thats what I want. Do you think that I, brought up to regard myself as the son of a great and holy Church, can bear to see her begging her bread from the ignorance and superstition of men like you? I would have her as high above worldly want as I would have her above worldly pride or ambition. Aye; and I would have Ireland compete with Rome itself for the chair of St. Peter and the citadel of the Church; for Rome, in spite of all the blood of the martyrs, is pagan at heart to this day, while in Ireland the people is the Church and the Church the people.

FATHER DEMPSEY (*startled, but not at all displeased*). Whisht, man! youre worse than mad Pether Keegan himself.

BROADBENT (*who has listened in the greatest astonishment*). You amaze me, Larry. Who would have thought of your coming out like this! (*Solemnly.*) But much as I appreciate your really brilliant eloquence, I implore you not to desert the great Liberal principle of Disestablishment.

LARRY. I am not a Liberal: Heaven forbid! A disestablished Church is the worst tyranny a nation can groan under.

BROADBENT (*making a wry face*). Dont be paradoxical, Larry. It really gives me a pain in my stomach.

LARRY. Youll soon find out the truth of it here. Look at Father Dempsey! he is disestablished: he has nothing to hope or fear from the State; and the result is that hes the most powerful man in Rosscullen. The member for Rosscullen would shake in his shoes if Father Dempsey looked crooked at him. (*Father Dempsey smiles, by no means averse to this acknowledgment of his authority.*) Look at yourself! you would defy

the established Archbishop of Canterbury ten times a
day; but catch you daring to say a word that would
shock a Nonconformist! not you. The Conservative
party today is the only one thats not priestrid-
den—excuse the expression, Father (*Father Dempsey
nods tolerantly*)—because its the only one that has
established its Church and can prevent a clergyman
becoming a bishop if he's not a Statesman as well as a
Churchman.

*He stops. They stare at him dumbfounded, and leave
it to the priest to answer him.*

FATHER DEMPSEY (*judicially*). Young man: youll
not be the member for Rosscullen; but theres more in
your head than the comb will take out.

LARRY. I'm sorry to disappoint you, father; but I
told you it would be no use. And now I think the
candidate had better retire and leave you to discuss his
successor. (*He takes a newspaper from the table and
goes away through the shrubbery amid dead silence, all
turning to watch him until he passes out of sight round
the corner of the house.*)

DORAN (*dazed*). Hwat sort of a fella is he at all at
all?

FATHER DEMPSEY. He's a clever lad: theres the
making of a man in him yet.

MATTHEW (*in consternation*). D'ye mane to say dhat
yll put him into parliament to bring back Nick Le-
sthrange on me, and to put tithes on me, and to rob
me for the like o Patsy Farrll, because hes Corny Doyle's
only son?

DORAN (*brutally*). Arra hould your whisht: who's
goin to send him into parliament? Maybe youd like us
to send y o u dhere to thrate them to a little o your
anxiety about dhat dirty little podato patch o yours.

MATTHEW (*plaintively*). Am I to be towld dhis
afther all me sufferins?

DORAN. Och, I'm tired o your sufferins. Weve been

hearin nothin else ever since we was childher but sufferins. Hwen it wasnt yours it was somebody else's;
and hwen it was nobody else's it was ould Irelan's. How
the divil are we to live on wan anodher's sufferins?

FATHER DEMPSEY. Thats a thrue word, Barney
Doarn; only your tongue's a little too familiar wi dhe
divil. (*To Mat.*) If youd think a little more o the
sufferins of the blessed saints, Mat, an a little less o
your own, youd find the way shorter from your farm
to heaven. (*Mat is about to reply.*) Dhere now! dhats
enough! we know you mean well; an I'm not angry with
you.

BROADBENT. Surely, Mr. Haffigan, you can see the
simple explanation of all this. My friend Larry Doyle
is a most brilliant speaker; but he's a Tory: an ingrained
old-fashioned Tory.

CORNELIUS. N how d'ye make dhat out, if I might
ask you, Mr. Broadbent?

BROADBENT (*collecting himself for a political deliver-
ance*). Well, you know, Mr. Doyle, theres a strong
dash of Toryism in the Irish character. Larry himself
says that the great Duke of Wellington was the most
typical Irishman that ever lived. Of course thats an
absurd paradox; but still theres a great deal of truth
in it. Now I am a Liberal. You know the great principles of the Liberal party. Peace—

FATHER DEMPSEY (*piously*). Hear! hear!

BROADBENT (*encouraged*). Thank you. Retrench-
ment— (*he waits for further applause*).

MATTHEW (*timidly*). What might rethrenchment
mane now?

BROADBENT. It means an immense reduction in the
burden of the rates and taxes.

MATTHEW (*respectfully approving*). Dhats right.
Dhats right, sir.

BROADBENT (*perfunctorily*). And, of course, Reform.

CORNELIUS
FATHER DEMPSEY } (*conventionally*).   Of course.
DORAN

MATTHEW (*still suspicious*). Hwat does Reform mane, sir? Does it mane altherin annythin dhats as it is now?

BROADBENT (*impressively*). It means, Mr. Haffigan, maintaining those reforms which have already been conferred on humanity by the Liberal Party, and trusting for future developments to the free activity of a free people on the basis of those reforms.

DORAN. Dhats right. No more meddlin. We're all right now: all we want is to be let alone.

CORNELIUS. Hwat about Home Rule?

BROADBENT (*rising so as to address them more imposingly*). I really cannot tell you what I feel about Home Rule without using the language of hyperbole.

DORAN. Savin Fadher Dempsey's presence, eh?

BROADBENT (*not understanding him*). Quite so—er —oh yes. All I can say is that as an Englishman I blush for the Union. It is the blackest stain on our national history. I look forward to the time—and it cannot be far distant, gentlemen, because Humanity is looking forward to it too, and insisting on it with no uncertain voice— I look forward to the time when an Irish legislature shall arise once more on the emerald pasture of College Green, and the Union Jack—that detestable symbol of a decadent Imperialism—be replaced by a flag as green as the island over which it waves—a flag on which we shall ask for England only a modest quartering in memory of our great party and of the immortal name of our grand old leader.

DORAN (*enthusiastically*). Dhats the style, begob! (*He smites his knee, and winks at Mat.*)

MATTHEW. More power to you, sir!

BROADBENT. I shall leave you now, gentlemen, to

your deliberations. I should like to have enlarged on the services rendered by the Liberal Party to the religious faith of the great majority of the people of Ireland; but I shall content myself with saying that in my opinion you should choose no representative who— no matter what his personal creed may be—is not an ardent supporter of freedom of conscience, and is not prepared to prove it by contributions, as lavish as his means will allow, to the great and beneficent work which you, Father Dempsey (*Father Dempsey bows*), are doing for the people of Rosscullen. Nor should the lighter, but still most important question of the sports of the people be forgotten. The local cricket club—

CORNELIUS. The hwat!

DORAN. Nobody plays batn ball here, if dhats what you mean.

BROADBENT. Well, let us say quoits. I saw two men, I think, last night—but after all, these are questions of detail. The main thing is that your candidate, whoever he may be, shall be a man of some means, able to help the locality instead of burdening it. And if he were a countryman of my own, the moral effect on the House of Commons would be immense! tremendous! Pardon my saying these few words: nobody feels their impertinence more than I do. Good morning, gentlemen.

He turns impressively to the gate, and trots away, congratulating himself, with a little twist of his head and cock of his eye, on having done a good stroke of political business.

HAFFIGAN (*awestruck*). Good morning, sir.

THE REST. Good morning. (*They watch him vacantly until he is out of earshot.*)

CORNELIUS. Hwat d'ye think, Father Dempsey?

FATHER DEMPSEY (*indulgently*). Well, he hasnt much sense, God help him; but for the matter o that, neither has our present member.

DORAN.   Arra musha hes good enough for parliament: what is there to do there but gas a bit, an chivy the Government, an vote wi dh Irish party?

CORNELIUS (*ruminatively*).   He's the queerest Englishman *I* ever met.   When he opened the paper dhis mornin tho first thing he saw was that an English expedition had been bet in a battle in Inja somewhere; an he was as pleased as Punch! Larry told him that if he'd been alive when the news o Waterloo came, he'd a died o grief over it.   Bedad I dont think hes quite right in his head.

DORAN.   Divil a matther if he has plenty o money. He'll do for us right enough.

MATTHEW (*deeply impressed by Broadbent, and unable to understand their levity concerning him*).   Did you mind what he said about rethrenchment?   That was very good, I thought.

FATHER DEMPSEY.   You might find out from Larry, Corny, what his means are.   God forgive us all! it's poor work spoiling the Egyptians, though we have good warrant for it; so I'd like to know how much spoil there is before I commit meself.   (*He rises.   They all rise respectfully.*)

CORNELIUS (*ruefully*).   I'd set me mind on Larry himself for the seat; but I suppose it cant be helped.

FATHER DEMPSEY (*consoling him*).   Well, the boy's young yet; an he has a head on him.   Goodbye, all. (*He goes out through the gate.*)

DORAN.   I must be goin, too.   (*He directs Cornelius's attention to what is passing in the road.*)   Look at me bould Englishman shakin hans wid Fadher Dempsey for all the world like a candidate on election day.   And look at Fadher Dempsey givin him a squeeze an a wink as much as to say Its all right, me boy.   You watch him shakin hans with me too: hes waitn for me.   I'll tell him hes as good as elected.   (*He goes, chuckling mischievously.*)

CORNELIUS. Come in with me, Mat. I think I'll sell you the pig after all. Come in an wet the bargain.

MATTHEW (*instantly dropping into the old whine of the tenant*). I'm afeerd I cant afford the price, sir. (*He follows Cornelius into the house.*)

Larry, newspaper still in hand, comes back through the shrubbery. Broadbent returns through the gate.

LARRY. Well? What has happened.

BROADBENT (*hugely self-satisfied*). I think Ive done the trick this time. I just gave them a bit of straight talk; and it went home. They were greatly impressed: everyone of those men believes in me and will vote for me when the question of selecting a candidate comes up. After all, whatever you say, Larry, they like an Englishman. They feel they can trust him, I suppose.

LARRY. Oh! theyve transferred the honor to you, have they?

BROADBENT (*complacently*). Well, it was a pretty obvious move, I should think. You know, these fellows have plenty of shrewdness in spite of their Irish oddity. (*Hodson comes from the house. Larry sits in Doran's chair and reads.*) Oh, by the way, Hodson—

HODSON (*coming between Broadbent and Larry*). Yes, sir?

BROADBENT. I want you to be rather particular as to how you treat the people here.

HODSON. I havnt treated any of em yet, sir. If I was to accept all the treats they offer me I shouldnt be able to stand at this present moment, sir.

BROADBENT. Oh well, dont be too stand-offish, you know, Hodson. I should like you to be popular. If it costs anything I'll make it up to you. It doesnt matter if you get a bit upset at first: theyll like you all the better for it.

HODSON. I'm sure youre very kind, sir; but it dont seem to matter to me whether they like me or not. I'm not going to stand for parliament here, sir.

BROADBENT. Well, I am. Now do you understand?

HODSON (*waking up at once*). Oh, I beg your pardon, sir, I'm sure. I understand, sir.

CORNELIUS (*appearing at the house door with Mat*). Patsy'll drive the pig over this evenin, Mat. Goodbye. (*He goes back into the house. Mat makes for the gate. Broadbent stops him. Hodson, pained by the derelict basket, picks it up and carries it away behind the house.*)

BROADBENT (*beaming candidatorially*). I must thank you very particularly, Mr. Haffigan, for your support this morning. I value it because I know that the real heart of a nation is the class you represent, the yeomanry.

MATTHEW (*aghast*). The yeomanry!!!

LARRY (*looking up from his paper*). Take care, Tom! In Rosscullen a yeoman means a sort of Orange Bashi-Bazouk. In England, Mat, they call a freehold farmer a yeoman.

MATTHEW (*huffily*). I dont need to be insthructed be you, Larry Doyle. Some people think no one knows anythin but dhemselves. (*To Broadbent, deferentially.*) Of course I know a gentleman like you would not compare me to thc yeomanry. Me own granfather was flogged in the sthreets of Athenmullet be them when they put a gun in the thatch of his house an then went and found it there, bad cess to them!

BROADBENT (*with sympathetic interest*). Then you are not the first martyr of your family, Mr. Haffigan?

MATTHEW. They turned me out o the farm I made out of the stones o Little Rosscullen hill wid me own hans.

BROADBENT. I have heard about it; and my blood still boils at the thought. (*Calling.*) Hodson—

HODSON (*behind the corner of the house*). Yes, sir. (*He hurries forward.*)

BROADBENT. Hodson: this gentleman's sufferings

should make every Englishman think. It is want of thought rather than want of heart that allows such iniquities to disgrace society.

HODSON (*prosaically*). Yes sir.

MATTHEW. Well, I'll be goin. Good morning to you kindly, sir.

BROADBENT. You have some distance to go, Mr. Haffigan: will you allow me to drive you home?

MATTHEW. Oh sure it'd be throublin your honor.

BROADBENT. I insist: it will give me the greatest pleasure, I assure you. My car is in the stable: I can get it round in five minutes.

MATTHEW. Well, sir, if you wouldnt mind, we could bring the pig Ive just bought from Corny—

BROADBENT (*with enthusiasm*). Certainly, Mr. Haffigan: it will be quite delightful to drive with a pig in the car: I shall feel quite like an Irishman. Hodson: stay with Mr. Haffigan; and give him a hand with the pig if necessary. Come, Larry; and help me. (*He rushes away through the shrubbery.*)

LARRY (*throwing the paper ill-humoredly on the chair*). Look here, Tom! here, I say! confound it! (*he runs after him*).

MATTHEW (*glowering disdainfully at Hodson, and sitting down on Cornelius's chair as an act of social self-assertion*). N are you the valley?

HODSON. The valley? Oh, I follow you: yes: I'm Mr. Broadbent's valet.

MATTHEW. Ye have an aisy time of it: you look purty sleek. (*With suppressed ferocity.*) Look at m e! Do *I* look sleek?

HODSON (*sadly*). I wish I ad your ealth: you look as hard as nails. I suffer from an excess of uric acid.

MATTHEW. Musha what sort o disease is zhouragassid? Didjever suffer from injustice and starvation? Dhats the Irish disease. Its aisy for you to talk o sufferin, an you livin on the fat o the land wid money wrung from us.

HODSON (*coolly*). Wots wrong with you, old chap? Has ennybody been doin ennything to you?

MATTHEW. Anythin timme! Didnt your English masther say that the blood biled in him to hear the way they put a rint on me for the farm I made wid me own hans, and turned me out of it to give it to Billy Byrne?

HODSON. Ow, Tom Broadbent's blood boils pretty easy over ennything that appens out of his own country. Dont you be taken in by my ole man, Paddy.

MATTHEW (*indignantly*). Paddy yourself! How dar you call me Paddy?

HODSON (*unmoved*). You just keep your hair on and listen to me. You Irish people are too well off: thats whats the matter with y o u. (*With sudden passion.*) Y o u talk of your rotten little farm because you made it by chuckin a few stownes dahn a hill! Well, wot price my grenfawther, I should like to know, that fitted up a fuss clawss shop and built up a fuss clawss drapery business in London by sixty years work, and then was chucked aht of it on is ed at the end of is lease withaht a penny for his goodwill. Y o u talk of evictions! you that cawnt be moved until youve run up eighteen months rent. I once ran up four weeks in Lambeth when I was aht of a job in winter. They took the door off its inges and the winder aht of its sashes on me, and gave my wife pnoomownia. I'm a widower now. (*Between his teeth.*) Gawd! when I think of the things we Englishmen av to put up with, and hear you Irish hahlin abaht your silly little grievances, and see the way you make it worse for us by the rotten wages youll come over and take and the rotten places youll sleep in, I jast feel that I could take the oul bloomin British awland and make you a present of it, jast to let you find out wot real ardship's like.

MATTHEW (*starting up, more in scandalized incre-
dulity than in anger*). D'ye have the face to set up England agen Ireland for injustices an wrongs an disthress
an sufferin?

HODSON (*with intense disgust and contempt, but with
Cockney coolness*). Ow, chuck it, Paddy. Cheese it.
You danno wot ardship is over ere: all you know is ah
to ahl abaht it. You take the biscuit at that, you do.
I'm a Owm Ruler, I am. Do you know why?

MATTHEW (*equally contemptuous*). D'ye know, yourself?

HODSON. Yes I do. It's because I want a little attention paid to my own country; and thetll never be as
long as your chaps are ollerin at Wesminister as if now-
body mettered but your own bloomin selves. Send em
back to hell or C'naught, as good oul English Cromwell
said. I'm jast sick of Ireland. Let it gow. Cut the
cable. Make it a present to Germany to keep the oul
Kyzer busy for a while; and give poor owld England a
chawnce: thets wot *I* say.

MATTHEW (*full of scorn for a man so ignorant as to
be unable to pronounce the word Connaught, which practically rhymes with bonnet in Ireland, though in Hodson's dialect it rhymes with untaught*). Take care we
dont cut the cable ourselves some day, bad scran to you!
An tell me dhis: have yanny Coercion Acs in England?
Have yanny removables? Have you Dublin Castle to
suppress every newspaper dhat takes the part o your
own counthry?

HODSON. We can beyave ahrselves withaht sich
things.

MATTHEW. Bedad youre right. It'd only be waste
o time to muzzle a sheep. Here! where's me pig? God
forgimme for talkin to a poor ignorant craycher like
you.

HODSON (*grinning with good-humored malice, too
convinced of his own superiority to feel his withers*

wrung). Your pigll ave a rare doin in that car, Paddy.
Forty miles an ahr dahn that rocky lane will strike it
pretty pink, you bet.

MATTHEW (*scornfully*). Hwy cant you tell a raison-
able lie when youre about it? What horse can go forty
mile an hour?

HODSON. Orse! Wy, you silly oul rotter, it's not a
orse: it's a mowtor. Do you suppose Tom Broadbent
would gow off himself to arness a orse?

MATTHEW (*in consternation*). Holy Moses! dont tell
me its the ingine he wants to take me on.

HODSON. Wot else?

MATTHEW. Your sowl to Morris Kelly! why didnt
you tell me that before? The divil an ingine he'll get
me on this day. (*His ear catches an approaching teuf-
teuf.*) Oh murdher! its comin afther me: I hear the
puff-puff of it. (*He runs away through the gate, much
to Hodson's amusement. The noise of the motor ceases;
and Hodson, anticipating Broadbent's return, throws off
the politician and recomposes himself as a valet. Broadbent and Larry come through the shrubbery. Hodson
moves aside to the gate.*)

BROADBENT. Where is Mr. Haffigan? Has he gone
for the pig?

HODSON. Bolted, sir? Afraid of the motor, sir.

BROADBENT (*much disappointed*). Oh, thats very
tiresome. Did he leave any message?

HODSON. He was in too great a hurry, sir. Started
to run home, sir, and left his pig behind him.

BROADBENT (*eagerly*). Left the pig! Then it's all
right. The pig's the thing: the pig will win over every
Irish heart to me. We'll take the pig home to Haffigan's
farm in the motor: it will have a tremendous effect.
Hodson!

HODSON. Yes sir?

BROADBENT. Do you think you could collect a crowd
to see the motor?

HODSON. Well, I'll try, sir.

BROADBENT. Thank you, Hodson: do.

Hodson goes out through the gate.

LARRY (*desperately*). Once more, Tom, will you listen to me?

BROADBENT. Rubbish! I tell you it will be all right.

LARRY. Only this morning you confessed how surprised you were to find that the people here shewed no sense of humor.

BROADBENT (*suddenly very solemn*). Yes: their sense of humor is in abeyance: I noticed it the moment we landed. Think of that in a country where every man is a born humorist! Think of what it means! (*Impressively.*) Larry: we are in the presence of a great national grief.

LARRY. Whats to grieve them?

BROADBENT. I divined it, Larry: I saw it in their faces. Ireland has never smiled since her hopes were buried in the grave of Gladstone.

LARRY. Oh, whats the use of talking to such a man? Now look here, Tom. Be serious for a moment if you can.

BROADBENT (*stupent*). Serious! I!!!

LARRY. Yes, you. You say the Irish sense of humor is in abeyance. Well, if you drive through Rosscullen in a motor car with Haffigan's pig, it wont stay in abeyance. Now I warn you.

BROADBENT (*breezily*). Why, so much the better! I shall enjoy the joke myself more than any of them. (*Shouting.*) Hallo, Patsy Farrell, where are you?

PATSY (*appearing in the shrubbery*). Here I am, your honor.

BROADBENT. Go and catch the pig and put it into the car: we're going to take it to Mr. Haffigan's. (*He gives Larry a slap on the shoulders that sends him staggering off through the gate, and follows him buoyantly, ex-*

claiming) Come on, you old croaker! I'll shew you how to win an Irish seat.

PATSY (*meditatively*). Bedad, if dhat pig gets a howlt o the handle o the machine— (*He shakes his head ominously and drifts away to the pigsty.*)

END OF ACT III.

ACT IV

The parlor in Cornelius Doyle's house. It communicates with the garden by a half glazed door. The fireplace is at the other side of the room, opposite the door and windows, the architect not having been sensitive to draughts. The table, rescued from the garden, is in the middle; and at it sits Keegan, the central figure in a rather crowded apartment. Nora, sitting with her back to the fire at the end of the table, is playing backgammon across its corner with him, on his left hand. Aunt Judy, a little further back, sits facing the fire knitting, with her feet on the fender. A little to Keegan's right, in front of the table, and almost sitting on it, is Barney Doran. Half a dozen friends of his, all men, are between him and the open door, supported by others outside. In the corner behind them is the sofa, of mahogany and horsehair, made up as a bed for Broadbent. Against the wall behind Keegan stands a mahogany sideboard. A door leading to the interior of the house is near the fireplace, behind Aunt Judy. There are chairs against the wall, one at each end of the sideboard. Keegan's hat is on the one nearest the inner door; and his stick is leaning against it. A third chair, also against the wall, is near the garden door.

There is a strong contrast of emotional atmosphere between the two sides of the room. Keegan is extraordinarily stern: no game of backgammon could possibly make a man's face so grim. Aunt Judy is quietly busy. Nora is trying to ignore Doran and attend to her game.

On the other hand Doran is reeling in an ecstasy of

mischievous mirth which has infected all his friends.
They are screaming with laughter, doubled up, leaning
on the furniture and against the walls, shouting, screech-
ing, crying.

AUNT JUDY (*as the noise lulls for a moment*). Arra
hold your noise, Barney. What is there to laugh at?

DORAN. It got its fut into the little hweel— (*he is
overcome afresh; and the rest collapse again*).

AUNT JUDY. Ah, have some sense: youre like a parcel
o childher. Nora, hit him a thump on the back: he'll
have a fit.

DORAN (*with squeezed eyes, exsufflicate with cachin-
nation*). Frens, he sez to dhem outside Doolan's: I'm
takin the gintleman that pays the rint for a dhrive.

AUNT JUDY. Who did he mean be that?

DORAN. They call a pig that in England. Thats
their notion of a joke.

AUNT JUDY. Musha God help them if they can joke
no better than that!

DORAN (*with renewed symptoms*). Thin—

AUNT JUDY. Ah now dont be tellin it all over and
settin yourself off again, Barney.

NORA. Youve told us three times, Mr. Doran.

DORAN. Well but whin I think of it—!

AUNT JUDY. Then dont think of it, alanna.

DORAN. There was Patsy Farrll in the back sate wi
dhe pig between his knees, n me bould English boyoh
in front at the machinery, n Larry Doyle in the road
startin the injine wid a bed winch. At the first puff of
it the pig lep out of its skin and bled Patsy's nose wi
dhe ring in its snout. (*Roars of laughter: Keegan
glares at them.*) Before Broadbint knew hwere he was,
the pig was up his back and over into his lap; and
bedad the poor baste did credit to Corny's thrainin of
it; for it put in the fourth speed wid its right crubeen
as if it was enthered for the Gordn Bennett.

NORA (*reproachfully*). And Larry in front of it and all! It's nothin to laugh at, Mr. Doran.

DORAN. Bedad, Miss Reilly, Larry cleared six yards backwards at wan jump if he cleared an inch; and he'd a cleared seven if Doolan's granmother hadnt cotch him in her apern widhout intindin to. (*Immense merriment.*)

AUNT JUDY. Ah, for shame, Barney! the poor old woman! An she was hurt before, too, when she slipped on the stairs.

DORAN. Bedad, maam, shes hurt behind now; for Larry bouled her over like a skittle. (*General delight at this typical stroke of Irish Rabelaisianism.*)

NORA. It's well the lad wasnt killed.

DORAN. Faith it wasnt o Larry we were thinkin jus dhen, wi dhe pig takin the main sthreet o Rosscullen on market day at a mile a minnit. Dh ony thing Broadbint could get at wi dhe pig in front of him was a fut brake; n the pig's tail was undher dhat; so that whin he thought he was putn non the brake he was ony squeezin the life out o the pig's tail. The more he put the brake on the more the pig squealed n the fasther he dhruv.

AUNT JUDY. Why couldnt he throw the pig out into the road?

DORAN. Sure he couldnt stand up to it, because he was spanchelled-like between his seat and dhat thing like a wheel on top of a stick between his knees.

AUNT JUDY. Lord have mercy on us!

NORA. I dont know how you can laugh. Do you, Mr. Keegan?

KEEGAN (*grimly*). Why not? There is danger, destruction, torment! What more do we want to make us merry? Go on, Barney: the last drops of joy are not squeezed from the story yet. Tell us again how our brother was torn asunder.

DORAN (*puzzled*). Whose bruddher?

KEEGAN. Mine.

NORA. He means the pig, Mr. Doran. You know his way.

DORAN (*rising gallantly to the occasion*). Bedad I'm sorry for your poor bruddher, Misther Keegan; but I recommend you to thry him wid a couple o fried eggs for your breakfast tomorrow. It was a case of Excelsior wi dhat ambitious baste; for not content wid jumpin from the back seat into the front wan, he jumped from the front wan into the road in front of the car. And—

KEEGAN. And everybody laughed!

NORA. Dont go over that again, p l e a s e, Mr. Doran.

DORAN. Faith be the time the car went over the poor pig dhere was little left for me or anywan else to go over except wid a knife an fork.

AUNT JUDY. Why didnt Mr. Broadbent stop the car when the pig was gone?

DORAN. Stop the car! He might as well ha thried to stop a mad bull. First it went wan way an made fireworks o Molly Ryan's crockery stall; an dhen it slewed round an ripped ten fut o wall out o the corner o the pound. (*With enormous enjoyment.*) Begob, it just tore the town in two and sent the whole dam market to blazes. (*Nora offended, rises.*)

KEEGAN (*indignantly*). Sir!

DORAN (*quickly*). Savin your presence, Miss Reilly, and Misther Keegan's. Dhere! I wont say anuddher word.

NORA. I'm surprised at you, Mr. Doran. (*She sits down again.*)

DORAN (*reflectively*). He has the divil's own luck, that Englishman, annyway; for when they picked him up he hadnt a scratch on him, barrn hwat the pig did to his cloes. Patsy had two fingers out o jynt; but the smith pulled them sthraight for him. Oh, you never heard such a hullaballoo as there was. There was Molly cryin Me chaney, me beautyful chaney! n oul Mat shoutin Me pig, me pig! n the polus takin the number o the car, n not a man in the town able to speak for laughin—

KEEGAN (*with intense emphasis*). It is hell: it is hell. Nowhere else could such a scene be a burst of happiness for the people.

Cornelius comes in hastily from the garden, pushing his way through the little crowd.

CORNELIUS. Whisht your laughin, boys! Here he is. (*He puts his hat on the sideboard, and goes to the fireplace, where he posts himself with his back to the chimneypiece.*)

AUNT JUDY. Remember your behavior, now.

Everybody becomes silent, solemn, concerned, sympathetic. Broadbent enters, soiled and disordered as to his motoring coat: immensely important and serious as to himself. He makes his way to the end of the table nearest the garden door, whilst Larry, who accompanies him, throws his motoring coat on the sofa bed, and sits down, watching the proceedings.

BROADBENT (*taking off his leather cap with dignity and placing it on the table*). I hope you have not been anxious about me.

AUNT JUDY. Deedn we have, Mr. Broadbent. Its a mercy you werent killed.

DORAN. Kilt! Its a mercy dheres two bones of you left houldin together. How dijjescape at all at all? Well, I never thought I'd be so glad to see you safe and sound again. Not a man in the town would say less (*murmurs of kindly assent*). Wont you come down to Doolan's and have a dhrop o brandy to take the shock off?

BROADBENT. Youre all really too kind; but the shock has quite passed off.

DORAN (*jovially*). Never mind. Come along all the same and tell us about it over a frenly glass.

BROADBENT. May I say how deeply I feel the kindness with which I have been overwhelmed since my accident? I can truthfully declare that I am glad it happened, because it has brought out the kindness and sympathy of the Irish character to an extent I had no conception of.

SEVERAL PRESENT. Oh, sure youre welcome!
Sure its only natural.
Sure you might have been kilt.

A young man, on the point of bursting, hurries out. Barney puts an iron constraint on his features.

BROADBENT. All I can say is that I wish I could drink the health of everyone of you.

DORAN. Dhen come an do it.

BROADBENT (*very solemnly*). No: I am a teetotaller.

AUNT JUDY (*incredulously*). Arra since when?

BROADBENT. Since this morning, Miss Doyle. I have had a lesson (*he looks at Nora significantly*) that I shall not forget. It may be that total abstinence has already saved my life; for I was astonished at the steadiness of my nerves when death stared me in the face today. So I will ask you to excuse me. (*He collects himself for a speech.*) Gentlemen: I hope the gravity of the peril through which we have all passed—for I know that the danger to the bystanders was as great as to the occupants of the car—will prove an earnest of closer and more serious relations between us in the future. We have had a somewhat agitating day: a valuable and innocent animal has lost its life: a public building has been wrecked: an aged and infirm lady has suffered an impact for which I feel personally responsible, though my old friend Mr. Laurence Doyle unfortunately incurred the first effects of her very natural resentment. I greatly regret the damage to Mr. Patrick Farrell's fingers; and I have of course taken care that he shall not suffer pecuniarily by his mishap. (*Murmurs of admiration at his magnanimity, and A Voice* "Youre a gentleman, sir.") I am glad to say that Patsy took it like an Irishman, and, far from expressing any vin-

dictive feeling, declared his willingness to break all his
fingers and toes for me on the same terms (*subdued
applause, and* " More power to Patsy! "). Gentlemen:
I felt at home in Ireland from the first (*rising excitement among his hearers*). In every Irish breast I have
found that spirit of liberty (*A cheery voice* " Hear
Hear "), that instinctive mistrust of the Government
(*A small pious voice, with intense expression,* " God
bless you, sir! "), that love of independence (*A defiant
voice,* " Thats it! Independence! "), that indignant sympathy with the cause of oppressed nationalities abroad
(*A threatening growl from all: the ground-swell of
patriotic passion*), and with the resolute assertion of
personal rights at home, which is all but extinct in' my
own country. If it were legally possible I should become a naturalized Irishman; and if ever it be my good
fortune to represent an Irish constituency in parliament,
it shall be my first care to introduce a Bill legalizing
such an operation. I believe a large section of the Liberal party would avail themselves of it. (*Momentary
scepticism.*) I do. (*Convulsive cheering.*) Gentlemen: I have said enough. (*Cries of* " Go on.") No:
I have as yet no right to address you at all on political
subjects; and we must not abuse the warmhearted Irish
hospitality of Miss Doyle by turning her sittingroom
into a public meeting.

DORAN (*energetically*). Three cheers for Tom
Broadbent, the future member for Rosscullen!

AUNT JUDY (*waving a half knitted sock*). Hip hip
hurray!

*The cheers are given with great heartiness, as it is
by this time, for the more humorous spirits present, a
question of vociferation or internal rupture.*

BROADBENT. Thank you from the bottom of my
heart, friends.

NORA (*whispering to Doran*). Take them away, Mr.
Doran (*Doran nods*).

DORAN. Well, good evenin, Mr. Broadbent; an may you never regret the day you wint dhrivin wid Haffigan's pig! (*They shake hands.*) Good evenin, Miss Doyle.

General handshaking, Broadbent shaking hands with everybody effusively. He accompanies them to the garden and can be heard outside saying Goodnight in every inflexion known to parliamentary candidates. Nora, Aunt Judy, Keegan, Larry, and Cornelius are left in the parlor. Larry goes to the threshold and watches the scene in the garden.

NORA. It's a shame to make game of him like that. Hes a gradle more good in him than Barney Doran.

CORNELIUS. It's all up with his candidature. He'll be laughed out o the town.

LARRY (*turning quickly from the doorway*). Oh no he wont: hes not an Irishman. He'll never know theyre laughing at him; and while theyre laughing he'll win the seat.

CORNELIUS. But he cant prevent the story getting about.

LARRY. He wont want to. He'll tell it himself as one of the most providential episodes in the history of England and Ireland.

AUNT JUDY. Sure he wouldnt make a fool of himself like that.

LARRY. Are you sure hes such a fool after all, Aunt Judy? Suppose you had a vote! which would you rather give it to? the man that told the story of Haffigan's pig Barney Doran's way or Broadbent's way?

AUNT JUDY. Faith I wouldnt give it to a man at all. It's a few women they want in parliament to stop their foolish blather.

BROADBENT (*bustling into the room, and taking off his damaged motoring overcoat, which he puts down on the sofa*). Well, that's over. I must apologize for making that speech, Miss Doyle; but they like it, you know. Everything helps in electioneering.

Larry takes the chair near the door; draws it near the table; and sits astride it, with his elbows folded on the back.

AUNT JUDY. I'd no notion you were such an orator, Mr. Broadbent.

BROADBENT. Oh, it's only a knack. One picks it up on the platform. It stokes up their enthusiasm.

AUNT JUDY. Oh, I forgot. Youve not met Mr. Keegan. Let me introjooce you.

BROADBENT (*shaking hands effusively*). Most happy to meet you, Mr. Keegan. I have heard of you, though I have not had the pleasure of shaking your hand before. And now may I ask you—for I value no man's opinion more—what you think of my chances here.

KEEGAN (*coldly*). Your chances, sir, are excellent. You will get into parliament.

BROADBENT (*delighted*). I hope so. I think so. (*Fluctuating.*) You really think so? You are sure you are not allowing your enthusiasm for our principles to get the better of your judgment?

KEEGAN. I have no enthusiasm for your principles, sir. You will get into parliament because you w a n t to get into it badly enough to be prepared to take the necessary steps to induce the people to vote for you. That is how people usually get into that fantastic assembly.

BROADBENT (*puzzled*). Of course. (*Pause.*) Quite so. (*Pause.*) Er—yes. (*Buoyant again.*) I think they will vote for me. Eh? Yes?

AUNT JUDY. Arra why shouldnt they? Look at the people they d o vote for!

BROADBENT (*encouraged*). Thats true: thats very true. When I see the windbags, the carpet-baggers, the charlatans, the — the — the fools and ignoramuses who corrupt the multitude by their wealth, or seduce them by spouting balderdash to them, I cannot help thinking that an honest man with no humbug about him, who will

talk straight common sense and take his stand on the
solid ground of principle and public duty, m u s t win his
way with men of all classes.

KEEGAN (*quietly*). Sir: there was a time, in my
ignorant youth, when I should have called you a hypocrite.

BROADBENT (*reddening*). A hypocrite!

NORA (*hastily*). Oh I'm sure you dont think anything of the sort, Mr. Keegan.

BROADBENT (*emphatically*). Thank you, Miss Reilly:
thank you.

CORNELIUS (*gloomily*). We all have to stretch it a
bit in politics: hwats the use o pretendin we dont?

BROADBENT (*stiffly*). I hope I have said or done
nothing that calls for any such observation, Mr. Doyle.
If there is a vice I detest—or against which my whole
public life has been a protest—it is the vice of hypocrisy.
I would almost rather be inconsistent than insincere.

KEEGAN. Do not be offended, sir: I know that you
are quite sincere. There is a saying in the Scripture
which runs—so far as the memory of an oldish man
can carry the words—Let not the right side of your
brain know what the left side doeth. I learnt at Oxford
that this is the secret of the Englishman's strange power
of making the best of both worlds.

BROADBENT. Surely the text refers to our right and
left hands. I am somewhat surprised to hear a member
of your Church quote so essentially Protestant a docu-
ment as the Bible; but at least you might quote it accurately.

LARRY. Tom: with the best intentions youre making
an ass of yourself. You dont understand Mr. Keegan's
peculiar vein of humor.

BROADBENT (*instantly recovering his confidence*).
Ah! it was only your delightful Irish humor, Mr.
Keegan. Of course, of course. How stupid of me!
I'm so sorry. (*He pats Keegan consolingly on the*

back.) John Bull's wits are still slow, you see. Besides, calling m e a hypocrite was too big a joke to swallow all at once, you know.

KEEGAN. You must also allow for the fact that I am mad.

NORA. Ah, dont talk like that, Mr. Keegan.

BROADBENT (*encouragingly*). Not at all, not at all. Only a whimsical Irishman, eh?

LARRY. Are you really mad, Mr. Keegan?

AUNT JUDY (*shocked*). Oh, Larry, how could you ask him such a thing?

LARRY. I dont think Mr. Keegan minds. (*To Keegan.*) Whats the true version of the story of that black man you confessed on his deathbed?

KEEGAN. What story have you heard about that?

LARRY. I am informed that when the devil came for the black heathen, he took off your head and turned it three times round before putting it on again; and that your head's been turned ever since.

NORA (*reproachfully*). Larry!

KEEGAN (*blandly*). That is not quite what occurred. (*He collects himself for a serious utterance: they attend involuntarily.*) I heard that a black man was dying, and that the people were afraid to go near him. When I went to the place I found an elderly Hindoo, who told me one of those tales of unmerited misfortune, of cruel ill luck, of relentless persecution by destiny, which sometimes wither the commonplaces of consolation on the lips of a priest. But this man did not complain of his misfortunes. They were brought upon him, he said, by sins committed in a former existence. Then, without a word of comfort from me, he died with a clear-eyed resignation that my most earnest exhortations have rarely produced in a Christian, and left me sitting there by his bedside with the mystery of this world suddenly revealed to me.

BROADBENT. That is a remarkable tribute to the

liberty of conscience enjoyed by the subjects of our Indian Empire.

LARRY. No doubt; but may we venture to ask what is the mystery of this world?

KEEGAN. This world, sir, is very clearly a place of torment and penance, a place where the fool flourishes and the good and wise are hated and persecuted, a place where men and women torture one another in the name of love; where children are scourged and enslaved in the name of parental duty and education; where the weak in body are poisoned and mutilated in the name of healing, and the weak in character are put to the horrible torture of imprisonment, not for hours but for years, in the name of justice. It is a place where the hardest toil is a welcome refuge from the horror and tedium of pleasure, and where charity and good works are done only for hire to ransom the souls of the spoiler and the sybarite. Now, sir, there is only one place of horror and torment known to my religion; and that place is hell. Therefore it is plain to me that this earth of ours must be hell, and that we are all here, as the Indian revealed to me—perhaps he was sent to reveal it to me—to expiate crimes committed by us in a former existence.

AUNT JUDY (*awestruck*). Heaven save us, what a thing to say!

CORNELIUS (*sighing*). It's a queer world: thats certain.

BROADBENT. Your idea is a very clever one, Mr. Keegan: really most brilliant: *I* should never have thought of it. But it seems to me—if I may say so—that you are overlooking the fact that, of the evils you describe, some are absolutely necessary for the preservation of society, and others are encouraged only when the Tories are in office.

LARRY. I expect you were a Tory in a former existence; and that is why you are here.

BROADBENT (*with conviction*). Never, Larry, never. But leaving politics out of the question, I find the world quite good enough for me: rather a jolly place, in fact.

KEEGAN (*looking at him with quiet wonder*). You are satisfied?

BROADBENT. As a reasonable man, yes. I see no evils in the world—except, of course, natural evils—that cannot be remedied by freedom, self-government, and English institutions. I think so, not because I am an Englishman, but as a matter of common sense.

KEEGAN. You feel at home in the world, then?

BROADBENT. Of course. Dont you?

KEEGAN (*from the very depths of his nature*). No.

BROADBENT (*breezily*). Try phosphorus pills. I always take them when my brain is overworked. I'll give you the address in Oxford Street.

KEEGAN (*enigmatically: rising*). Miss Doyle: my wandering fit has come on me: will you excuse me?

AUNT JUDY. To be sure: you know you can come in n nout as you like.

KEEGAN. We can finish the game some other time, Miss Reilly. (*He goes for his hat and stick.*)

NORA. No: I'm out with you (*she disarranges the pieces and rises.*) I was too wicked in a former existence to play backgammon with a good man like you.

AUNT JUDY (*whispering to her*). Whisht, whisht, child! Dont set him back on that again.

KEEGAN (*to Nora*). When I look at you, I think that perhaps Ireland is only purgatory, after all. (*He passes on to the garden door.*)

NORA. Galong with you!

BROADBENT (*whispering to Cornelius*). Has he a vote?

CORNELIUS (*nodding*). Yes. An theres lotsle vote the way he tells them.

KEEGAN (*at the garden door, with gentle gravity*).

Good evening, Mr. Broadbent.   You have set me thinking.   Thank you.

BROADBENT (*delighted, hurrying across to him to
shake hands*).   No, really?   You find that contact with
English ideas is stimulating, eh?

KEEGAN.   I am never tired of hearing you talk, Mr.
Broadbent.

BROADBENT (*modestly remonstrating*).   Oh come!
come!

KEEGAN.   Yes, I assure you.   You are an extremely
interesting man.   (*He goes out.*)

BROADBENT (*enthusiastically*).   What a nice chap!
What an intelligent, interesting fellow!   By the way,
I'd better have a wash.   (*He takes up his coat and cap,
and leaves the room through the inner door.*)

*Nora returns to her chair and shuts up the backgam-
mon board.*

AUNT JUDY.   Keegan's very queer to-day.   He has
his mad fit on him.

CORNELIUS (*worried and bitter*).   I wouldnt say but
hes right after all.   It's a contrairy world.   (*To Larry.*)
Why would you be such a fool as to let him take the
seat in parliament from you?

LARRY (*glancing at Nora*).   He will take more than
that from me before hes done here.

CORNELIUS.   I wish he'd never set foot in my house,
bad luck to his fat face!   D'ye think he'd lend me £300
on the farm, Larry?   When I'm so hard up, it seems
a waste o money not to mortgage it now its me
own.

LARRY.   *I* can lend you £300 on it.

CORNELIUS.   No, no: I wasnt putn in for that.   When
I die and leave you the farm I should like to be able to
feel that it was all me own, and not half yours to start
with.   Now I'll take me oath Barney Doarn's goin to
ask Broadbent to lend him £500 on the mill to put in
a new hweel; for the old one'll harly hol together.   An

Haffigan cant sleep with covetn that corner o land at the foot of his medda that belongs to Doolan. He'll have to mortgage to buy it. I may as well be first as last. D'ye think Broadbent'd len me a little?

LARRY. I'm quite sure he will.

CORNELIUS. Is he as ready as that? Would he len me five hunderd, d'ye think?

LARRY. He'll lend you more than the landll ever be worth to you; so for Heaven's sake be prudent.

CORNELIUS (*judicially*). All right, all right, me son: I'll be careful. I'm goin into the office for a bit. (*He withdraws through the inner door, obviously to prepare his application to Broadbent.*)

AUNT JUDY (*indignantly*). As if he hadnt seen enough o borryin when he was an agent without beginnin borryin himself! (*She rises.*) I'll borry him, so I will. (*She puts her knitting on the table and follows him out, with a resolute air that bodes trouble for Cornelius.*)

Larry and Nora are left together for the first time since his arrival. She looks at him with a smile that perishes as she sees him aimlessly rocking his chair, and reflecting, evidently not about her, with his lips pursed as if he were whistling. With a catch in her throat she takes up Aunt Judy's knitting, and makes a pretence of going on with it.

NORA. I suppose it didnt seem very long to you.

LARRY (*starting*). Eh? What didnt?

NORA. The eighteen years youve been away.

LARRY. Oh, that! No: it seems hardly more than a week. I've been so busy—had so little time to think.

NORA. Ive had nothin else to do but think.

LARRY. That was very bad for you. Why didnt you give it up? Why did you stay here?

NORA. Because nobody sent for me to go anywhere else, I suppose. Thats why.

LARRY. Yes: one does stick frightfully in the same

place, unless some external force comes and routs one out. (*He yawns slightly; but as she looks up quickly at him, he pulls himself together and rises with an air of waking up and setting to work cheerfully to make himself agreeable.*) And how have you been all this time?

NORA. Quite well, thank you.

LARRY. Thats right. (*Suddenly finding that he has nothing else to say, and being ill at ease in consequence, he strolls about the room humming a certain tune from Offenbach's Whittington.*)

NORA (*struggling with her tears*). Is that all you have to say to me, Larry?

LARRY. Well, what is there to say? You see, we know each other so well.

NORA (*a little consoled*). Yes: of course we do. (*He does not reply.*) I wonder you came back at all.

LARRY. I couldnt help it. (*She looks up affectionately.*) Tom made me. (*She looks down again quickly to conceal the effect of this blow. He whistles another stave; then resumes.*) I had a sort of dread of returning to Ireland. I felt somehow that my luck would turn if I came back. And now here I am, none the worse.

NORA. Praps it's a little dull for you.

LARRY. No: I havnt exhausted the interest of strolling about the old places and remembering and romancing about them.

NORA (*hopefully*). Oh! You do remember the places, then?

LARRY. Of course. They have associations.

NORA (*not doubting that the associations are with her*). I suppose so.

LARRY. M'yes. I can remember particular spots where I had long fits of thinking about the countries I meant to get to when I escaped from Ireland. America and London, and sometimes Rome and the east.

NORA (*deeply mortified*). Was that all you used to be thinking about?

LARRY. Well, there was precious little else to think about here, my dear Nora, except sometimes at sunset, when one got maudlin and called Ireland Erin, and imagined one was remembering the days of old, and so forth. (*He whistles Let Erin remember.*)

NORA. Did jever get a letter I wrote you last February?

LARRY. Oh yes; and I really intended to answer it. But I havnt had a moment; and I knew you wouldnt mind. You see, I am so afraid of boring you by writing about affairs you dont understand and people you dont know! And yet what else have I to write about? I begin a letter; and then I tear it up again. The fact is, fond as we are of one another, Nora, we have so little in common——I mean of course the things one can put in a letter——that correspondence is apt to become the hardest of hard work.

NORA. Yes: it's hard for me to know anything about you if you never tell me anything.

LARRY (*pettishly*). Nora: a man cant sit down and write his life day by day when hes tired enough with having lived it.

NORA. I'm not blaming you.

LARRY (*looking at her with some concern*). You seem rather out of spirits. (*Going closer to her, anxiously and tenderly.*) You havnt got neuralgia, have you?

NORA. No.

LARRY (*reassured*). I get a touch of it sometimes when I am below par. (*Absently, again strolling about.*) Yes, yes. (*He begins to hum again, and soon breaks into articulate melody.*)

> Though summer smiles on here for ever,
> Though not a leaf falls from the tree,
> Tell England I'll forget her never,

(Nora puts down the knitting and stares at him.)

O wind that blows across the sea.

(With much expression.)

Tell England I'll forget her ne-e-e-e-ver
O wind that blows acro-oss—

(Here the melody soars out of his range. He continues falsetto, but changes the tune to Let Erin remember.) I'm afraid I'm boring you, Nora, though youre too kind to say so.

NORA. Are you wanting to get back to England already?

LARRY. Not at all. Not at all.

NORA. Thats a queer song to sing to me if youre not.

LARRY. The song! Oh, it doesnt mean anything: its by a German Jew, like most English patriotic sentiment. Never mind me, my dear: go on with your work; and dont let me bore you.

NORA *(bitterly)*. Rosscullen isnt such a lively place that I am likely to be bored by you at our first talk together after eighteen years, though you dont seem to have much to say to me after all.

LARRY. Eighteen years is a devilish long time, Nora. Now if it had been eighteen minutes, or even eighteen months, we should be able to pick up the interrupted thread, and chatter like two magpies. But as it is, I have simply nothing to say; and you seem to have less.

NORA. I— *(her tears choke her; but she keeps up appearances desperately).*

LARRY *(quite unconscious of his cruelty)*. In a week or so we shall be quite old friends again. Meanwhile, as I feel that I am not making myself particularly entertaining, I'll take myself off. Tell Tom Ive gone for a stroll over the hill.

NORA. You seem very fond of Tom, as you call him.

LARRY (*the triviality going suddenly out of his voice*). Yes: I'm fond of Tom.

NORA. Oh, well, dont let me keep you from him.

LARRY. I know quite well that my departure will be a relief. Rather a failure, this first meeting after eighteen years, eh? Well, never mind: these great sentimental events always a r e failures; and now the worst of it's over anyhow. (*He goes out through the garden door.*)

Nora, left alone, struggles wildly to save herself from breaking down, and then drops her face on the table and gives way to a convulsion of crying. Her sobs shake her so that she can hear nothing; and she has no suspicion that she is no longer alone until her head and breast are raised by Broadbent, who, returning newly washed and combed through the inner door, has seen her condition, first with surprise and concern, and then with an emotional disturbance that quite upsets him.

BROADBENT. Miss Reilly. Miss Reilly. Whats the matter? Dont cry: I cant stand it: you mustnt cry. (*She makes a choked effort to speak, so painful that he continues with impulsive sympathy.*) No: dont try to speak: it's all right now. Have your cry out: never mind me: trust me. (*Gathering her to him, and babbling consolatorily.*) Cry on my chest: the only really comfortable place for a woman to cry is a man's chest: a real man, a real friend. A good broad chest, eh? not less than forty-two inches—no: dont fuss: never mind the conventions: we're two friends, arnt we? Come now, come, come! Its all right and comfortable and happy now, isnt it?

NORA (*through her tears*). Let me go. I want me hankerchief.

BROADBENT (*holding her with one arm and producing a large silk handkerchief from his breast pocket*). Heres a handkerchief. Let me (*he dabs her tears dry with it*).

Never mind your own: it's too small: it's one of those wretched little cambric handkerchiefs—

NORA (*sobbing*). Indeed it's a common cotton one.

BROADBENT. Of course it's a common cotton one— silly little cotton one—not good enough for the dear eyes of Nora Cryna—

NORA (*spluttering into a hysterical laugh and clutching him convulsively with her fingers while she tries to stifle her laughter against his collar bone*). Oh dont make me laugh: please dont make me laugh.

BROADBENT (*terrified*). I didnt mean to, on my soul. What is it? What is it?

NORA. Nora Creena, Nora Creena.

BROADBENT (*patting her*). Yes, yes, of course, Nora Creena, Nora acushla (*he makes cush rhyme to plush*)—

NORA. Acushla (*she makes cush rhyme to bush*).

BROADBENT. Oh, confound the language! Nora darling—my Nora—the Nora I love—

NORA (*shocked into propriety*). You mustnt talk like that to me.

BROADBENT (*suddenly becoming prodigiously solemn and letting her go*). No, of course not. I dont mean it —at least I d o mean it; but I know it's premature. I had no right to take advantage of your being a little upset; but I lost my self-control for a moment.

NORA (*wondering at him*). I think youre a very kindhearted man, Mr. Broadbent; but you seem to me to have no self-control at all (*she turns her face away with a keen pang of shame and adds*) no more than myself.

BROADBENT (*resolutely*). Oh yes, I have: you should see me when I am really roused: then I have T R E - M E N D O U S self-control. Remember: we have been alone together only once before; and then, I regret to say, I was in a disgusting state.

NORA. Ah no, Mr. Broadbent: you wernt disgusting.

BROADBENT (*mercilessly*). Yes I was: nothing can

excuse it: perfectly beastly. It must have made a most unfavorable impression on you.

NORA. Oh, sure it's all right. Say no more about that.

BROADBENT. I must, Miss Reilly: it is my duty. I shall not detain you long. May I ask you to sit down. (*He indicates her chair with oppressive solemnity. She sits down wondering. He then, with the same portentous gravity, places a chair for himself near her; sits down; and proceeds to explain.*) First, Miss Reilly, may I say that I have tasted nothing of an alcoholic nature today.

NORA. It doesnt seem to make as much difference in you as it would in an Irishman, somehow.

BROADBENT. Perhaps not. Pcrhaps not. I never quite lose myself.

NORA (*consolingly*). Well, anyhow, youre all right now.

BROADBENT (*fervently*). Thank you, Miss Reilly: I am. Now we shall get along. (*Tenderly, lowering his voice.*) Nora: I was in earnest last night. (*Nora moves as if to rise.*) No: one moment. You must not think I am going to press you for an answer before you have known me for 24 hours. I am a reasonable man, I hope; and I am prepared to wait as long as you like, provided you will give me some small assurance that the answer will not be unfavorable.

NORA. How could I go back from it if I did? I sometimes think youre not quite right in your head, Mr. Broadbent, you say such funny things.

BROADBENT. Yes: I know I have a strong sense of humor which sometimes makes people doubt whether I am quite serious. That is why I have always thought I should like to marry an Irishwoman. She would always understand my jokes. For instance, you would understand them, eh?

NORA (*uneasily*). Mr. Broadbent, I couldnt.

BROADBENT (*soothingly*). Wait: let me break this to you gently, Miss Reilly: hear me out. I daresay you have noticed that in speaking to you I have been putting a very strong constraint on myself, so as to avoid wounding your delicacy by too abrupt an avowal of my feelings. Well, I feel now that the time has come to be open, to be frank, to be explicit. Miss Reilly: you have inspired in me a very strong attachment. Perhaps, with a woman's intuition, you have already guessed that.

NORA (*rising distractedly*). Why do you talk to me in that unfeeling nonsensical way?

BROADBENT (*rising also, much astonished*). Unfeeling! Nonsensical!

NORA. Dont you know that you have said things to me that no man ought to say unless—unless— (*she suddenly breaks down again and hides her face on the table as before.*) Oh, go away from me: I wont get married at all: what is it but heartbreak and disappointment?

BROADBENT (*developing the most formidable symptoms of rage and grief*). Do you mean to say that you are going to refuse me? that you dont care for me?

NORA (*looking at him in consternation*). Oh, dont take it to heart, Mr. Br—

BROADBENT (*flushed and almost choking*). I dont want to be petted and blarneyed. (*With childish rage.*) I love you. I want you for my wife. (*In despair.*) I cant help your refusing. I'm helpless: I can do nothing. You have no right to ruin my whole life. You— (*a hysterical convulsion stops him*).

NORA (*almost awestruck*). Youre not going to cry, are you? I never thought a man c o u l d cry. Dont.

BROADBENT. I'm not crying. I—I—I leave that sort of thing to your damned sentimental Irishmen. You think I have no feeling because I am a plain unemotional Englishman, with no powers of expression.

NORA. I dont think you know the sort of man you

are at all. Whatever may be the matter with you, it's
not want of feeling.

BROADBENT (*hurt and petulant*). It's you who have
no feeling. Youre as heartless as Larry.

NORA. What do you expect me to do? Is it to throw
meself at your head the minute the word is out o your
mouth?

BROADBENT (*striking his silly head with his fists*).
Oh, what a fool! what a brute I am! It's only your
Irish delicacy: of course, of course. You mean Yes.
Eh? What? Yes, yes, yes?

NORA. I think you might understand that though I
might choose to be an old maid, I could never marry
anybody but you now.

BROADBENT (*clasping her violently to his breast,
with a crow of immense relief and triumph*). Ah, thats
right, thats right: thats magnificent. I knew you would
see what a first-rate thing this will be for both of us.

NORA (*incommoded and not at all enraptured by his
ardor*). Youre dreadfully strong, an a gradle too free
with your strength. An I never thought o whether it'd
be a good thing for us or not. But when you found
me here that time, I let you be kind to me, and cried
in your arms, because I was too wretched to think of
anything but the comfort of it. An how could I let
any other man touch me after that?

BROADBENT (*touched*). Now thats very nice of you,
Nora: thats really most delicately womanly (*he kisses
her hand chivalrously*).

NORA (*looking earnestly and a little doubtfully at
him*). Surely if you let one woman cry on you like
that youd never let another touch you.

BROADBENT (*conscientiously*). One should not. One
o u g h t not, my dear girl. But the honest truth is, if
a chap is at all a pleasant sort of chap, his chest becomes
a fortification that has to stand many assaults: at least
it is so in England.

Nora (*curtly, much disgusted*). Then youd better marry an Englishwoman.

Broadbent (*making a wry face*). No, no: the Englishwoman is too prosaic for my taste, too material, too much of the animated beefsteak about her. The ideal is what I like. Now Larry's taste is just the opposite: he likes em solid and bouncing and rather keen about him. It's a very convenient difference; for weve never been in love with the same woman.

Nora. An d'ye mean to tell me to me face that youve ever been in love before?

Broadbent. Lord! yes.

Nora. I'm not your first love?

Broadbent. First love is only a little foolishness and a lot of curiosity: no really self-respecting woman would take advantage of it. No, my dear Nora: Ive done with all that long ago. Love affairs always end in rows. We're not going to have any rows: we're going to have a solid four-square home: man and wife: comfort and common sense—and plenty of affection, eh (*he puts his arm round her with confident proprietorship*)?

Nora (*coldly, trying to get away*). I dont want any other woman's leavings.

Broadbent (*holding her*). Nobody asked you to, maam. I never asked any woman to marry me before.

Nora (*severely*). Then why didnt you if youre an honorable man?

Broadbent. Well, to tell you the truth, they were mostly married already. But never mind! there was nothing wrong. Come! dont take a mean advantage of me. After all, you must have had a fancy or two yourself, eh?

Nora (*conscience-stricken*). Yes. I suppose Ive no right to be particular.

Broadbent (*humbly*). I know I'm not good enough for you, Nora. But no man is, you know, when the woman is a really nice woman.

NORA. Oh, I'm no better than yourself. I may as well tell you about it.

BROADBENT. No, no: lets have no telling: much better not. *I* shant tell y o u anything; dont y o u tell m e anything. Perfect confidence in one another and no tellings: thats the way to avoid rows.

NORA. Dont think it was anything I need be ashamed of.

BROADBENT. I dont.

NORA. It was only that I'd never known anybody else that I could care for; and I was foolish enough once to think that Larry—

BROADBENT (*disposing of the idea at once*). Larry! Oh, that wouldnt have done at all, not at all. You dont know Larry as I do, my dear. He has absolutely no capacity for enjoyment: he couldnt make any woman happy. He's as clever as be-blowed; but life's too earthly for him: he doesnt really care for anything or anybody.

NORA. Ive found that out.

BROADBENT. Of course you have. No, my dear: take my word for it, youre jolly well out of that. There! (*swinging her round against his breast*) thats much more comfortable for you.

NORA (*with Irish peevishness*). Ah, you mustnt go on like that. I dont like it.

BROADBENT (*unabashed*). Youll acquire the taste by degrees. You mustnt mind me: it's an absolute necessity of my nature that I should have somebody to hug occasionally. Besides, it's good for you: itll plump out your muscles and make em elastic and set up your figure.

NORA. Well, I'm sure! if this is English manners! Arnt you ashamed to talk about such things?

BROADBENT (*in the highest feather*). Not a bit. By George, Nora, its a tremendous thing to be able to enjoy oneself. Lets go off for a walk out of this stuffy little room. I want the open air to expand in. Come along. Co-o-o-me along. (*He puts her arm into his and sweeps her out into the garden as an equinoctial gale might sweep a dry leaf.*)

Later in the evening, the grasshopper is again enjoying the sunset by the great stone on the hill; but this time he enjoys neither the stimulus of Keegan's conversation nor the pleasure of terrifying Patsy Farrell. He is alone until Nora and Broadbent come up the hill arm in arm. Broadbent is still breezy and confident; but she has her head averted from him and is almost in tears.

BROADBENT (*stopping to snuff up the hillside air*). Ah! I like this spot. I like this view. This would be a jolly good place for a hotel and a golf links. Friday to Tuesday, railway ticket and hotel all inclusive. I tell you, Nora, I'm going to develop this place. (*Looking at her.*) Hallo! Whats the matter? Tired?

NORA (*unable to restrain her tears*). I'm ashamed out o me life.

BROADBENT (*astonished*). Ashamed! What of?

NORA. Oh, how could you drag me all round the place like that, telling everybody that we're going to be married, and introjoocing me to the lowest of the low, and letting them shake hans with me, and encouraging them to make free with us? I little thought I should live to be shaken hans with be Doolan in broad daylight in the public street of Rosscullen.

BROADBENT. But, my dear, Doolan's a publican: a most influential man. By the way, I asked him if his wife would be at home tomorrow. He said she would; so you must take the motor car round and call on her.

NORA (*aghast*). Is it me call on Doolan's wife!

BROADBENT. Yes, of course: call on all their wives. We must get a copy of the register and a supply of canvassing cards. No use calling on people who havnt votes. Youll be a great success as a canvasser, Nora:

they call you the heiress; and theyll be flattered no end by your calling, especially as youve never cheapened yourself by speaking to them before—have you?

NORA (*indignantly*). Not likely, indeed.

BROADBENT. Well, we mustnt be stiff and stand-off, you know. We must be thoroughly democratic, and patronize everybody without distinction of class. I tell you I'm a jolly lucky man, Nora Cryna. I get engaged to the most delightful woman in Ireland; and it turns out that I couldnt have done a smarter stroke of electioneering.

NORA. An would you let me demean meself like that, just to get yourself into parliament?

BROADBENT (*buoyantly*). Aha! Wait till you find out what an exciting game electioneering is: youll be mad to get me in. Besides, youd like people to say that Tom Broadbent's wife had been the making of him— that she got him into parliament—into the Cabinet, perhaps, eh?

NORA. God knows I dont grudge you me money! But to lower meself to the level of common people—

BROADBENT. To a member's wife, Nora, nobody is common provided hes on the register. Come, my dear! its all right: do you think I'd let you do it if it wasnt? The best people do it. Everybody does it.

NORA (*who has been biting her lip and looking over the hill, disconsolate and unconvinced*). Well, praps you know best what they do in England. They must have very little respect for themselves. I think I'll go in now. I see Larry and Mr. Keegan coming up the hill; and I'm not fit to talk to them.

BROADBENT. Just wait and say something nice to Keegan. They tell me he controls nearly as many votes as Father Dempsey himself.

NORA. You little know Peter Keegan. He'd see through me as if I was a pane o glass.

BROADBENT. Oh, he wont like it any the less for

that. What really flatters a man is that you think him
worth flattering. Not that I would flatter any man:
dont think that. I'll just go and meet him. (*He goes
down the hill with the eager forward look of a man
about to greet a valued acquaintance. Nora dries her
eyes, and turns to go as Larry strolls up the hill to her.*)

LARRY. Nora. (*She turns and looks at him hardly,
without a word. He continues anxiously, in his most
conciliatory tone.*) When I left you that time, I was
just as wretched as you. I didnt rightly know what I
wanted to say; and my tongue kept clacking to cover
the loss I was at. Well, Ive been thinking ever since;
and now I know what I ought to have said. Ive come
back to say it.

NORA. Youve come too late, then. You thought
eighteen years was not long enough, and that you might
keep me waiting a day longer. Well, you were mistaken.
I'm engaged to your friend Mr. Broadbent; and I'm
done with you.

LARRY (*naïvely*). But that was the very thing I was
going to advise you to do.

NORA (*involuntarily*). Oh you brute! to tell me that
to me face.

LARRY (*nervously relapsing into his most Irish manner*). Nora, dear, dont you understand that I'm an
Irishman, and hes an Englishman. He wants you; and
he grabs you. *I* want you; and I quarrel with you and
have to go on wanting you.

NORA. So you may. Youd better go back to England
to the animated beefsteaks youre so fond of.

LARRY (*amazed*). Nora! (*Guessing where she got
the metaphor.*) Hes been talking about me, I see. Well,
never mind: we must be friends, you and I. I dont
want his marriage to you to be his divorce from me.

NORA. You care more for him than you ever did for
me.

LARRY (*with curt sincerity*). Yes of course I do:

why should I tell you lies about it? Nora Reilly was a person of very little consequence to me or anyone else outside this miserable little hole. But Mrs. Tom Broadbent will be a person of very considerable consequence indeed. Play your new part well, and there will be no more neglect, no more loneliness, no more idle regrettings and vain-hopings in the evenings by the round tower, but real life and real work and real cares and real joys among real people: solid English life in London, the very centre of the world. You will find your work cut out for you keeping Tom's house and entertaining Tom's friends and getting Tom into parliament; but it will be worth the effort.

NORA.   You talk as if I were under an obligation to him for marrying me.

LARRY.   I talk as I think. Youve made a very good match, let me tell you.

NORA.   Indeed!   Well, some people might say hes not done so badly himself.

LARRY.   If you mean that you will be a treasure to him, he thinks so now; and you can keep him thinking so if you like.

NORA.   I wasnt thinking o meself at all.

LARRY.   Were you thinking of your money, Nora?

NORA.   I didnt say so.

LARRY.   Your money will not pay your cook's wages in London.

NORA (*flaming up*).   If thats true—and the more shame for you to throw it in my face if it i s true—at all events itll make us independent; for if the worst comes to the worst, we can always come back here an live on it. An if I have to keep his house for him, at all events I can keep y o u out of it; for Ive done with you; and I wish I'd never seen you. So goodbye to you, Mister Larry Doyle. (*She turns her back on him and goes home.*)

LARRY (*watching her as she goes*).   Goodbye. Good-

bye. Oh, thats so Irish! Irish both of us to the backbone: Irish, Irish, Irish—

*Broadbent arrives, conversing energetically with
Keegan.*

BROADBENT. Nothing pays like a golfing hotel, if
you hold the land instead of the shares, and if the furniture people stand in with you, and if you are a good
man of business.

LARRY. Nora's gone home.

BROADBENT (*with conviction*). You were right this
morning, Larry. I must feed up Nora. She's weak;
and it makes her fanciful. Oh, by the way, did I tell
you that we're engaged?

LARRY. She told me herself.

BROADBENT (*complacently*). She's rather full of it,
as you may imagine. Poor Nora! Well, Mr. Keegan,
as I said, I begin to see my way here. I begin to see
my way.

KEEGAN (*with a courteous inclination*). The con-
quering Englishman, sir. Within 24 hours of your arrival you have carried off our only heiress, and practically secured the parliamentary seat. And you have
promised me that when I come here in the evenings to
meditate on my madness; to watch the shadow of the
round tower lengthening in the sunset; to break my
heart uselessly in the curtained gloaming over the dead
heart and blinded soul of the island of the saints, you
will comfort me with the bustle of a great hotel, and
the sight of the little children carrying the golf clubs
of your tourists as a preparation for the life to come.

BROADBENT (*quite touched, mutely offering him a
cigar to console him, at which he smiles and shakes his
head*). Yes, Mr. Keegan: youre quite right. Theres
poetry in everything, even (*looking absently into the
cigar case*) in the most modern prosaic things, if you
know how to extract it (*he extracts a cigar for himself
and offers one to Larry, who takes it*). If I was to be

shot for it I couldnt extract it myself; but thats where y o u come in, you see (*roguishly, waking up from his reverie and bustling Keegan goodhumoredly*). And then I shall wake you up a bit. Thats where *I* come in: eh? d'ye see? Eh? eh? (*He pats him very pleasantly on the shoulder, half admiringly, half pityingly.*) Just so, just so. (*Coming back to business.*) By the way, I believe I can do better than a light railway here. There seems to be no question now that the motor boat has come to stay. Well, look at your magnificent river there, going to waste.

KEEGAN (*closing his eyes*). " Silent, O Moyle, be the roar of thy waters."

BROADBENT. You know, the roar of a motor boat is quite pretty.

KEEGAN. Provided it does not drown the Angelus.

BROADBENT (*reassuringly*). Oh no: it wont do that: not the least danger. You know, a church bell can make a devil of a noise when it likes.

KEEGAN. You have an answer for everything, sir. But your plans leave one question still unanswered: how to get butter out of a dog's throat.

BROADBENT. Eh?

KEEGAN. You cannot build your golf links and hotels in the air. For that you must own our land. And how will you drag our acres from the ferret's grip of Matthew Haffigan? How will you persuade Cornelius Doyle to forego the pride of being a small landowner? How will Barney Doran's millrace agree with your motor boats? Will Doolan help you to get a license for your hotel?

BROADBENT. My dear sir: to all intents and purposes the syndicate I represent already owns half Rosscullen. Doolan's is a tied house; and the brewers are in the syndicate. As to Haffigan's farm and Doran's mill and Mr. Doyle's place and half a dozen others, they will be mortgaged to me before a month is out.

KEEGAN.   But pardon me, you will not lend them more on their land than the land is worth; so they will be able to pay you the interest.

BROADBENT.   Ah, you are a poet, Mr. Keegan, not a man of business.

LARRY.   We will lend everyone of these men half as much again on their land as it is worth, or ever can be worth, t o t h e m.

BROADBENT.   You forget, sir, that we, with our capital, our knowledge, our organization, and may I say our English business habits, can make or lose ten pounds out of land that Haffigan, with all his industry, could not make or lose ten shillings out of.   Doran's mill is a superannuated folly: I shall want it for electric lighting.

LARRY.   What is the use of giving land to such men? they are too small, too poor, too ignorant, too simple-minded to hold it against us: you might as well give a dukedom to a crossing sweeper.

BROADBENT.   Yes, Mr. Keegan: this place may have an industrial future, or it may have a residential future: I cant tell yet; but it's not going to be a future in the hands of your Dorans and Haffigans, poor devils!

KEEGAN.   It may have no future at all.   Have you thought of that?

BROADBENT.   Oh, I'm not afraid of that.   I have faith in Ireland, great faith, Mr. Keegan.

KEEGAN.   And we have none: only empty enthusiasms and patriotisms, and emptier memories and regrets.   Ah yes: you have some excuse for believing that if there be any future, it will be yours; for our faith seems dead, and our hearts cold and cowed.   An island of dreamers who wake up in your jails, of critics and cowards whom you buy and tame for your own service, of bold rogues who help you to plunder us that they may plunder you afterwards.   Eh?

BROADBENT (*a little impatient of this unbusinesslike*

view). Yes, yes; but you know you might say that of any country. The fact is, there are only two qualities in the world: efficiency and inefficiency, and only two sorts of people: the efficient and the inefficient. It dont matter whether theyre English or Irish. I shall collar this place, not because I'm an Englishman and Haffigan and Co. are Irishmen, but because theyre duffers and I know my way about.

Kᴇᴇɢᴀɴ. Have you considered what is to become of Haffigan?

Lᴀʀʀʏ. Oh, we'll employ him in some capacity or other, and probably pay him more than he makes for himself now.

Bʀᴏᴀᴅʙᴇɴᴛ (*dubiously*). Do you think so? No no: Haffigan's too old. It really doesnt pay now to take on men over forty even for unskilled labor, which I suppose is all Haffigan would be good for. No: Haffigan had better go to America, or into the Union, poor old chap! Hes worked out, you know: you can see it.

Kᴇᴇɢᴀɴ. Poor lost soul, so cunningly fenced in with invisible bars!

Lᴀʀʀʏ. Haffigan doesnt matter much. He'll die presently.

Bʀᴏᴀᴅʙᴇɴᴛ (*shocked*). Oh come, Larry! Dont be unfeeling. Its hard on Haffigan. It's always hard on the inefficient.

Lᴀʀʀʏ. Pah! what does it matter where an old and broken man spends his last days, or whether he has a million at the bank or only the workhouse dole? It's the young men, the able men, that matter. The real tragedy of Haffigan is the tragedy of his wasted youth, his stunted mind, his drudging over his clods and pigs until he has become a clod and a pig himself—until the soul within him has smouldered into nothing but a dull temper that hurts himself and all around him. I say let him die, and let us have no more of his like. And let young Ireland take care that it doesnt share his fate,

instead of making another empty grievance of it.   Let
your syndicate come—

BROADBENT.   Your syndicate too, old chap.   You
have your bit of the stock.

LARRY.   Yes, mine if you like.   Well, our syndicate
has no conscience: it has no more regard for your Haffigans and Doolans and Dorans than it has for a gang of
Chinee coolies.   It will use your patriotic blatherskite
and balderdash to get parliamentary powers over you as
cynically as it would bait a mousetrap with toasted
cheese.   It will plan, and organize, and find capital
while you slave like bees for it and revenge yourselves
by paying politicians and penny newspapers out of your
small wages to write articles and report speeches against
its wickedness and tyranny, and to crack up your own
Irish heroism, just as Haffigan once paid a witch a penny
to put a spell on Billy Byrne's cow.   In the end it will
grind the nonsense out of you, and grind strength and
sense into you.

BROADBENT (*out of patience*).   Why cant you say a
simple thing simply, Larry, without all that Irish ex-
aggeration and talky-talky?   The syndicate is a perfectly respectable body of responsible men of good
position.   We'll take Ireland in hand, and by straightforward business habits teach it efficiency and self-help on
sound Liberal principles.   You agree with me, Mr.
Keegan, dont you?

KEEGAN.   Sir: I may even vote for you.

BROADBENT (*sincerely moved, shaking his hand
warmly*).   You shall never regret it, Mr. Keegan: I give
you my word for that.   I shall bring money here: I
shall raise wages: I shall found public institutions, a
library, a Polytechnic (undenominational, of course), a
gymnasium, a cricket club, perhaps an art school.   I
shall make a Garden city of Rosscullen: the round tower
shall be thoroughly repaired and restored.

KEEGAN.   And our place of torment shall be as clean

and orderly as the cleanest and most orderly place I know in Ireland, which is our poetically named Mountjoy prison. Well, perhaps I had better vote for an efficient devil that knows his own mind and his own business than for a foolish patriot who has no mind and no business.

BROADBENT (*stiffly*). Devil is rather a strong expression in that connexion, Mr. Keegan.

KEEGAN. Not from a man who knows that this world is hell. But since the word offends you, let me soften it, and compare you simply to an ass. (*Larry whitens with anger.*)

BROADBENT (*reddening*). An ass!

KEEGAN (*gently*). You may take it without offence from a madman who calls the ass his brother—and a very honest, useful and faithful brother too. The ass, sir, is the most efficient of beasts, matter-of-fact, hardy, friendly when you treat him as a fellow-creature, stubborn when you abuse him, ridiculous only in love, which sets him braying, and in politics, which move him to roll about in the public road and raise a dust about nothing. Can you deny these qualities and habits in yourself, sir?

BROADBENT (*goodhumoredly*). Well, yes, I'm afraid I do, you know.

KEEGAN. Then perhaps you will confess to the ass's one fault.

BROADBENT. Perhaps so: what is it?

KEEGAN. That he wastes all his virtues—his efficiency, as you call it—in doing the will of his greedy masters instead of doing the will of Heaven that is in himself. He is efficient in the service of Mammon, mighty in mischief, skilful in ruin, heroic in destruction. But he comes to browse here without knowing that the soil his hoof touches is holy ground. Ireland, sir, for good or evil, is like no other place under heaven; and no man can touch its sod or breathe its air without becoming better or worse. It produces two kinds of men in strange perfection: saints and traitors. It is called the island of the saints; but indeed in these later years it might be more fitly called the island of the traitors; for our harvest of these is the fine flower of the world's crop of infamy. But the day may come when these islands shall live by the quality of their men rather than by the abundance of their minerals; and then we shall see.

LARRY. Mr. Keegan: if you are going to be sentimental about Ireland, I shall bid you good evening. We have had enough of that, and more than enough of cleverly proving that everybody who is not an Irishman is an ass. It is neither good sense nor good manners. It will not stop the syndicate; and it will not interest young Ireland so much as my friend's gospel of efficiency.

BROADBENT. Ah, yes, yes: efficiency is the thing. I dont in the least mind your chaff, Mr. Keegan; but Larry's right on the main point. The world belongs to the efficient.

KEEGAN (*with polished irony*). I stand rebuked, gentlemen. But believe me, I do every justice to the efficiency of you and your syndicate. You are both, I am told, thoroughly efficient civil engineers; and I have no doubt the golf links will be a triumph of your art. Mr. Broadbent will get into parliament most efficiently, which is more than St. Patrick could do if he were alive now. You may even build the hotel efficiently if you can find enough efficient masons, carpenters, and plumbers, which I rather doubt. (*Dropping his irony, and beginning to fall into the attitude of the priest rebuking sin.*) When the hotel becomes insolvent (*Broadbent takes his cigar out of his mouth, a little taken aback*), your English business habits will secure the thorough efficiency of the liquidation. You will reorganize the scheme efficiently; you will liquidate its second bankruptcy efficiently

(*Broadbent and Larry look quickly at one another; for this, unless the priest is an old financial hand, must be inspiration*); you will get rid of its original shareholders efficiently after efficiently ruining them; and you will finally profit very efficiently by getting that hotel for a few shillings in the pound. (*More and more sternly.*) Besides these efficient operations, you will foreclose your mortgages most efficiently (*his rebuking forefinger goes up in spite of himself*); you will drive Haffigan to America very efficiently; you will find a use for Barney Doran's foul mouth and bullying temper by employing him to slave-drive your laborers very efficiently; and (*low and bitter*) when at last this poor desolate country-side becomes a busy mint in which we shall all slave to make money for you, with our Polytechnic to teach us how to do it efficiently, and our library to fuddle the few imaginations your distilleries will spare, and our repaired round tower with admission sixpence, and refreshments and penny-in-the-slot mutoscopes to make it interesting, then no doubt your English and American shareholders will spend all the money we make for them very efficiently in shooting and hunting, in operations for cancer and appendicitis, in gluttony and gambling; and you will devote what they save to fresh land development schemes. For four wicked centuries the world has dreamed this foolish dream of efficiency; and the end is not yet. But the end will come.

BROADBENT (*seriously*). Too true, Mr. Keegan, only too true. And most eloquently put. It reminds me of poor Ruskin—a great man, you know. I sympathize. Believe me, I'm on your side. Dont sneer, Larry: I used to read a lot of Shelley years ago. Let us be faithful to the dreams of our youth (*he wafts a wreath of cigar smoke at large across the hill*).

KEEGAN. Come, Mr. Doyle! is this English sentiment so much more efficient than our Irish sentiment, after all? Mr. Broadbent spends his life inefficiently admiring the thoughts of great men, and efficiently serving the cupidity of base money hunters. We spend o u r lives efficiently sneering at him and doing nothing. Which of us has any right to reproach the other?

BROADBENT (*coming down the hill again to Keegan's right hand*). But you know, something m u s t be done.

KEEGAN. Yes: when we cease to do, we cease to live. Well, what shall we do?

BROADBENT. Why, what lies to our hand.

KEEGAN. Which is the making of golf links and hotels to bring idlers to a country which workers have left in millions because it is a hungry land, a naked land, an ignorant and oppressed land.

BROADBENT. But, hang it all, the idlers will bring money from England to Ireland!

KEEGAN. Just as o u r idlers have for so many generations taken money from Ireland to England. Has that saved England from poverty and degradation more horrible than we have ever dreamed of? When I went to England, sir, I hated England. Now I pity it. (*Broadbent can hardly conceive an Irishman pitying England; but as Larry intervenes angrily, he gives it up and takes to the hill and his cigar again.*)

LARRY. Much good your pity will do it!

KEEGAN. In the accounts kept in heaven, Mr. Doyle, a heart purified of hatred may be worth more even than a Land Development Syndicate of Anglicized Irishmen and Gladstonized Englishman.

LARRY. Oh, in heaven, no doubt! I have never been there. Can you tell me where it is?

KEEGAN. Could you have told me this morning where hell is? Yet you know now that it is here. Do not despair of finding heaven: it may be no farther off.

LARRY (*ironically*). On this holy ground, as you call it, eh?

KEEGAN (*with fierce intensity*). Yes, perhaps, even

on this holy ground which such Irishmen as you have turned into a Land of Derision.

BROADBENT (*coming between them*). Take care! you will be quarrelling presently. Oh, you Irishmen, you Irishmen! Toujours Ballyhooly, eh? (*Larry, with a shrug, half comic, half impatient, turns away up the hill, but presently strolls back on Keegan's right. Broadbent adds, confidentially to Keegan*) Stick to the Englishman, Mr. Keegan: he has a bad name here; but at least he can forgive you for being an Irishman.

KEEGAN. Sir: when you speak to me of English and Irish you forget that I am a Catholic. My country is not Ireland nor England, but the whole mighty realm of my Church. For me there are but two countries: heaven and hell; but two conditions of men: salvation and damnation. Standing here between you the Englishman, so clever in your foolishness, and this Irishman, so foolish in his cleverness, I cannot in my ignorance be sure which of you is the more deeply damned; but I should be unfaithful to my calling if I opened the gates of my heart less widely to one than to the other.

LARRY. In either case it would be an impertinence, Mr. Keegan, as your approval is not of the slightest consequence to us. What use do you suppose all this drivel is to men with serious practical business in hand?

BROADBENT. I dont agree with that, Larry. I think these things cannot be said too often: they keep up the moral tone of the community. As you know, I claim the right to think for myself in religious matters: in fact, I am ready to avow myself a bit of a—of a—well, I dont care who knows it—a bit of a Unitarian; but if the Church of England contained a few men like Mr. Keegan, I should certainly join it.

KEEGAN. You do me too much honor, sir. (*With priestly humility to Larry.*) Mr. Doyle: I am to blame for having unintentionally set your mind somewhat on edge against me. I beg your pardon.

LARRY (*unimpressed and hostile*). I didnt stand on ceremony with you: you neednt stand on it with me. Fine manners and fine words are cheap in Ireland: you can keep both for my friend here, who is still imposed on by them. *I* know their value.

KEEGAN. You mean you dont know their value.

LARRY (*angrily*). I mean what I say.

KEEGAN (*turning quietly to the Englishman*). You see, Mr. Broadbent, I only make the hearts of my countrymen harder when I preach to them: the gates of hell still prevail against me. I shall wish you good evening. I am better alone, at the round tower, dreaming of heaven. (*He goes up the hill.*)

LARRY. Aye, thats it! there you are! dreaming, dreaming, dreaming, dreaming!

KEEGAN (*halting and turning to them for the last time*). Every dream is a prophecy: every jest is an earnest in the womb of Time.

BROADBENT (*reflectively*). Once, when I was a small kid, I dreamt I was in heaven. (*They both stare at him.*) It was a sort of pale blue satin place, with all the pious old ladies in our congregation sitting as if they were at a service; and there was some awful person in the study at the other side of the hall. I didnt enjoy it, you know. What is it like in y o u r dreams?

KEEGAN. In my dreams it is a country where the State is the Church and the Church the people: three in one and one in three. It is a commonwealth in which work is play and play is life: three in one and one in three. It is a temple in which the priest is the worshipper and the worshipper the worshipped: three in one and one in three. It is a godhead in which all life is human and all humanity divine: three in one and one in three. It is, in short, the dream of a madman. (*He goes away across the hill.*)

BROADBENT (*looking after him affectionately*). What a regular old Church and State Tory he is! Hes a

character: he'll be an attraction here. Really almost
equal to Ruskin and Carlyle.

LARRY. Yes; and much good t h e y did with all their
talk!

BROADBENT. Oh tut, tut, Larry! They improved my
mind: they raised my tone enormously. I feel sincerely
obliged to Keegan: he has made me feel a better man:
distinctly better. (*With sincere elevation.*) I feel now
as I never did before that I am right in devoting my
life to the cause of Ireland. Come along and help me
to choose the site for the hotel.

CURTAIN.

HOW HE LIED TO HER HUSBAND

1904

PREFACE

LIKE many other works of mine, this playlet is a *pièce d'occasion*. In 1905 it happened that Mr. Arnold Daly, who was then playing the part of Napoleon in The Man of Destiny in New York, found that whilst the play was too long to take a secondary place in the evening's performance, it was too short to suffice by itself. I therefore took advantage of four days continuous rain during a holiday in the north of Scotland to write How He Lied To Her Husband for Mr. Daly. In his hands, it served its turn very effectively.

I print it here as a sample of what can be done with even the most hackneyed stage framework by filling it in with an observed touch of actual humanity instead of with doctrinaire romanticism. Nothing in the theatre is staler than the situation of husband, wife and lover, or the fun of knockabout farce. I have taken both, and got an original play out of them, as anybody else can if only he will look about him for his material instead of plagiarizing Othello and the thousand plays that have proceeded on Othello's romantic assumptions and false point of honor.

A further experiment made by Mr. Arnold Daly with this play is worth recording. In 1905 Mr. Daly produced Mrs. Warren's Profession in New York. The press of that city instantly raised a cry that such persons as Mrs. Warren are " ordure," and should not be mentioned in the presence of decent people. This hideous repudiation of humanity and social conscience so took possession of the New York journalists that the few among them who kept their feet morally and intellectually could do nothing to check the epidemic of foul language, gross suggestion, and raving obscenity of word and thought that broke out. The writers abandoned all self-restraint under the impression that they were upholding virtue instead of outraging it. They infected each other with their hysteria until they were for all practical purposes indecently mad. They finally forced the police to arrest Mr. Daly and his company, and led the magistrate to express his loathing of the duty thus forced upon him of reading an unmentionable and abominable play. Of course the convulsion soon exhausted itself. The magistrate, naturally somewhat impatient when he found that what he had to read was a strenuously ethical play forming part of a book which had been in circulation unchallenged for eight years, and had been received without protest by the whole London and New York press, gave the journalists a piece of his mind as to their moral taste in plays. By consent, he passed the case on to a higher court, which declared that the play was not immoral; acquitted Mr. Daly; and made an end of the attempt to use the law to declare living women to be " ordure," and thus enforce silence as to the far-reaching fact that you cannot cheapen women in the market for industrial purposes without cheapening them for other purposes as well. I hope Mrs. Warren's Profession will be played everywhere, in season and out of season, until Mrs. Warren has bitten that fact into the public conscience, and shamed the newspapers which support a tariff to keep up the price of every American commodity except American manhood and womanhood.

Unfortunately, Mr. Daly had already suffered the usual fate of those who direct public attention to the profits of the sweater or the pleasures of the voluptuary. He was morally lynched side by side with me. Months elapsed before the decision of the courts vindicated him;

and even then, since his vindication implied the condemnation of the press, which was by that time sober again, and ashamed of its orgie, his triumph received a rather sulky and grudging publicity. In the meantime he had hardly been able to approach an American city, including even those cities which had heaped applause on him as the defender of hearth and home when he produced Candida, without having to face articles discussing whether mothers could allow their daughters to attend such plays as You Never Can Tell, written by the infamous author of Mrs. Warren's Profession, and acted by the monster who produced it. What made this harder to bear was that though no fact is better established in theatrical business than the financial disastrousness of moral discredit, the journalists who had done all the mischief kept paying vice the homage of assuming that it is enormously popular and lucrative, and that I and Mr. Daly, being exploiters of vice, must therefore be making colossal fortunes out of the abuse heaped on us, and had in fact provoked it and welcomed it with that express object. Ignorance of real life could hardly go further.

One consequence was that Mr. Daly could not have kept his financial engagements or maintained his hold on the public had he not accepted engagements to appear for a season in the vaudeville theatres (the American equivalent of our music halls), where he played How He Lied to Her Husband comparatively unhampered by the press censorship of the theatre, or by that sophistication of the audience through press suggestion from which I suffer more, perhaps, than any other author. Vaudeville authors are fortunately unknown: the audiences see what the play contains and what the actor can do, not what the papers have told them to expect. Success under such circumstances had a value both for Mr. Daly and myself which did something to console us for the very unsavory mobbing which the New York press organized for us, and which was not the less disgusting because we suffered in a good cause and in the very best company.

Mr. Daly, having weathered the storm, can perhaps shake his soul free of it as he heads for fresh successes with younger authors.   But I have certain sensitive places in my soul: I do not like that word " ordure." Apply it to my work, and I can afford to smile, since the world, on the whole, will smile with me.   But to apply it to the woman in the street, whose spirit is of one substance with our own and her body no less holy: to look your womenfolk in the face afterwards and not go out and hang yourself: that is not on the list of pardonable sins.

HOW HE LIED TO HER HUSBAND

It is eight o'clock in the evening. The curtains are drawn and the lamps lighted in the drawing room of Her flat in Cromwell Road. Her lover, a beautiful youth of eighteen, in evening dress and cape, with a bunch of flowers and an opera hat in his hands, comes in alone. The door is near the corner; and as he appears in the doorway, he has the fireplace on the nearest wall to his right, and the grand piano along the opposite wall to his left. Near the fireplace a small ornamental table has on it a hand mirror, a fan, a pair of long white gloves, and a little white woollen cloud to wrap a woman's head in. On the other side of the room, near the piano, is a broad, square, softly upholstered stool. The room is furnished in the most approved South Kensington fashion: that is, it is as like a show room as possible, and is intended to demonstrate the social position and spending powers of its owners, and not in the least to make them comfortable.

He is, be it repeated, a very beautiful youth, moving as in a dream, walking as on air. He puts his flowers down carefully on the table beside the fan; takes off his cape, and, as there is no room on the table for it, takes it to the piano; puts his hat on the cape; crosses to the hearth; looks at his watch; puts it up again; notices the things on the table; lights up as if he saw heaven opening before him; goes to the table and takes the cloud in both hands, nestling his nose into its softness and kissing it; kisses the gloves one after another; kisses

133

*the fan; gasps a long shuddering sigh of ecstasy; sits
down on the stool and presses his hands to his eyes to
shut out reality and dream a little; takes his hands down
and shakes his head with a little smile of rebuke for his
folly; catches sight of a speck of dust on his shoes and
hastily and carefully brushes it off with his handkerchief; rises and takes the hand mirror from the table
to make sure of his tie with the gravest anxiety; and is
looking at his watch again when She comes in, much
flustered. As she is dressed for the theatre; has spoilt,
petted ways; and wears many diamonds, she has an air
of being a young and beautiful woman; but as a matter
of hard fact, she is, dress and pretensions apart, a very
ordinary South Kensington female of about 37, hope-
lessly inferior in physical and spiritual distinction to the
beautiful youth, who hastily puts down the mirror as she
enters.*

He (*kissing her hand*). At last!

She. Henry: something dreadful has happened.

He. Whats the matter?

She. I have lost your poems.

He. They were unworthy of you. I will write you
some more.

She. No, thank you. Never any more poems for
me. Oh, how could I have been so mad! so rash! so
imprudent!

He. Thank Heaven for your madness, your rashness,
your imprudence!

She (*impatiently*). Oh, be sensible, Henry. Cant
you see what a terrible thing this is for me? Suppose
anybody finds these poems! what will they think?

He. They will think that a man once loved a woman
more devotedly than ever man loved woman before. But
they will not know what man it was.

She. What good is that to me if everybody will know
what woman it was?

He. But how will they know?

She. How will they know! Why, my name is all over them: my silly, unhappy name. Oh, if I had only been christened Mary Jane, or Gladys Muriel, or Beatrice, or Francesca, or Guinevere, or something quite common! But Aurora! Aurora! I'm the only Aurora in London; and everybody knows it. I believe I'm the only Aurora in the world. And it's so horribly easy to rhyme to it! Oh, Henry, why didn't you try to restrain your feelings a little in common consideration for me? Why didnt you write with some little reserve?

He. Write poems to you with reserve! You ask me that!

She (*with perfunctory tenderness*). Yes, dear, of course it was very nice of you; and I know it was my own fault as much as yours. I ought to have noticed that your verses ought never to have been addressed to a married woman.

He. Ah, how I wish they had been addressed to an u n-married woman! h o w I wish they had!

She. Indeed you have no right to wish anything of the sort. They are quite unfit for anybody but a married woman. Thats just the difficulty. What will my sisters-in-law think of them?

He (*painfully jarred*). Have y o u got sisters-in-law?

She. Yes, of course I have. Do you suppose I am an angel?

He (*biting his lips*). I do. Heaven help me, I do— or I did—or (*he almost chokes a sob*).

She (*softening and putting her hand caressingly on his shoulder*). Listen to me, dear. Its very nice of you to live with me in a dream, and to love me, and so on; but I cant help my husband having disagreeable relatives, can I?

He (*brightening up*). Ah, of course they are your husband's relatives: I forgot that. Forgive me, Aurora.

(*He takes her hand from his shoulder and kisses it. She sits down on the stool. He remains near the table, with his back to it, smiling fatuously down at her.*)

SHE. The fact is, Teddy's got nothing but relatives. He has eight sisters and six half-sisters, and ever so many brothers—but I dont mind his brothers. Now if you only knew the least little thing about the world, Henry, youd know that in a large family, though the sisters quarrel with one another like mad all the time, yet let one of the brothers marry, and they all turn on their unfortunate sister-in-law and devote the rest of their lives with perfect unanimity to persuading him that his wife is unworthy of him. They can do it to her very face without her knowing it, because there are always a lot of stupid low family jokes that nobody understands but themselves. Half the time you cant tell what theyre talking about: it just drives you wild. There ought to be a law against a man's sister ever entering his house after hes married. I'm as certain as that I'm sitting here that Georgina stole those poems out of my workbox.

HE. She will not understand them, I think.

SHE. Oh, wont she! She'll understand them only too well. She'll understand more harm than ever was in them: nasty vulgar-minded cat!

HE (*going to her*). Oh dont, dont think of people in that way. Dont think of her at all. (*He takes her hand and sits down on the carpet at her feet.*) Aurora: do you remember the evening when I sat here at your feet and read you those poems for the first time?

SHE. I shouldnt have let you: I see that now. When I think of Georgina sitting there at Teddy's feet and reading them to h i m for the first time, I feel I shall just go distracted.

HE. Yes, you are right. It will be a profanation.

SHE. Oh, I dont care about the profanation; but

what will Teddy think? what will he do? (*Suddenly
throwing his head away from her knee.*) You dont seem
to think a bit about Teddy. (*She jumps up, more and
more agitated.*)

HE (*supine on the floor; for she has thrown him off
his balance*). To me Teddy is nothing, and Georgina
less than nothing.

SHE. Youll soon find out how much less than nothing
she is. If you think a woman cant do any harm because
shes only a scandalmongering dowdy ragbag, youre
greatly mistaken. (*She flounces about the room. He
gets up slowly and dusts his hands. Suddenly she runs
to him and throws herself into his arms.*) Henry: help
me. Find a way out of this for me; and I'll bless you
as long as you live. Oh, how wretched I am! (*She sobs
on his breast.*)

HE. And oh! how happy I am!

SHE (*whisking herself abruptly away*). Dont be
selfish.

HE (*humbly*). Yes: I deserve that. I think if I were
going to the stake with you, I should still be so happy
with you that I could hardly feel your danger more
than my own.

SHE (*relenting and patting his hand fondly*). Oh,
you are a dear darling boy, Henry; but (*throwing his
hand away fretfully*) youre no u s e. I want somebody
to tell me what to do.

HE (*with quiet conviction*). Your heart will tell you
at the right time. I have thought deeply over this; and
I know what we two m u s t do, sooner or later.

SHE. No, Henry. I will do nothing improper, nothing dishonorable. (*She sits down plump on the stool
and looks inflexible.*)

HE. If you did, you would no longer be Aurora. Our
course is perfectly simple, perfectly straightforward,
perfectly stainless and true. We love one another. I
am not ashamed of that: I am ready to go out and pro-

claim it to all London as simply as I will declare it to your husband when you see—as you soon will see—that this is the only way honorable enough for your feet to tread. Let us go out together to our own house, this evening, without concealment and without shame. Remember! we owe something to your husband. We are his guests here: he is an honorable man: he has been kind to us: he has perhaps loved you as well as his prosaic nature and his sordid commercial environment permitted. We owe it to him in all honor not to let him learn the truth from the lips of a scandalmonger. Let us go to him now quietly, hand in hand; bid him farewell; and walk out of the house without concealment and subterfuge, freely and honestly, in full honor and self-respect.

SHE (*staring at him*). And where shall we go to?

HE. We shall not depart by a hair's breadth from the ordinary natural current of our lives. We were going to the theatre when the loss of the poems compelled us to take action at once. We shall go to the theatre still; but we shall leave your diamonds here; for we cannot afford diamonds, and do not need them.

SHE (*fretfully*). I have told you already that I hate diamonds; only Teddy insists on hanging me all over with them. You need not preach simplicity to me.

HE. I never thought of doing so, dearest: I know that these trivialities are nothing to you. What was I saying?—oh yes. Instead of coming back here from the theatre, you will come with me to my home—now and henceforth o u r home—and in due course of time, when you are divorced, we shall go through whatever idle legal ceremony you may desire. *I* attach no importance to the law: my love was not created in me by the law, nor can it be bound or loosed by it. That is simple enough, and sweet enough, is it not? (*He takes the flowers from the table.*) Here are flowers for you:

I have the tickets: we will ask your husband to lend us the carriage to shew that there is no malice, no grudge, between us. Come!

SHE (*spiritlessly, taking the flowers without looking at them, and temporizing*). Teddy isnt in yet.

HE. Well, let us take that calmly. Let us go to the theatre as if nothing had happened, and tell him when we come back. Now or three hours hence: to-day or to-morrow: what does it matter, provided all is done in honor, without shame or fear?

SHE. What did you get tickets for? Lohengrin?

HE. I tried; but Lohengrin was sold out for to-night. (*He takes out two Court Theatre tickets.*)

SHE. Then what did you get?

HE. Can you ask me? What is there besides Lohengrin that we two could endure, except Candida?

SHE (*springing up*). Candida! No, I wont go to it again, Henry (*tossing the flowers on the piano*). It is that play that has done all the mischief. I'm very sorry I ever saw it: it ought to be stopped.

HE (*amazed*). Aurora!

SHE. Yes: I mean it.

HE. That divinest love poem! the poem that gave us courage to speak to one another! that revealed to us what we really felt for one another! that—

SHE. Just so. It put a lot of stuff into my head that I should never have dreamt of for myself. I imagined myself just like Candida.

HE (*catching her hands and looking earnestly at her*). You were right. You a r e like Candida.

SHE (*snatching her hands away*). Oh, stuff! And I thought you were just like Eugene. (*Looking critically at him.*) Now that I come to look at you, you a r e rather like him, too. (*She throws herself discontentedly into the nearest seat, which happens to be the bench at the piano. He goes to her.*)

HE (*very earnestly*). Aurora: if Candida had loved

Eugene she would have gone out into the night with him without a moment's hesitation.

SHE (*with equal earnestness*). Henry: do you know whats wanting in that play?

HE. There is nothing wanting in it.

SHE. Yes there is. Theres a Georgina wanting in it. If Georgina had been there to make trouble, that play would have been a true-to-life tragedy. Now I'll tell you something about it that I have never told you before.

HE. What is that?

SHE. I took Teddy to it. I thought it would do him good; and so it would if I could only have kept him awake. Georgina came too; and you should have heard the way she went on about it. She said it was downright immoral, and that s h e knew the sort of woman that encourages boys to sit on the hearthrug and make love to her. She was just preparing Teddy's mind to poison it about me.

HE. Let us be just to Georgina, dearest—

SHE. Let her deserve it first. Just to Georgina, indeed!

HE. She really sees the world in that way. That is her punishment.

SHE. How can it be her punishment when she likes it? Itll be my punishment when she brings that budget of poems to Teddy. I wish youd have some sense, and sympathize with my position a little.

HE (*going away from the piano and beginning to walk about rather testily*). My dear: I really dont care about Georgina or about Teddy. All these squabbles belong to a plane on which I am, as you say, no use. I have counted the cost; and I do not fear the consequences. After all, what is there to fear? Where is the difficulty? What can Georgina do? What can your husband do? What can anybody do?

SHE. Do you mean to say that you propose that we

should walk right bang up to Teddy and tell him we're going away together?

HE. Yes. What can be simpler?

SHE. And do you think for a moment he'd stand it, like that half-baked clergyman in the play? He'd just kill you.

HE (*coming to a sudden stop and speaking with considerable confidence*). You dont understand these things, my darling: how could you? In one respect I am unlike the poet in the play. I have followed the Greek ideal and not neglected the culture of my body. Your husband would make a tolerable second-rate heavy weight if he were in training and ten years younger. As it is, he could, if strung up to a great effort by a burst of passion, give a good account of himself for perhaps fifteen seconds. But I am active enough to keep out of his reach for fifteen seconds; and after that I should be simply all over him.

SHE (*rising and coming to him in consternation*). What do you mean by all over him?

HE (*gently*). Dont ask me, dearest. At all events, I swear to you that you need not be anxious about me.

SHE. And what about Teddy? Do you mean to tell me that you are going to beat Teddy before my face like a brutal prizefighter?

HE. All this alarm is needless, dearest. Believe me, nothing will happen. Your husband knows that I am capable of defending myself. Under such circumstances nothing ever does happen. And of course I shall do nothing. The man who once loved you is sacred to me.

SHE (*suspiciously*). Doesnt he love me still? Has he told you anything?

HE. No, no. (*He takes her tenderly in his arms.*) Dearest, dearest: how agitated you are! how unlike yourself! All these worries belong to the lower plane. Come up with me to the higher one. The heights, the solitudes, the soul world!

SHE (*avoiding his gaze*). No: stop: it's no use, Mr. Apjohn.

HE (*recoiling*). Mr. Apjohn!!!

SHE. Excuse me: I meant Henry, of course.

HE. How could you even think of m e as Mr. Apjohn? I never think of you as Mrs. Bompas: it is always Cand— I mean Aurora, Aurora, Auro—

SHE. Yes, yes: thats all very well, Mr. Apjohn (*he is about to interrupt again: but she wont have it*) no: it's no use: Ive suddenly begun to think of you as Mr. Apjohn; and it's ridiculous to go on calling you Henry. I thought you were only a boy, a child, a dreamer. I thought you would be too much afraid to do anything. And now you want to beat Teddy and to break up my home and disgrace me and make a horrible scandal in the papers. It's cruel, unmanly, cowardly.

HE (*with grave wonder*). Are you afraid?

SHE. Oh, of course I'm afraid. So would you be if you had any common sense. (*She goes to the hearth, turning her back to him, and puts one tapping foot on the fender.*)

HE (*watching her with great gravity*). Perfect love casteth out fear. That is why I am not afraid. Mrs. Bompas: you do not love me.

SHE (*turning to him with a gasp of relief*). Oh, thank you, thank you! You really can be very nice, Henry.

HE. Why do you thank me?

SHE (*coming prettily to him from the fireplace*). For calling me Mrs. Bompas again. I feel now that you are going to be reasonable and behave like a gentleman. (*He drops on the stool; covers his face with his hands; and groans.*) Whats the matter?

HE. Once or twice in my life I have dreamed that I was exquisitely happy and blessed. But oh! the misgiving at the first stir of consciousness! the stab of reality! the prison walls of the bedroom! the bitter,

bitter disappointment of waking! And this time! oh,
this time I thought I was awake.

SHE. Listen to me, Henry: we really havnt time for
all that sort of flapdoodle now. (*He starts to his feet
as if she had pulled a trigger and straightened him by
the release of a powerful spring, and goes past her with
set teeth to the little table.*) Oh, take care: you nearly
hit me in the chin with the top of your head.

HE (*with fierce politeness*). I beg your pardon.
What is it you want me to do? I am at your service. I
am ready to behave like a gentleman if you will be kind
enough to explain exactly how.

SHE (*a little frightened*). Thank you, Henry: I was
sure you would. Youre not angry with me, are you?

HE. Go on. Go on quickly. Give me something to
think about, or I will—I will— (*he suddenly snatches
up her fan and is about to break it in his clenched fists*).

SHE (*running forward and catching at the fan, with
loud lamentation*). Dont break my fan—no, dont. (*He
slowly relaxes his grip of it as she draws it anxiously
out of his hands.*) No, really, thats a stupid trick. I
dont like that. Youve no right to do that. (*She opens
the fan, and finds that the sticks are disconnected.*) Oh,
how could you be so inconsiderate?

HE. I beg your pardon. I will buy you a new one.

SHE (*querulously*). You will never be able to match
it. And it was a particular favorite of mine.

HE (*shortly*). Then you will have to do without it:
thats all.

SHE. Thats not a very nice thing to say after breaking my pet fan, I think.

HE. If you knew how near I was to breaking Teddy's
pet wife and presenting him with the pieces, you would
be thankful that you are alive instead of—of—of howling about fiveshillingsworth of ivory. Damn your fan!

SHE. Oh! Dont you dare swear in my presence.
One would think you were my husband.

HE (*again collapsing on the stool*). This is some horrible dream. What has become of you? Y o u are not my Aurora.

SHE. Oh, well, if you come to that, what has become of y o u? Do you think I would ever have encouraged you if I had known you were such a little devil?

HE. Dont drag me down—dont—dont. Help me to find the way back to the heights.

SHE (*kneeling beside him and pleading*). If you would only be reasonable, Henry. If you would only remember that I am on the brink of ruin, and not go on calmly saying it's all quite simple.

HE. It seems so to me.

SHE (*jumping up distractedly*). If you say that again I shall do something I'll be sorry for. Here we are, standing on the edge of a frightful precipice. No doubt it's quite simple to go over and have done with it. But cant you suggest anything more agreeable?

HE. I can suggest nothing now. A chill black darkness has fallen: I can see nothing but the ruins of our dream. (*He rises with a deep sigh.*)

SHE. Cant you? Well, I can. I can see Georgina rubbing those poems into Teddy. (*Facing him determinedly.*) And I tell you, Henry Apjohn, that y o u got me into this mess: and y o u must get me out of it again.

HE (*polite and hopeless*). All I can say is that I am entirely at your service. What do you wish me to do?

SHE. Do you know anybody else named Aurora?

HE. No.

SHE. Theres no use in saying No in that frozen pigheaded way. You m u s t know some Aurora or other somewhere.

HE. You said you were the only Aurora in the world. And (*lifting his clasped fists with a sudden return of his emotion*) oh God! you were the only Aurora in the world to me. (*He turns away from her, hiding his face.*)

SHE (*petting him*). Yes, yes, dear: of course. It's very nice of you; and I appreciate it: indeed I do; but it's not seasonable just at present. Now just listen to me. I suppose you know all those poems by heart.

HE. Yes, by h e a r t. (*Raising his head and looking at her with a sudden suspicion.*) Dont you?

SHE. Well, I never can remember verses; and besides, Ive been so busy that Ive not had time to read them all; though I intend to the very first moment I can get: I promise you that most faithfully, Henry. But now try and remember very particularly. Does the name of Bompas occur in any of the poems?

HE (*indignantly*). No.

SHE. Youre quite sure?

HE. Of course I am quite sure. How could I use such a name in a poem?

SHE. Well, I dont see why not. It rhymes to rumpus, which seems appropriate enough at present, goodness knows! However, youre a poet, and you ought to know.

HE. What does it matter—now?

SHE. It matters a lot, I can tell you. If theres nothing about Bompas in the poems, we can say that they were written to some other Aurora, and that you shewed them to me because my name was Aurora too. So youve got to invent another Aurora for the occasion.

HE (*very coldly*). Oh, if you wish me to tell a lie—

SHE. Surely, as a man of honor—as a gentleman, you wouldnt tell the truth, would you?

HE. Very well. You have broken my spirit and desecrated my dreams. I will lie and protest and stand on my honor: oh, I will play the gentleman, never fear.

SHE. Yes, put it all on me, of course. Dont be mean, Henry.

HE (*rousing himself with an effort*). You are

quite right, Mrs. Bompas: I beg your pardon. You must excuse my temper. I have got growing pains, I think.

SHE. Growing pains!

HE. The process of growing from romantic boyhood into cynical maturity usually takes fifteen years. When it is compressed into fifteen minutes, the pace is too fast; and growing pains are the result.

SHE. Oh, is this a time for cleverness? It's settled, isnt it, that youre going to be nice and good, and that youll brazen it out to Teddy that you have some other Aurora?

HE. Yes: I'm capable of anything now. I should not have told him the truth by halves; and now I will not lie by halves. I'll wallow in the honor of a gentleman.

SHE. Dearest boy, I knew you would. I— Sh! (*she rushes to the door, and holds it ajar, listening breathlessly*).

HE. What is it?

SHE (*white with apprehension*). It's Teddy: I hear him tapping the new barometer. He cant have anything serious on his mind or he wouldnt do that. Perhaps Georgina hasnt said anything. (*She steals back to the hearth.*) Try and look as if there was nothing the matter. Give me my gloves, quick. (*He hands them to her. She pulls on one hastily and begins buttoning it with ostentatious unconcern.*) Go further away from me, quick. (*He walks doggedly away from her until the piano prevents his going farther.*) If I button my glove, and you were to hum a tune, dont you think that—

HE. The tableau would be complete in its guiltiness. For Heaven's sake, Mrs. Bompas, let that glove alone: you look like a pickpocket.

Her husband comes in: a robust, thicknecked, well groomed city man, with a strong chin but a blithering

*eye and credulous mouth. He has a momentous air, but
shews no sign of displeasure: rather the contrary.*

HER HUSBAND. Hallo! I thought you two were at
the theatre.

SHE. I felt anxious about you, Teddy. Why didnt
you come home to dinner?

HER HUSBAND. I got a message from Georgina. She
wanted me to go to her.

SHE. Poor dear Georgina! I'm sorry I havnt been
able to call on her this last week. I hope theres nothing
the matter with her.

HER HUSBAND. Nothing, except anxiety for my welfare—and yours. (*She steals a terrified look at Henry.*)
By the way, Apjohn, I should like a word with you this
evening, if Aurora can spare you for a moment.

HE (*formally*). I am at your service.

HER HUSBAND. No hurry. After the theatre will do.

HE. We have decided not to go.

HER HUSBAND. Indeed! Well, then, shall we ad-
journ to my snuggery?

SHE. You neednt move. I shall go and lock up my
diamonds since I'm not going to the theatre. Give me
my things.

HER HUSBAND (*as he hands her the cloud and the
mirror*). Well, we shall have more room here.

HE (*looking about him and shaking his shoulders
loose*). I think I should prefer plenty of room.

HER HUSBAND. So, if its not disturbing you, Rory—?

SHE. Not at all. (*She goes out.*)

*When the two men are alone together, Bompas de-
liberately takes the poems from his breast pocket; looks
at them reflectively; then looks at Henry, mutely in-
viting his attention. Henry refuses to understand, doing
his best to look unconcerned.*

HER HUSBAND. Do these manuscripts seem at all
familiar to you, may I ask?

HE. Manuscripts?

HER HUSBAND. Yes. Would you like to look at them a little closer? (*He proffers them under Henry's nose.*)

HE (*as with a sudden illumination of glad surprise*). Why, these are my poems!

HER HUSBAND. So I gather.

HE. What a shame! Mrs. Bompas has shewn them to you! You must think me an utter ass. I wrote them years ago after reading Swinburne's Songs Before Sunrise. Nöthing would do me then but I must reel off a set of Songs to the Sunrise. Aurora, you know: the rosy fingered Aurora. Theyre all about Aurora. When Mrs. Bompas told me her name was Aurora, I couldnt resist the temptation to lend them to her to read. But I didnt bargain for your unsympathetic eyes.

HER HUSBAND (*grinning*). Apjohn: thats really very ready of you. You are cut out for literature; and the day will come when Rory and I will be proud to have you about the house. I have heard far thinner stories from much older men.

HE (*with an air of great surprise*). Do you mean to imply that you dont believe me?

HER HUSBAND. Do you expect me to believe you?

HE. Why not? I dont understand.

HER HUSBAND. Come! Dont underrate your own cleverness, Apjohn. I think you understand pretty well.

HE. I assure you I am quite at a loss. Can you not be a little more explicit?

HER HUSBAND. Dont overdo it, old chap. However, I will just be so far explicit as to say that if you think these poems read as if they were addressed, not to a live woman, but to a shivering cold time of day at which you were never out of bed in your life, you hardly do justice to your own literary powers—which I admire and appreciate, mind you, as much as any man. Come! own up. You wrote those poems to my wife. (*An internal struggle prevents Henry from answering.*) Of course you did. (*He throws the poems on the table;*

*and goes to the hearthrug, where he plants himself
solidly, chuckling a little and waiting for the next
move.)*

HE (*formally and carefully*).   Mr. Bompas: I pledge
you my word you are mistaken.   I need not tell you
that Mrs. Bompas is a lady of stainless honor, who has
never cast an unworthy thought on me.   The fact that
she has shewn you my poems—

HER HUSBAND.   Thats not a fact.   I came by them
without her knowledge.   She didnt show them to me.

HE.   Does not that prove their perfect innocence?
She would have shewn them to you at once if she had
taken your quite unfounded view of them.

HER HUSBAND (*shaken*).   Apjohn: play fair.   Dont
abuse your intellectual gifts.   Do you really mean that
I am making a fool of myself?

HE (*earnestly*).   Believe me, you are.   I assure you,
on my honor as a gentleman, that I have never had the
slightest feeling for Mrs. Bompas beyond the ordinary
esteem and regard of a pleasant acquaintance.

HER HUSBAND (*shortly, showing ill humor for the
first time*).   Oh, indeed.   (*He leaves his hearth and begins to approach Henry slowly, looking him up and
down with growing resentment.*)

HE (*hastening to improve the impression made by his
mendacity*).   I should never have dreamt of writing
poems to her.   The thing is absurd.

HER HUSBAND (*reddening ominously*).   Why is it absurd?

HE (*shrugging his shoulders*).   Well, it happens that
I do not admire Mrs. Bompas—in that way.

HER HUSBAND (*breaking out in Henry's face*).   Let
me tell you that Mrs. Bompas has been admired by better men than you, you soapy headed little puppy, you.

HE (*much taken aback*).   There is no need to insult
me like this.   I assure you, on my honor as a—

HER HUSBAND (*too angry to tolerate a reply, and

boring Henry more and more towards the piano). Y o u
dont admire Mrs. Bompas! Y o u would never dream
of writing poems to Mrs. Bompas! My wife's not good
enough for you, isnt she. (*Fiercely.*) Who are you,
pray, that you should be so jolly superior?

HE.   Mr. Bompas: I can make allowances for your
jealousy—

HER HUSBAND.   Jealousy! do you suppose I'm jealous of y o u? No, nor of ten like you. But if you
think I'll stand here and let you insult my wife in her
own house, youre mistaken.

HE (*very uncomfortable with his back against the
piano and Teddy standing over him threateningly*). How
can I convince you? Be reasonable. I tell you my relations with Mrs. Bompas are relations of perfect coldness—of indifference—

HER HUSBAND (*scornfully*). Say it again: say it
again. Youre proud of it, arnt you? Yah! youre not
worth kicking.

*Henry suddenly executes the feat known to pugilists
as slipping, and changes sides with Teddy, who is now
between Henry and the piano.*

HE.   Look here: I'm not going to stand this.

HER HUSBAND.   Oh, you h a v e some blood in your
body after all! Good job!

HE.   This is ridiculous. I assure you Mrs. Bompas
is quite—

HER HUSBAND.   What is Mrs. Bompas to you, I'd
like to know. I'll tell you what Mrs. Bompas is. Shes
the smartest woman in the smartest set in South Kensington, and the handsomest, and the cleverest, and the
most fetching to experienced men who know a good
thing when they see it, whatever she may be to con-
ceited penny-a-lining puppies who think nothing good
enough for them. It's admitted by the best people;
and not to know it argues yourself unknown. Three
of our first actor-managers have offered her a hundred

a week if she'll go on the stage when they start a
repertory theatre; and I think they know what theyre
about as well as you.   The only member of the present
Cabinet that you might call a handsome man has
neglected the business of the country to dance with her,
though he dont belong to our set as a regular thing.
One of the first professional poets in Bedford Park
wrote a sonnet to her, worth all your amateur trash.   At
Ascot last season the eldest son of a duke excused himself from calling on me on the ground that his feelings
for Mrs. Bompas were not consistent with his duty to
me as host; and it did him honor and me too.   But
(*with gathering fury*) she isnt good enough for y o u,
it seems.   You regard her with coldness, with indifference; and you have the cool cheek to tell me so to my
face.   For two pins I'd flatten your nose in to teach you
manners.   Introducing a fine woman to you is casting
pearls before swine (*yelling at him*) before s w i n e!
d'ye hear?

HE (*with a deplorable lack of polish*).   You call me
a swine again and I'll land you one on the chin thatll
make your head sing for a week.

HER HUSBAND (*exploding*).   What—!

*He charges at Henry with bull-like fury.   Henry
places himself on guard in the manner of a well taught
boxer, and gets away smartly, but unfortunately forgets
the stool which is just behind him.   He falls backwards
over it, unintentionally pushing it against the shins of
Bompas, who falls forward over it.   Mrs. Bompas, with
a scream, rushes into the room between the sprawling
champions, and sits down on the floor in order to get
her right arm round her husband's neck.*

SHE.   You shant, Teddy: you shant.   You will be
killed: he is a prizefighter.

HER HUSBAND (*vengefully*).   I'll prizefight him.
(*He struggles vainly to free himself from her embrace.*)

SHE.   Henry: dont let him fight you.   Promise me that you wont.

HE (*ruefully*).   I have got a most frightful bump on the back of my head.   (*He tries to rise.*)

SHE (*reaching out her left hand to seize his coat tail, and pulling him down again, whilst keeping fast hold of Teddy with the other hand*).   Not until you have promised: not until you both have promised. (*Teddy rises to rise: she pulls him back again.*) Teddy: you promise, dont you?   Yes, yes.   Be good: you promise.

HER HUSBAND.   I wont, unless he takes it back.

SHE.   He will: he does.   You take it back, Henry? —yes.

HE (*savagely*).   Yes.   I take it back.   (*She lets go his coat.   He gets up.   So does Teddy.*)   I take it all back, all, without reserve.

SHE (*on the carpet*).   Is nobody going to help me up? (*They each take a hand and pull her up.*)   Now wont you shake hands and be good?

HE (*recklessly*).   I shall do nothing of the sort. I have steeped myself in lies for your sake; and the only reward I get is a lump on the back of my head the size of an apple.   Now I will go back to the straight path.

SHE.   Henry: for Heaven's sake—

HE.   It's no use.   Your husband is a fool and a brute—

HER HUSBAND.   Whats that you say?

HE.   I say you are a fool and a brute; and if youll step outside with me I'll say it again.   (*Teddy begins to take off his coat for combat.*)   Those poems w e r e written to your wife, every word of them, and to no-body else.   (*The scowl clears away from Bompas's countenance.   Radiant, he replaces his coat.*)   I wrote them because I loved her.   I thought her the most beautiful woman in the world; and I told her so over

and over again. I adored her: do you hear? I told her
that you were a sordid commercial chump, utterly unworthy of her; and so you are.

HER HUSBAND (*so gratified, he can hardly believe his
ears*). You dont mean it!

HE. Yes, I do mean it, and a lot more too. I asked
Mrs. Bompas to walk out of the house with me—to
leave you—to get divorced from you and marry me. I
begged and implored her to do it this very night. It
was her refusal that ended everything between us.
(*Looking very disparagingly at him.*) What she can
see in you, goodness only knows!

HER HUSBAND (*beaming with remorse*). My dear
chap, why didnt you say so before? I apologize. Come!
dont bear malice: shake hands. Make him shake hands,
Rory.

SHE. For my sake, Henry. After all, hes my husband. Forgive him. Take his hand. (*Henry, dazed,
lets her take his hand and place it in Teddy's.*)

HER HUSBAND (*shaking it heartily*). Youve got to
own that none of your literary heroines can touch my
Rory. (*He turns to her and claps her with fond pride
on the shoulder.*) Eh, Rory? They cant resist you:
none of em. Never knew a man yet that could hold out
three days.

SHE. Dont be foolish, Teddy. I hope you were not
really hurt, Henry. (*She feels the back of his head.
He flinches.*) Oh, poor boy, what a bump! I must get
some vinegar and brown paper. (*She goes to the bell
and rings.*)

HER HUSBAND. Will you do me a great favor, Ap-
. I hardly like to ask; but it would be a real kindness to us both.

HE. What can I do?

HER HUSBAND (*taking up the poems*). Well, may I
get these printed? It shall be done in the best style.
The finest paper, sumptuous binding, everything first

class. Theyre beautiful poems. I should like to shew them about a bit.

SHE (*running back from the bell, delighted with the idea, and coming between them*). Oh Henry, if you wouldnt mind!

HE. Oh, *I* dont mind. I am past minding anything. I have grown too fast this evening.

SHE. How old are you, Henry?

HE. This morning I was eighteen. Now I am—confound it! I'm quoting that beast of a play (*he takes the Candida tickets out of his pocket and tears them up viciously*).

HER HUSBAND. What shall we call the volume. To Aurora, or something like that, eh?

HE. I should call it How He Lied to Her Husband.

CURTAIN.

MAJOR BARBARA

1905

PREFACE TO MAJOR BARBARA

FIRST AID TO CRITICS

BEFORE dealing with the deeper aspects of Major Barbara, let me, for the credit of English literature, make a protest against an unpatriotic habit into which many of my critics have fallen. Whenever my view strikes them as being at all outside the range of, say, an ordinary suburban churchwarden, they conclude that I am echoing Schopenhauer, Nietzsche, Ibsen, Strindberg, Tolstoy, or some other heresiarch in northern or eastern Europe.

I confess there is something flattering in this simple faith in my accomplishment as a linguist and my erudition as a philosopher. But I cannot tolerate the assumption that life and literature is so poor in these islands that we must go abroad for all dramatic material that is not common and all ideas that are not superficial. I therefore venture to put my critics in possession of certain facts concerning my contact with modern ideas.

About half a century ago, an Irish novelist, Charles Lever, wrote a story entitled A Day's Ride: A Life's Romance. It was published by Charles Dickens in Household Words, and proved so strange to the public taste that Dickens pressed Lever to make short work of it. I read scraps of this novel when I was a child; and it made an enduring impression on me. The hero was a very romantic hero, trying to live bravely, chivalrously, and powerfully by dint of mere romance-fed imagination, without courage, without means, without knowledge, without skill, without anything real except his bodily appetites. Even in my childhood I found in this poor devil's unsuccessful encounters with the facts of life, a poignant quality that romantic fiction lacked. The book, in spite of its first failure, is not dead: I saw its title the other day in the catalogue of Tauchnitz.

Now why is it that when I also deal in the tragi-comic irony of the conflict between real life and the romantic imagination, no critic ever affiliates me to my countryman and immediate forerunner, Charles Lever, whilst they confidently derive me from a Norwegian author of whose language I do not know three words, and of whom I knew nothing until years after the Shavian *Anschauung* was already unequivocally declared in books full of what came, ten years later, to be per-functorily labelled Ibsenism. I was not Ibsenist even at second hand; for Lever, though he may have read Henri Beyle, *alias* Stendhal, certainly never read Ibsen. Of the books that made Lever popular, such as Charles O'Malley and Harry Lorrequer, I know nothing but the names and some of the illustrations. But the story of the day's ride and life's romance of Potts (claiming alliance with Pozzo di Borgo) caught me and fascinated me as something strange and significant, though I al-ready knew all about Alnaschar and Don Quixote and Simon Tappertit and many another romantic hero mocked by reality. From the plays of Aristophanes to the tales of Stevenson that mockery has been made familiar to all who are properly saturated with letters.

Where, then, was the novelty in Lever's tale? Partly, I think, in a new seriousness in dealing with Potts's disease. Formerly, the contrast between madness and sanity was deemed comic: Hogarth shews us how fash-ionable people went in parties to Bedlam to laugh at the lunatics. I myself have had a village idiot exhibited to

me as something irresistibly funny. On the stage the
madman was once a regular comic figure: that was how
Hamlet got his opportunity before Shakespear touched
him. The originality of Shakespear's version lay in his
taking the lunatic sympathetically and seriously, and
thereby making an advance towards the eastern consciousness of the fact that lunacy may be inspiration in
disguise, since a man who has more brains than his fellows necessarily appears as mad to them as one who
has less. But Shakespear did not do for Pistol and
Parolles what he did for Hamlet. The particular sort
of madman they represented, the romantic make-be-
liever, lay outside the pale of sympathy in literature:
he was pitilessly despised and ridiculed here as he was
in the east under the name of Alnaschar, and was doomed
to be, centuries later, under the name of Simon Tappertit. When Cervantes relented over Don Quixote, and
Dickens relented over Pickwick, they did not become
impartial: they simply changed sides, and became
friends and apologists where they had formerly been
mockers.

In Lever's story there is a real change of attitude.
There is no relenting towards Potts: he never gains our
affections like Don Quixote and Pickwick: he has not
even the infatuate courage of Tappertit. But we dare
not laugh at him, because, somehow, we recognize ourselves in Potts. We may, some of us, have enough nerve,
enough muscle, enough luck, enough tact or skill or
address or knowledge to carry things off better than he
did; to impose on the people who saw through him; to
fascinate Katinka (who cut Potts so ruthlessly at the
end of the story); but for all that, we know that Potts
plays an enormous part in ourselves and in the world,
and that the social problem is not a problem of story-
book heroes of the older pattern, but a problem of
Pottses, and of how to make men of them. To fall
back on my old phrase, we have the feeling—one that

Alnaschar, Pistol, Parolles, and Tappertit never gave us—that Potts is a piece of really scientific natural history as distinguished from comic story telling. His author is not throwing a stone at a creature of another and inferior order, but making a confession, with the effect that the stone hits everybody full in the conscience and causes their self-esteem to smart very sorely. Hence the failure of Lever's book to please the readers of Household Words. That pain in the self-esteem nowadays causes critics to raise a cry of Ibsenism. I therefore assure them that the sensation first came to me from Lever and may have come to him from Beyle, or at least out of the Stendhalian atmosphere. I exclude the hypothesis of complete originality on Lever's part, because a man can no more be completely original in that sense than a tree can grow out of air.

Another mistake as to my literary ancestry is made whenever I violate the romantic convention that all women are angels when they are not devils; that they are better looking than men; that their part in courtship is entirely passive; and that the human female form is the most beautiful object in nature. Schopenhauer wrote a splenetic essay which, as it is neither polite nor profound, was probably intended to knock this nonsense violently on the head. A sentence denouncing the idolized form as ugly has been largely quoted. The English critics have read that sentence; and I must here affirm, with as much gentleness as the implication will bear, that it has yet to be proved that they have dipped any deeper. At all events, whenever an English playwright represents a young and marriageable woman as being anything but a romantic heroine, he is disposed of without further thought as an echo of Schopenhauer. My own case is a specially hard one, because, when I implore the critics who are obsessed with the Schopenhaurian formula to remember that playwrights, like sculptors, study their figures from life, and not from philosophic essays, they reply passionately that I am not a playwright and that my stage figures do not live. But even so, I may and do ask them why, if they must give the credit of my plays to a philosopher, they do not give it to an English philosopher? Long before I ever read a word by Schopenhauer, or even knew whether he was a philosopher or a chemist, the Socialist revival of the eighteen-eighties brought me into contact, both literary and personal, with Mr. Ernest Belfort Bax, an English Socialist and philosophic essayist, whose handling of modern feminism would provoke romantic protests from Schopenhauer himself, or even Strindberg. At a matter of fact I hardly noticed Schopenhauer's disparagements of women when they came under my notice later on, so thoroughly had Mr. Bax familiarized me with the homoist attitude, and forced me to recognize the extent to which public opinion, and consequently legislation and jurisprudence, is corrupted by feminist sentiment.

But Mr. Bax's essays were not confined to the Feminist question. He was a ruthless critic of current morality. Other writers have gained sympathy for dramatic criminals by eliciting the alleged " soul of goodness in things evil "; but Mr. Bax would propound some quite undramatic and apparently shabby violation of our commercial law and morality, and not merely defend it with the most disconcerting ingenuity, but actually prove it to be a positive duty that nothing but the certainty of police persecution should prevent every right-minded man from at once doing on principle. The Socialists were naturally shocked, being for the most part morbidly moral people; but at all events they were saved later on from the delusion that nobody but Nietzsche had ever challenged our mercanto-Christian morality. I first heard the name of Nietzsche from a German mathematician, Miss Borchardt, who had read my Quintessence of Ibsenism, and told me that she saw

what I had been reading: namely, Nietzsche's Jenseits
von Gut und Böse. Which I protest I had never seen,
and could not have read with any comfort, for want of
the necessary German, if I had seen it.

Nietzsche, like Schopenhauer, is the victim in England of a single much quoted sentence containing the
phrase " big blonde beast." On the strength of this
alliteration it is assumed that Nietzsche gained his European reputation by a senseless glorification of selfish
bullying as the rule of life, just as it is assumed, on
the strength of the single word Superman (Übermensch)
borrowed by me from Nietzsche, that I look for the
salvation of society to the despotism of a single Napo-
leonic Superman, in spite of my careful demonstration
of the folly of that outworn infatuation. But even the
less recklessly superficial critics seem to believe that
the modern objection to Christianity as a pernicious
slave-morality was first put forward by Nietzsche. It
was familiar to me before I ever heard of Nietzsche.
The late Captain Wilson, author of several queer
pamphlets, propagandist of a metaphysical system called
Comprehensionism, and inventor of the term " Crosstianity " to distinguish the retrograde element in Christendom, was wont thirty years ago, in the discussions of
the Dialectical Society, to protest earnestly against the
beatitudes of the Sermon on the Mount as excuses for
cowardice and servility, as destructive of our will, and
consequently of our honor and manhood. Now it is
true that Captain Wilson's moral criticism of Christianity was not a historical theory of it, like Nietzsche's;
but this objection cannot be made to Mr. Stuart-Glennie, the successor of Buckle as a philosophic historian,
who has devoted his life to the elaboration and propagation of his theory that Christianity is part of an epoch
(or rather an aberration, since it began as recently as
6000 B.C. and is already collapsing) produced by the
necessity in which the numerically inferior white races

found themselves to impose their domination on the colored races by priestcraft, making a virtue and a popular religion of drudgery and submissiveness in this world not only as a means of achieving saintliness of character but of securing a reward in heaven. Here you have the slave-morality view formulated by a Scotch philosopher long before English writers began chattering about Nietzsche.

As Mr. Stuart-Glennie traced the evolution of society to the conflict of races, his theory made some sensation among Socialists—that is, among the only people who were seriously thinking about historical evolution at all —by its collision with the class-conflict theory of Karl Marx. Nietzsche, as I gather, regarded the slave-morality as having been invented and imposed on the world by slaves making a virtue of necessity and a religion of their servitude. Mr. Stuart-Glennie regards the slave-morality as an invention of the superior white race to subjugate the minds of the inferior races whom they wished to exploit, and who would have destroyed them by force of numbers if their minds had not been subjugated. As this process is in operation still, and can be studied at first hand not only in our Church schools and in the struggle between our modern proprietary classes and the proletariat, but in the part played by Christian missionaries in reconciling the black races of Africa to their subjugation by European Capitalism, we can judge for ourselves whether the initiative came from above or below. My object here is not to argue the historical point, but simply to make our theatre critics ashamed of their habit of treating Britain as an intellectual void, and assuming that every philosophical idea, every historic theory, every criticism of our moral, religious and juridical institutions, must necessarily be either imported from abroad, or else a fantastic sally (in rather questionable taste) totally unrelated to the existing body of thought. I urge them to remember that this body of thought is the slowest of growths and the rarest of blossomings, and that if there is such a thing on the philosophic plane as a matter of course, it is that no individual can make more than a minute contribution to it. In fact, their conception of clever persons parthenogenetically bringing forth complete original cosmogonies by dint of sheer " brilliancy " is part of that ignorant credulity which is the despair of the honest philosopher, and the opportunity of the religious impostor.

THE GOSPEL OF ST. ANDREW UNDERSHAFT.

It is this credulity that drives me to help my critics out with Major Barbara by telling them what to say about it. In the millionaire Undershaft I have represented a man who has become intellectually and spiritually as well as practically conscious of the irresistible natural truth which we all abhor and repudiate: to wit, that the greatest of evils and the worst of crimes is poverty, and that our first duty—a duty to which every other consideration should be sacrificed—is not to be poor. " Poor but honest," " the respectable poor," and such phrases are as intolerable and as immoral as " drunken but amiable," " fraudulent but a good after-dinner speaker," " splendidly criminal," or the like. Security, the chief pretence of civilization, cannot exist where the worst of dangers, the danger of poverty, hangs over everyone's head, and where the alleged protection of our persons from violence is only an accidental result of the existence of a police force whose real business is to force the poor man to see his children starve whilst idle people overfeed pet dogs with the money that might feed and clothe them.

It is exceedingly difficult to make people realize that an evil is an evil. For instance, we seize a man and deliberately do him a malicious injury: say, imprison him for years. One would not suppose that it needed any exceptional clearness of wit to recognize in this an act of diabolical cruelty. But in England such a recognition provokes a stare of surprise, followed by an explanation that the outrage is punishment or justice or something else that is all right, or perhaps by a heated attempt to argue that we should all be robbed and murdered in our beds if such senseless villainies as sentences of imprisonment were not committed daily. It is useless to argue that even if this were true, which it is not, the alternative to adding crimes of our own to the crimes from which we suffer is not helpless submission. Chickenpox is an evil; but if I were to declare that we must either submit to it or else repress it sternly by seizing everyone who suffers from it and punishing them by inoculation with smallpox, I should be laughed at; for though nobody could deny that the result would be to prevent chickenpox to some extent by making people avoid it much more carefully, and to effect a further apparent prevention by making them conceal it very anxiously, yet people would have sense enough to see that the deliberate propagation of smallpox was a creation of evil, and must therefore be ruled out in favor of purely humane and hygienic measures. Yet in the precisely parallel case of a man breaking into my house and stealing my wife's diamonds I am expected as a matter of course to steal ten years of his life, torturing him all the time. If he tries to defeat that monstrous retaliation by shooting me, my survivors hang him. The net result suggested by the police statistics is that we inflict atrocious injuries on the burglars we catch in order to make the rest take effectual precautions against detection; so that instead of saving our wives' diamonds from burglary we only greatly decrease our chances of ever getting them back, and increase our chances of being shot by the robber if we are unlucky enough to disturb him at his work.

But the thoughtless wickedness with which we scatter sentences of imprisonment, torture in the solitary cell and on the plank bed, and flogging, on moral invalids and energetic rebels, is as nothing compared to the stupid levity with which we tolerate poverty as if it were either a wholesome tonic for lazy people or else a virtue to be embraced as St. Francis embraced it. If a man is indolent, let him be poor. If he is drunken, let him be poor. If he is not a gentleman, let him be poor. If he is addicted to the fine arts or to pure science instead of to trade and finance, let him be poor. If he chooses to spend his urban eighteen shillings a week or his agricultural thirteen shillings a week on his beer and his family instead of saving it up for his old age, let him be poor. Let nothing be done for " the undeserving ": let him be poor. Serve him right! Also—somewhat inconsistently—blessed are the poor!

Now what does this Let Him Be Poor mean? It means let him be weak. Let him be ignorant. Let him become a nucleus of disease. Let him be a standing exhibition and example of ugliness and dirt. Let him have rickety children. Let him be cheap and let him drag his fellows down to his price by selling himself to do their work. Let his habitations turn our cities into poisonous congeries of slums. Let his daughters infect our young men with the diseases of the streets and his sons revenge him by turning the nation's manhood into scrofula, cowardice, cruelty, hypocrisy, political imbecility, and all the other fruits of oppression and malnutrition. Let the undeserving become still less deserving; and let the deserving lay up for himself, not treasures in heaven, but horrors in hell upon earth. This being so, is it really wise to let him be poor? Would he not do ten times less harm as a prosperous burglar, incendiary, ravisher or murderer, to the utmost limits of humanity's comparatively negligible impulses in these directions? Suppose we were to abolish all penalties for such activities, and decide that poverty is the one thing we will not tolerate—that every adult with less than, say, £365 a year, shall be painlessly but inexorably killed, and every hungry half naked child forcibly fattened and clothed, would not that be an enormous improvement on our existing system, which has already destroyed so many civilizations, and is visibly destroying ours in the same way?

Is there any radicle of such legislation in our parliamentary system? Well, there are two measures just sprouting in the political soil, which may conceivably grow to something valuable. One is the institution of a Legal Minimum Wage. The other, Old Age Pensions. But there is a better plan than either of these. Some time ago I mentioned the subject of Universal Old Age Pensions to my fellow Socialist Mr. Cobden-Sanderson, famous as an artist-craftsman in bookbinding and printing. "Why not Universal Pensions for Life?" said Cobden-Sanderson. In saying this, he solved the industrial problem at a stroke. At present we say callously to each citizen: "If you want money, earn it," as if his having or not having it were a matter that concerned himself alone. We do not even secure for him the opportunity of earning it; on the contrary, we allow our industry to be organized in open dependence on the maintenance of "a reserve army of unemployed" for the sake of "elasticity." The sensible course would be Cobden-Sanderson's: that is, to give every man enough to live well on, so as to guarantee the community against the possibility of a case of the malignant disease of poverty, and then (necessarily) to see that he earned it.

Undershaft, the hero of Major Barbara, is simply a man who, having grasped the fact that poverty is a crime, knows that when society offered him the alternative of poverty or a lucrative trade in death and destruction, it offered him, not a choice between opulent villainy and humble virtue, but between energetic enterprise and cowardly infamy. His conduct stands the Kantian test, which Peter Shirley's does not. Peter Shirley is what we call the honest poor man. Undershaft is what we call the wicked rich one: Shirley is Lazarus, Undershaft Dives. Well, the misery of the world is due to the fact that the great mass of men act and believe as Peter Shirley acts and believes. If they acted and believed as Undershaft acts and believes, the immediate result would be a revolution of incalculable beneficence. To be wealthy, says Undershaft, is with me a point of honor for which I am prepared to kill at the risk of my own life. This preparedness is, as he says, the final test of sincerity. Like Froissart's medieval hero, who saw that "to rob and pill was a good life," he is not the dupe of that public sentiment against killing which is propagated and endowed by people who would otherwise be killed themselves, or of the mouth-honor paid to poverty and obedience by rich and insubordinate do-nothings who want to rob the poor without courage and command them without superiority. Froissart's knight, in placing the achievement of a good life before all the other duties—which indeed are not duties at all when they conflict with it, but plain wickednesses—behaved bravely, admirably, and, in the final analysis, public-spiritedly. Medieval society, on the other hand, behaved very badly indeed in organizing itself so stupidly that a good life could be achieved by robbing and pilling. If the knight's contemporaries had been all as resolute as he, robbing and pilling would have been the shortest way to the gallows, just as, if we were all as resolute and clearsighted as Undershaft, an attempt to live by means of what is called " an independent income " would be the shortest way to the lethal chamber. But as, thanks to our political imbecility and personal cowardice (fruits of poverty, both), the best imitation of a good life now procurable is life on an independent income, all sensible people aim at securing such an income, and are, of course, careful to legalize and moralize both it and all the actions and sentiments which lead to it and support it as an institution. What else can they do? They know, of course, that they are rich because others are poor. But they cannot help that: it is for the poor to repudiate poverty when they have had enough of it. The thing can be done easily enough: the demonstrations to the contrary made by the economists, jurists, moralists and sentimentalists hired by the rich to defend them, or even doing the work gratuitously out of sheer folly and abjectness, impose only on the hirers.

The reason why the independent income-tax payers are not solid in defence of their position is that since we are not medieval rovers through a sparsely populated country, the poverty of those we rob prevents our having the good life for which we sacrifice them. Rich men or aristocrats with a developed sense of life—men like Ruskin and William Morris and Kropotkin—have enormous social appetites and very fastidious personal ones. They are not content with handsome houses: they want handsome cities. They are not content with bediamonded wives and blooming daughters: they complain because the charwoman is badly dressed, because the laundress smells of gin, because the sempstress is anemic, because every man they meet is not a friend and every woman not a romance. They turn up their noses at their neighbors' drains, and are made ill by the architecture of their neighbors' houses. Trade patterns made to suit vulgar people do not please them (and they can get nothing else): they cannot sleep nor sit at ease upon " slaughtered " cabinet makers' furniture. The very air is not good enough for them: there is too much factory smoke in it. They even demand abstract conditions: justice, honor, a noble moral atmosphere, a mystic nexus to replace the cash nexus. Finally they declare that though to rob and pill with your own hand on horseback

and in steel coat may have been a good life, to rob and
pill by the hands of the policeman, the bailiff, and the
soldier, and to underpay them meanly for doing it, is
not a good life, but rather fatal to all possibility of even
a tolerable one. They call on the poor to revolt, and,
finding the poor shocked at their ungentlemanliness,
despairingly revile the proletariat for its " damned want-
lessness " (*verdammte Bedürfnislosigkeit*).

So far, however, their attack on society has lacked
simplicity. The poor do not share their tastes nor understand their art-criticisms. They do not want the
simple life, nor the esthetic life; on the contrary, they
want very much to wallow in all the costly vulgarities
from which the elect souls among the rich turn away
with loathing. It is by surfeit and not by abstinence
that they will be cured of their hankering after un-
wholesome sweets. What they do dislike and despise
and are ashamed of is poverty. To ask them to fight
for the difference between the Christmas number of the
Illustrated London News and the Kelmscott Chaucer
is silly: they prefer the News. The difference between
a stockbroker's cheap and dirty starched white shirt and
collar and the comparatively costly and carefully dyed
blue shirt of William Morris is a difference so disgraceful to Morris in their eyes that if they fought on the
subject at all, they would fight in defence of the starch.
" Cease to be slaves, in order that you may become
cranks " is not a very inspiring call to arms; nor is it
really improved by substituting saints for cranks. Both
terms denote men of genius; and the common man does
not want to live the life of a man of genius: he would
much rather live the life of a pet collie if that were the
only alternative. But he does want more money. Whatever else he may be vague about, he is clear about that.
He may or may not prefer Major Barbara to the Drury
Lane pantomime; but he always prefers five hundred
pounds to five hundred shillings.

Now to deplore this preference as sordid, and teach children that it is sinful to desire money, is to strain towards the extreme possible limit of impudence in lying, and corruption in hypocrisy. The universal regard for money is the one hopeful fact in our civilization, the one sound spot in our social conscience. Money is the most important thing in the world. It represents health, strength, honor, generosity and beauty as conspicuously and undeniably as the want of it represents illness, weakness, disgrace, meanness and ugliness. Not the least of its virtues is that it destroys base people as certainly as it fortifies and dignifies noble people. It is only when it is cheapened to worthlessness for some, and made impossibly dear to others, that it becomes a curse. In short, it is a curse only in such foolish social conditions that life itself is a curse. For the two things are inseparable: money is the counter that enables life to be distributed socially: it *is* life as truly as sovereigns and bank notes are money. The first duty of every citizen is to insist on having money on reasonable terms; and this demand is not complied with by giving four men three shillings each for ten or twelve hours' drudgery and one man a thousand pounds for nothing. The crying need of the nation is not for better morals, cheaper bread, temperance, liberty, culture, redemption of fallen sisters and erring brothers, nor the grace, love and fellowship of the Trinity, but simply for enough money. And the evil to be attacked is not sin, suffering, greed, priestcraft, kingcraft, demagogy, monopoly, ignorance, drink, war, pestilence, nor any other of the scapegoats which reformers sacrifice, but simply poverty.

Once take your eyes from the ends of the earth and fix them on this truth just under your nose; and Andrew Undershaft's views will not perplex you in the least. Unless indeed his constant sense that he is only the instrument of a Will or Life Force which uses him for purposes wider than his own, may puzzle you. If so, that is because you are walking either in artificial Darwinian darkness, or in mere stupidity. All genuinely religious people have that consciousness. To them Undershaft the Mystic will be quite intelligible, and his perfect comprehension of his daughter the Salvationist and her lover the Euripidean republican natural and inevitable. That, however, is not new, even on the stage. What is new, as far as I know, is that article in Undershaft's religion which recognizes in Money the first need and in poverty the vilest sin of man and society.

This dramatic conception has not, of course, been attained *per saltum*. Nor has it been borrowed from Nietzsche or from any man born beyond the Channel. The late Samuel Butler, in his own department the greatest English writer of the latter half of the XIX century, steadily inculcated the necessity and morality of a conscientious Laodiceanism in religion and of an earnest and constant sense of the importance of money. It drives one almost to despair of English literature when one sees so extraordinary a study of English life as Butler's posthumous Way of All Flesh making so little impression that when, some years later, I produce plays in which Butler's extraordinarily fresh, free and future-piercing suggestions have an obvious share, I am met with nothing but vague cacklings about Ibsen and Nietzsche, and am only too thankful that they are not about Alfred de Musset and Georges Sand. Really, the English do not deserve to have great men. They allowed Butler to die practically unknown, whilst I, a comparatively insignificant Irish journalist, was leading them by the nose into an advertisement of me which has made my own life a burden. In Sicily there is a Via Samuele Butler. When an English tourist sees it, he either asks " Who the devil was Samuele Butler?" or wonders why the Sicilians should perpetuate the memory of the author of Hudibras.

Well, it cannot be denied that the English are only

too anxious to recognize a man of genius if somebody will kindly point him out to them. Having pointed myself out in this manner with some success, I now point out Samuel Butler, and trust that in consequence I shall hear a little less in future of the novelty and foreign origin of the ideas which are now making their way into the English theatre through plays written by Socialists. There are living men whose originality and power are as obvious as Butler's; and when they die that fact will be discovered. Meanwhile I recommend them to insist on their own merits as an important part of their own business.

THE SALVATION ARMY.

When Major Barbara was produced in London, the second act was reported in an important northern newspaper as a withering attack on the Salvation Army, and the despairing ejaculation of Barbara deplored by a London daily as a tasteless blasphemy. And they were set right, not by the professed critics of the theatre, but by religious and philosophical publicists like Sir Oliver Lodge and Dr. Stanton Coit, and strenuous Nonconformist journalists like Mr. William Stead, who not only understand the act as well as the Salvationists themselves, but also saw it in its relation to the religious life of the nation, a life which seems to lie not only outside the sympathy of many of our theatre critics, but actually outside their knowledge of society. Indeed nothing could be more ironically curious than the confrontation Major Barbara effected of the theatre enthusiasts with the religious enthusiasts. On the one hand was the playgoer, always seeking pleasure, paying exorbitantly for it, suffering unbearable discomforts for it, and hardly ever getting it. On the other hand was the Salvationist, repudiating gaiety and courting effort and sacrifice, yet always in the wildest spirits, laughing,

joking, singing, rejoicing, drumming, and tambourin-
ing: his life flying by in a flash of excitement, and his
death arriving as a climax of triumph. And, if you
please, the playgoer despising the Salvationist as a joy-
less person, shut out from the heaven of the theatre,
self-condemned to a life of hideous gloom; and the Salvationist mourning over the playgoer as over a prodigal
with vine leaves in his hair, careering outrageously to
hell amid the popping of champagne corks and the
ribald laughter of sirens! Could misunderstanding be
more complete, or sympathy worse misplaced?

Fortunately, the Salvationists are more accessible to
the religious character of the drama than the playgoers
to the gay energy and artistic fertility of religion. They
can see, when it is pointed out to them, that a theatre,
as a place where two or three are gathered together,
takes from that divine presence an inalienable sanctity
of which the grossest and profanest farce can no more
deprive it than a hypocritical sermon by a snobbish
bishop can desecrate Westminster Abbey. But in our
professional playgoers this indispensable preliminary
conception of sanctity seems wanting. They talk of
actors as mimes and mummers, and, I fear, think of
dramatic authors as liars and pandars, whose main business is the voluptuous soothing of the tired city specu-
lator when what he calls the serious business of the day
is over. Passion, the life of drama, means nothing to
them but primitive sexual excitement: such phrases as
" impassioned poetry " or " passionate love of truth "
have fallen quite out of their vocabulary and been replaced by " passional crime " and the like. They assume, as far as I can gather, that people in whom passion has a larger scope are passionless and therefore
uninteresting. Consequently they come to think of religious people as people who are not interesting and not
amusing. And so, when Barbara cuts the regular Salvation Army jokes, and snatches a kiss from her lover

across his drum, the devotees of the theatre think they
ought to appear shocked, and conclude that the whole
play is an elaborate mockery of the Army. And then
either hypocritically rebuke me for mocking, or foolishly take part in the supposed mockery!

Even the handful of mentally competent critics got
into difficulties over my demonstration of the economic
deadlock in which the Salvation Army finds itself. Some
of them thought that the Army would not have taken
money from a distiller and a cannon founder: others
thought it should not have taken it: all assumed more
or less definitely that it reduced itself to absurdity or
hypocrisy by taking it. On the first point the reply of
the Army itself was prompt and conclusive. As one of
its officers said, they would take money from the devil
himself and be only too glad to get it out of his hands
and into God's. They gratefully acknowledged that
publicans not only give them money but allow them to
collect it in the bar—sometimes even when there is a
Salvation meeting outside preaching teetotalism. In
fact, they questioned the verisimilitude of the play, not
because Mrs. Baines took the money, but because Barbara refused it.

On the point that the Army ought not to take such
money, its justification is obvious. It must take the
money because it cannot exist without money, and there
is no other money to be had. Practically all the spare
money in the country consists of a mass of rent, interest,
and profit, every penny of which is bound up with crime,
drink, prostitution, disease, and all the evil fruits of
poverty, as inextricably as with enterprise, wealth, commercial probity, and national prosperity. The notion
that you can earmark certain coins as tainted is an un-
practical individualist superstition. None the less the
fact that all our money is tainted gives a very severe
shock to earnest young souls when some dramatic instance of the taint first makes them conscious of it.

When an enthusiastic young clergyman of the Established Church first realizes that the Ecclesiastical Commissioners receive the rents of sporting public houses, brothels, and sweating dens; or that the most generous contributor at his last charity sermon was an employer trading in female labor cheapened by prostitution as unscrupulously as a hotel keeper trades in waiters' labor cheapened by tips, or commissionaire's labor cheapened by pensions; or that the only patron who can afford to rebuild his church or his schools or give his boys' brigade a gymnasium or a library is the son-in-law of a Chicago meat King, that young clergyman has, like Barbara, a very bad quarter hour. But he cannot help himself by refusing to accept money from anybody except sweet old ladies with independent incomes and gentle and lovely ways of life. He has only to follow up the income of the sweet ladies to its industrial source, and there he will find Mrs. Warren's profession and the poisonous canned meat and all the rest of it. His own stipend has the same root. He must either share the world's guilt or go to another planet. He must save the world's honor if he is to save his own. This is what all the Churches find just as the Salvation Army and Barbara find it in the play. Her discovery that she is her father's accomplice; that the Salvation Army is the accomplice of the distiller and the dynamite maker; that they can no more escape one another than they can escape the air they breathe; that there is no salvation for them through personal righteousness, but only through the redemption of the whole nation from its vicious, lazy, competitive anarchy: this discovery has been made by everyone except the Pharisees and (apparently) the professional playgoers, who still wear their Tom Hood shirts and underpay their washerwomen without the slightest misgiving as to the elevation of their private characters, the purity of their private atmospheres, and their right to repudiate as foreign to themselves the coarse depravity of the garret and the slum. Not that they mean any harm: they only desire to be, in their little private way, what they call gentlemen. They do not understand Barbara's lesson because they have not, like her, learnt it by taking their part in the larger life of the nation.

BARBARA'S RETURN TO THE COLORS.

Barbara's return to the colors may yet provide a subject for the dramatic historian of the future. To go back to the Salvation Army with the knowledge that even the Salvationists themselves are not saved yet; that poverty is not blessed, but a most damnable sin; and that when General Booth chose Blood and Fire for the emblem of Salvation instead of the Cross, he was perhaps better inspired than he knew: such knowledge, for the daughter of Andrew Undershaft, will clearly lead to something hopefuller than distributing bread and treacle at the expense of Bodger.

It is a very significant thing, this instinctive choice of the military form of organization, this substitution of the drum for the organ, by the Salvation Army. Does it not suggest that the Salvationists divine that they must actually fight the devil instead of merely praying at him? At present, it is true, they have not quite ascertained his correct address. When they do, they may give a very rude shock to that sense of security which he has gained from his experience of the fact that hard words, even when uttered by eloquent essayists and lecturers, or carried unanimously at enthusiastic public meetings on the motion of eminent reformers, break no bones. It has been said that the French Revolution was the work of Voltaire, Rousseau and the Encyclopedists. It seems to me to have been the work of men who had observed that virtuous indignation, caustic

criticism, conclusive argument and instructive pamphlet-
eering, even when done by the most earnest and witty
literary geniuses, were as useless as praying, things going steadily from bad to worse whilst the Social Con-
tract and the pamphlets of Voltaire were at the height
of their vogue. Eventually, as we know, perfectly
respectable citizens and earnest philanthropists con-
nived at the September massacres because hard experience had convinced them that if they contented themselves with appeals to humanity and patriotism, the
aristocracy, though it would read their appeals with the
greatest enjoyment and appreciation, flattering and admiring the writers, would none the less continue to
conspire with foreign monarchists to undo the revolution
and restore the old system with every circumstance of
savage vengeance and ruthless repression of popular
liberties.

The nineteenth century saw the same lesson repeated
in England. It had its Utilitarians, its Christian Socialists, its Fabians (still extant): it had Bentham, Mill,
Dickens, Ruskin, Carlyle, Butler, Henry George, and
Morris. And the end of all their efforts is the Chicago
described by Mr. Upton Sinclair, and the London in
which the people who pay to be amused by my dramatic
representation of Peter Shirley turned out to starve at
forty because there are younger slaves to be had for his
wages, do not take, and have not the slightest intention
of taking, any effective step to organize society in such
a way as to make that everyday infamy impossible. I,
who have preached and pamphleteered like any Ency-
clopedist, have to confess that my methods are no use,
and would be no use if I were Voltaire, Rousseau,
Bentham, Mill, Dickens, Carlyle, Ruskin, George, Butler, and Morris all rolled into one, with Euripides, More,
Molière, Shakespear, Beaumarchais, Swift, Goethe, Ibsen, Tolstoy, Moses and the prophets all thrown in (as
indeed in some sort I actually am, standing as I do on

all their shoulders). The problem being to make heroes out of cowards, we paper apostles and artist-magicians have succeeded only in giving cowards all the sensations of heroes whilst they tolerate every abomination, accept every plunder, and submit to every oppression. Christianity, in making a merit of such submission, has marked only that depth in the abyss at which the very sense of shame is lost. The Christian has been like Dickens' doctor in the debtor's prison, who tells the newcomer of its ineffable peace and security: no duns; no tyrannical collectors of rates, taxes, and rent; no importunate hopes nor exacting duties; nothing but the rest and safety of having no further to fall.

Yet in the poorest corner of this soul-destroying Christendom vitality suddenly begins to germinate again. Joyousness, a sacred gift long dethroned by the hellish laughter of derision and obscenity, rises like a flood miraculously out of the fetid dust and mud of the slums; rousing marches and impetuous dithyrambs rise to the heavens from people among whom the depressing noise called " sacred music " is a standing joke; a flag with Blood and Fire on it is unfurled, not in murderous rancor, but because fire is beautiful and blood a vital and splendid red; Fear, which we flatter by calling Self, vanishes; and transfigured men and women carry their gospel through a transfigured world, calling their leader General, themselves captains and brigadiers, and their whole body an Army: praying, but praying only for refreshment, for strength to fight, and for needful MONEY (a notable sign, that); preaching, but not preaching submission; daring ill-usage and abuse, but not putting up with more of it than is inevitable; and practising what the world will let them practise, including soap and water, color and music. There is danger in such activity; and where there is danger there is hope. Our present security is nothing, and can be nothing, but evil made irresistible.

Weaknesses of the Salvation Army.

For the present, however, it is not my business to flatter the Salvation Army. Rather must I point out to it that it has almost as many weaknesses as the Church of England itself. It is building up a business organization which will compel it eventually to see that its present staff of enthusiast-commanders shall be succeeded by a bureaucracy of men of business who will be no better than bishops, and perhaps a good deal more unscrupulous. That has always happened sooner or later to great orders founded by saints; and the order founded by St. William Booth is not exempt from the same danger. It is even more dependent than the Church on rich people who would cut off supplies at once if it began to preach that indispensable revolt against poverty which must also be a revolt against riches. It is hampered by a heavy contingent of pious elders who are not really Salvationists at all, but Evangelicals of the old school. It still, as Commissioner Howard affirms, " sticks to Moses," which is flat nonsense at this time of day if the Commissioner means, as I am afraid he does, that the Book of Genesis contains a trustworthy scientific account of the origin of species, and that the god to whom Jephthah sacrificed his daughter is any less obviously a tribal idol than Dagon or Chemosh.

Further, there is still too much other-worldliness about the Army. Like Frederick's grenadier, the Salvationist wants to live for ever (the most monstrous way of crying for the moon); and though it is evident to anyone who has ever heard General Booth and his best officers that they would work as hard for human salvation as they do at present if they believed that death would be the end of them individually, they and their followers have a bad habit of talking as if the Salvationists were heroically enduring a very bad time on earth as an investment which will bring them in divi-

dends later on in the form, not of a better life to come
for the whole world, but of an eternity spent by themselves personally in a sort of bliss which would bore
any active person to a second death. Surely the truth
is that the Salvationists are unusually happy people.
And is it not the very diagnostic of true salvation that
it shall overcome the fear of death? Now the man who
has come to believe that there is no such thing as death,
the change so called being merely the transition to an
exquisitely happy and utterly careless life, has not overcome the fear of death at all: on the contrary, it has
overcome him so completely that he refuses to die on
any terms whatever. I do not call a Salvationist really
saved until he is ready to lie down cheerfully on the
scrap heap, having paid scot and lot and something
over, and let his eternal life pass on to renew its youth
in the battalions of the future.

Then there is the nasty lying habit called confession,
which the Army encourages because it lends itself to
dramatic oratory, with plenty of thrilling incident. For
my part, when I hear a convert relating the violences
and oaths and blasphemies he was guilty of before he
was saved, making out that he was a very terrible fellow
then and is the most contrite and chastened of Christians
now, I believe him no more than I believe the millionaire
who says he came up to London or Chicago as a boy
with only three halfpence in his pocket. Salvationists
have said to me that Barbara in my play would never
have been taken in by so transparent a humbug as Snobby
Price; and certainly I do not think Snobby could have
taken in any experienced Salvationist on a point on
which the Salvationist did not wish to be taken in. But
on the point of conversion all Salvationists wish to be
taken in; for the more obvious the sinner the more obvious the miracle of his conversion. When you advertize
a converted burglar or reclaimed drunkard as one of the
attractions at an experience meeting, your burglar can

hardly have been too burglarious or your drunkard too drunken. As long as such attractions are relied on, you will have your Snobbies claiming to have beaten their mothers when they were as a matter of prosaic fact habitually beaten by them, and your Rummies of the tamest respectability pretending to a past of reckless and dazzling vice. Even when confessions are sincerely autobiographic there is no reason to assume at once that the impulse to make them is pious or the interest of the hearers wholesome. It might as well be assumed that the poor people who insist on shewing appalling ulcers to district visitors are convinced hygienists, or that the curiosity which sometimes welcomes such exhibitions is a pleasant and creditable one. One is often tempted to suggest that those who pester our police superintendents with confessions of murder might very wisely be taken at their word and executed, except in the few cases in which a real murderer is seeking to be relieved of his guilt by confession and expiation. For though I am not, I hope, an unmerciful person, I do not think that the inexorability of the deed once done should be disguised by any ritual, whether in the confessional or on the scaffold.

And here my disagreement with the Salvation Army, and with all propagandists of the Cross (to which I object as I object to all gibbets) becomes deep indeed. Forgiveness, absolution, atonement, are figments: punishment is only a pretence of cancelling one crime by another; and you can no more have forgiveness without vindictiveness than you can have a cure without a disease. You will never get a high morality from people who conceive that their misdeeds are revocable and pardonable, or in a society where absolution and expiation are officially provided for us all. The demand may be very real; but the supply is spurious. Thus Bill Walker, in my play, having assaulted the Salvation Lass, presently finds himself overwhelmed with an intolerable conviction of sin under the skilled treatment of Barbara. Straightway he begins to try to unassault the lass and deruffianize his deed, first by getting punished for it in kind, and, when that relief is denied him, by fining himself a pound to compensate the girl. He is foiled both ways. He finds the Salvation Army as inexorable as fact itself. It will not punish him: it will not take his money. It will not tolerate a redeemed ruffian: it leaves him no means of salvation except ceasing to be a ruffian. In doing this, the Salvation Army instinctively grasps the central truth of Christianity and discards its central superstition: that central truth being the vanity of revenge and punishment, and that central superstition the salvation of the world by the gibbet.

For, be it noted, Bill has assaulted an old and starving woman also; and for this worse offence he feels no remorse whatever, because she makes it clear that her malice is as great as his own. " Let her have the law of me, as she said she would," says Bill: " what I done to her is no more on what you might call my conscience than sticking a pig." This shews a perfectly natural and wholesome state of mind on his part. The old woman, like the law she threatens him with, is perfectly ready to play the game of retaliation with him: to rob him if he steals, to flog him if he strikes, to murder him if he kills. By example and precept the law and public opinion teach him to impose his will on others by anger, violence, and cruelty, and to wipe off the moral score by punishment. That is sound Crosstianity. But this Crosstianity has got entangled with something which Barbara calls Christianity, and which unexpectedly causes her to refuse to play the hangman's game of Satan casting out Satan. She refuses to prosecute a drunken ruffian; she converses on equal terms with a blackguard whom no lady could be seen speaking to in the public street: in short, she behaves as illegally and unbecomingly as possible under the circumstances. Bill's conscience reacts to this just as naturally as it does to the old woman's threats. He is placed in a position of unbearable moral inferiority, and strives by every means in his power to escape from it, whilst he is still quite ready to meet the abuse of the old woman by attempting to smash a mug on her face. And that is the triumphant justification of Barbara's Christianity as against our system of judicial punishment and the vindictive villain-thrashings and " poetic justice " of the romantic stage.

For the credit of literature it must be pointed out that the situation is only partly novel. Victor Hugo long ago gave us the epic of the convict and the bishop's candlesticks, of the Crosstian policeman annihilated by his encounter with the Christian Valjean. But Bill Walker is not, like Valjean, romantically changed from a demon into an angel. There are millions of Bill Walkers in all classes of society to-day; and the point which I, as a professor of natural psychology, desire to demonstrate, is that Bill, without any change in his character whatsoever, will react one way to one sort of treatment and another way to another.

In proof I might point to the sensational object lesson provided by our commercial millionaires to-day. They begin as brigands: merciless, unscrupulous, dealing out ruin and death and slavery to their competitors and employees, and facing desperately the worst that their competitors can do to them. The history of the English factories, the American trusts, the exploitation of African gold, diamonds, ivory and rubber, outdoes in villainy the worst that has ever been imagined of the buccaneers of the Spanish Main. Captain Kidd would have marooned a modern Trust magnate for conduct unworthy of a gentleman of fortune. The law every day seizes on unsuccessful scoundrels of this type and punishes them with a cruelty worse than their own, with the result that they come out of the torture house more dangerous than they went in, and renew their evil doing (nobody will employ them at anything else) until they are again seized, again tormented, and again let loose, with the same result.

But the successful scoundrel is dealt with very differently, and very Christianly. He is not only forgiven: he is idolized, respected, made much of, all but worshipped. Society returns him good for evil in the most extravagant overmeasure. And with what result? He begins to idolize himself, to respect himself, to live up to the treatment he receives. He preaches sermons; he writes books of the most edifying advice to young men, and actually persuades himself that he got on by taking his own advice; he endows educational institutions; he supports charities; he dies finally in the odor of sanctity, leaving a will which is a monument of public spirit and bounty. And all this without any change in his character. The spots of the leopard and the stripes of the tiger are as brilliant as ever; but the conduct of the world towards him has changed; and his conduct has changed accordingly. You have only to reverse your attitude towards him—to lay hands on his property, revile him, assault him, and he will be a brigand again in a moment, as ready to crush you as you are to crush him, and quite as full of pretentious moral reasons for doing it.

In short, when Major Barbara says that there are no scoundrels, she is right: there are no absolute scoundrels, though there are impracticable people of whom I shall treat presently. Every practicable man (and woman) is a potential scoundrel and a potential good citizen. What a man is depends on his character; but what he does, and what we think of what he does, depends on his circumstances. The characteristics that ruin a man in one class make him eminent in another. The characters that behave differently in different circumstances behave alike in similar circumstances. Take a common English character like that of Bill Walker.

We meet Bill everywhere: on the judicial bench, on the episcopal bench, in the Privy Council, at the War Office and Admiralty, as well as in the Old Bailey dock or in the ranks of casual unskilled labor. And the morality of Bill's characteristics varies with these various circumstances. The faults of the burglar are the qualities of the financier: the manners and habits of a duke would cost a city clerk his situation. In short, though character is independent of circumstances, conduct is not; and our moral judgments of character are not: both are circumstantial. Take any condition of life in which the circumstances are for a mass of men practically alike: felony, the House of Lords, the factory, the stables, the gipsy encampment or where you please! In spite of diversity of character and temperament, the conduct and morals of the individuals in each group are as predicable and as alike in the main as if they were a flock of sheep, morals being mostly only social habits and circumstantial necessities. Strong people know this and count upon it. In nothing have the master-minds of the world been distinguished from the ordinary suburban season-ticket holder more than in their straightforward perception of the fact that mankind is practically a single species, and not a menagerie of gentlemen and bounders, villains and heroes, cowards and daredevils, peers and peasants, grocers and aristocrats, artisans and laborers, washerwomen and duchesses, in which all the grades of income and caste represent distinct animals who must not be introduced to one another or intermarry. Napoleon constructing a galaxy of generals and courtiers, and even of monarchs, out of his collection of social nobodies; Julius Cæsar appointing as governor of Egypt the son of a freedman—one who but a short time before would have been legally disqualified for the post even of a private soldier in the Roman army; Louis XI. making his barber his privy councillor: all these had in their different ways a firm hold of the scientific fact of human equality, expressed by Barbara in the Christian formula that all men are children of one father. A man who believes that men are naturally divided into upper and lower and middle classes morally is making exactly the same mistake as the man who believes that they are naturally divided in the same way socially. And just as our persistent attempts to found political institutions on a basis of social inequality have always produced long periods of destructive friction relieved from time to time by violent explosions of revolution; so the attempt—will Americans please note—to found moral institutions on a basis of moral inequality can lead to nothing but unnatural Reigns of the Saints relieved by licentious Restorations; to Americans who have made divorce a public institution turning the face of Europe into one huge sardonic smile by refusing to stay in the same hotel with a Russian man of genius who has changed wives without the sanction of South Dakota; to grotesque hypocrisy, cruel persecution, and final utter confusion of conventions and compliances with benevolence and respectability. It is quite useless to declare that all men are born free if you deny that they are born good. Guarantee a man's goodness and his liberty will take care of itself. To guarantee his freedom on condition that you approve of his moral character is formally to abolish all freedom whatsoever, as every man's liberty is at the mercy of a moral indictment, which any fool can trump up against everyone who violates custom, whether as a prophet or as a rascal. This is the lesson Democracy has to learn before it can become anything but the most oppressive of all the priesthoods.

Let us now return to Bill Walker and his case of conscience against the Salvation Army. Major Barbara, not being a modern Tetzel, or the treasurer of a hospital, refuses to sell Bill absolution for a sovereign. Unfortunately, what the Army can afford to refuse in

the case of Bill Walker, it cannot refuse in the case of
Bodger. Bodger is master of the situation because he
holds the purse strings. " Strive as you will," says
Bodger, in effect: " me you cannot do without. You
cannot save Bill Walker without my money." And the
Army answers, quite rightly under the circumstances,
" We will take money from the devil himself sooner
than abandon the work of Salvation." So Bodger pays
his conscience-money and gets the absolution that is
refused to Bill. In real life Bill would perhaps never
know this. But I, the dramatist, whose business it is
to shew the connexion between things that seem apart
and unrelated in the haphazard order of events in real
life, have contrived to make it known to Bill, with the
result that the Salvation Army loses its hold of him at
once.

But Bill may not be lost, for all that. He is still in
the grip of the facts and of his own conscience, and
may find his taste for blackguardism permanently
spoiled. Still, I cannot guarantee that happy ending.
Let anyone walk through the poorer quarters of our
cities when the men are not working, but resting and
chewing the cud of their reflections; and he will find
that there is one expression on every mature face: the
expression of cynicism. The discovery made by Bill
Walker about the Salvation Army has been made by
everyone of them. They have found that every man
has his price; and they have been foolishly or corruptly
taught to mistrust and despise him for that necessary
and salutary condition of social existence. When they
learn that General Booth, too, has his price, they do
not admire him because it is a high one, and admit the
need of organizing society so that he shall get it in an
honorable way: they conclude that his character is un-
sound and that all religious men are hypocrites and
allies of their sweaters and oppressors. They know that
the large subscriptions which help to support the Army

are endowments, not of religion, but of the wicked doctrine of docility in poverty and humility under oppression; and they are rent by the most agonizing of all the doubts of the soul, the doubt whether their true salvation must not come from their most abhorrent passions, from murder, envy, greed, stubbornness, rage, and terrorism, rather than from public spirit, reasonableness, humanity, generosity, tenderness, delicacy, pity and kindness. The confirmation of that doubt, at which our newspapers have been working so hard for years past, is the morality of militarism; and the justification of militarism is that circumstances may at any time make it the true morality of the moment. It is by producing such moments that we produce violent and sanguinary revolutions, such as the one now in progress in Russia and the one which Capitalism in England and America is daily and diligently provoking.

At such moments it becomes the duty of the Churches to evoke all the powers of destruction against the existing order. But if they do this, the existing order must forcibly suppress them. Churches are suffered to exist only on condition that they preach submission to the State as at present capitalistically organized. The Church of England itself is compelled to add to the thirty-six articles in which it formulates its religious tenets, three more in which it apologetically protests that the moment any of these articles comes in conflict with the State it is to be entirely renounced, abjured, violated, abrogated and abhorred, the policeman being a much more important person than any of the Persons of the Trinity. And this is why no tolerated Church nor Salvation Army can ever win the entire confidence of the poor. It must be on the side of the police and the military, no matter what it believes or disbelieves; and as the police and the military are the instruments by which the rich rob and oppress the poor (on legal and moral principles made for the purpose), it is not possible to be on the side of the poor and of the police at the same time. Indeed the religious bodies, as the almoners of the rich, become a sort of auxiliary police, taking off the insurrectionary edge of poverty with coals and blankets, bread and treacle, and soothing and cheering the victims with hopes of immense and inexpensive happiness in another world when the process of working them to premature death in the service of the rich is complete in this.

CHRISTIANITY AND ANARCHISM.

Such is the false position from which neither the Salvation Army nor the Church of England nor any other religious organization whatever can escape except through a reconstitution of society. Nor can they merely endure the State passively, washing their hands of its sins. The State is constantly forcing the consciences of men by violence and cruelty. Not content with exacting money from us for the maintenance of its soldiers and policemen, its gaolers and executioners, it forces us to take an active personal part in its proceedings on pain of becoming ourselves the victims of its violence. As I write these lines, a sensational example is given to the world. A royal marriage has been celebrated, first by sacrament in a cathedral, and then by a bullfight having for its main amusement the spectacle of horses gored and disembowelled by the bull, after which, when the bull is so exhausted as to be no longer dangerous, he is killed by a cautious matador. But the ironic contrast between the bull fight and the sacrament of marriage does not move anyone. Another contrast— that between the splendor, the happiness, the atmosphere of kindly admiration surrounding the young couple, and the price paid for it under our abominable social arrangements in the misery, squalor and degradation of millions of other young couples—is drawn at the same moment by a novelist, Mr. Upton Sinclair, who chips a corner of the veneering from the huge meat packing industries of Chicago, and shews it to us as a sample of what is going on all over the world underneath the top layer of prosperous plutocracy. One man is sufficiently moved by that contrast to pay his own life as the price of one terrible blow at the responsible parties. Unhappily his poverty leaves him also ignorant enough to be duped by the pretence that the innocent young bride and bridegroom, put forth and crowned by plutocracy as the heads of a State in which they have less personal power than any policeman, and less influence than any chairman of a trust, are responsible. At them accordingly he launches his sixpennorth of fulminate, missing his mark, but scattering the bowels of as many horses as any bull in the arena, and slaying twenty-three persons, besides wounding ninetynine. And of all these, the horses alone are innocent of the guilt he is avenging: had he blown all Madrid to atoms with every adult person in it, not one could have escaped the charge of being an accessory, before, at, and after the fact, to poverty and prostitution, to such wholesale massacre of infants as Herod never dreamt of, to plague, pestilence and famine, battle, murder and lingering death—perhaps not one who had not helped, through example, precept, connivance, and even clamor, to teach the dynamiter his well-learnt gospel of hatred and vengeance, by approving every day of sentences of years of imprisonment so infernal in its unnatural stupidity and panic-stricken cruelty, that their advocates can disavow neither the dagger nor the bomb without stripping the mask of justice and humanity from themselves also.

Be it noted that at this very moment there appears the biography of one of our dukes, who, being Scotch, could argue about politics, and therefore stood out as a great brain among our aristocrats. And what, if you please, was his grace's favorite historical episode, which he de-

clared he never read without intense satisfaction? Why,
the young General Bonapart's pounding of the Paris
mob to pieces in 1795, called in playful approval by our
respectable classes " the whiff of grapeshot," though
Napoleon, to do him justice, took a deeper view of it,
and would fain have had it forgotten. And since the
Duke of Argyll was not a demon, but a man of like
passions with ourselves, by no means rancorous or cruel
as men go, who can doubt that all over the world pro-
letarians of the ducal kidney are now revelling in " the
whiff of dynamite " (the flavor of the joke seems to
evaporate a little, does it not?) because it was aimed at
the class they hate even as our argute duke hated what
he called the mob.

In such an atmosphere there can be only one sequel
to the Madrid explosion. All Europe burns to emulate
it. Vengeance! More blood! Tear " the Anarchist
beast " to shreds. Drag him to the scaffold. Imprison
him for life. Let all civilized States band together to
drive his like off the face of the earth; and if any State
refuses to join, make war on it. This time the leading
London newspaper, anti-Liberal and therefore anti-Rus-
sian in politics, does not say " Serve you right " to the
victims, as it did, in effect, when Bobrikoff, and De
Plehve, and Grand Duke Sergius, were in the same
manner unofficially fulminated into fragments. No: fulminate our rivals in Asia by all means, ye brave Russian
revolutionaries; but to aim at an English princess—
monstrous! hideous! hound down the wretch to his doom;
and observe, please, that we are a civilized and merciful
people, and, however much we may regret it, must not
treat him as Ravaillac and Damiens were treated. And
meanwhile, since we have not yet caught him, let us
soothe our quivering nerves with the bullfight, and com-
ment in a courtly way on the unfailing tact and good
taste of the ladies of our royal houses, who, though
presumably of full normal natural tenderness, have been

so effectually broken in to fashionable routine that they can be taken to see the horses slaughtered as helplessly as they could no doubt be taken to a gladiator show, if that happened to be the mode just now.

Strangely enough, in the midst of this raging fire of malice, the one man who still has faith in the kindness and intelligence of human nature is the fulminator, now a hunted wretch, with nothing, apparently, to secure his triumph over all the prisons and scaffolds of infuriate Europe except the revolver in his pocket and his readiness to discharge it at a moment's notice into his own or any other head. Think of him setting out to find a gentleman and a Christian in the multitude of human wolves howling for his blood. Think also of this: that at the very first essay he finds what he seeks, a veritable grandee of Spain, a noble, high-thinking, unterrified, malice-void soul, in the guise—of all masquerades in the world!—of a modern editor. The Anarchist wolf, flying from the wolves of plutocracy, throws himself on the honor of the man. The man, not being a wolf (nor a London editor), and therefore not having enough sympathy with his exploit to be made bloodthirsty by it, does not throw him back to the pursuing wolves—gives him, instead, what help he can to escape, and sends him off acquainted at last with a force that goes deeper than dynamite, though you cannot make so much of it for sixpence. That righteous and honorable high human deed is not wasted on Europe, let us hope, though it benefits the fugitive wolf only for a moment. The plutocratic wolves presently smell him out. The fugitive shoots the unlucky wolf whose nose is nearest; shoots himself; and then convinces the world, by his photograph, that he was no monstrous freak of reversion to the tiger, but a good looking young man with nothing abnormal about him except his appalling courage and resolution (that is why the terrified shriek Coward at him): one to whom murdering a happy young couple on their wedding morning would have been an unthink-ably unnatural abomination under rational and kindly human circumstances.

Then comes the climax of irony and blind stupidity. The wolves, balked of their meal of fellow-wolf, turn on the man, and proceed to torture him, after their manner, by imprisonment, for refusing to fasten his teeth in the throat of the dynamiter and hold him down until they came to finish him.

Thus, you see, a man may not be a gentleman nowadays even if he wishes to. As to being a Christian, he is allowed some latitude in that matter, because, I repeat, Christianity has two faces. Popular Christianity has for its emblem a gibbet, for its chief sensation a sanguinary execution after torture, for its central mystery an insane vengeance bought off by a trumpery expiation. But there is a nobler and profounder Christianity which affirms the sacred mystery of Equality, and forbids the glaring futility and folly of vengeance, often politely called punishment or justice. The gibbet part of Christianity is tolerated. The other is criminal felony. Connoisseurs in irony are well aware of the fact that the only editor in England who denounces punishment as radically wrong, also repudiates Christianity; calls his paper The Freethinker; and has been imprisoned for two years for blasphemy.

SANE CONCLUSIONS.

And now I must ask the excited reader not to lose his head on one side or the other, but to draw a sane moral from these grim absurdities. It is not good sense to propose that laws against crime should apply to principals only and not to accessories whose consent, counsel, or silence may secure impunity to the principal. If you institute punishment as part of the law, you must punish people for refusing to punish. If you have a police, part of its duty must be to compel everybody to assist the police. No doubt if your laws are unjust, and your policemen agents of oppression, the result will be an unbearable violation of the private consciences of citizens. But that cannot be helped: the remedy is, not to license everybody to thwart the law if they please, but to make laws that will command the public assent, and not to deal cruelly and stupidly with lawbreakers. Everybody disapproves of burglars; but the modern burglar, when caught and overpowered by a householder, usually appeals, and often, let us hope, with success, to his captor not to deliver him over to the useless horrors of penal servitude. In other cases the lawbreaker escapes because those who could give him up do not consider his breach of the law a guilty action. Sometimes, even, private tribunals are formed in opposition to the official tribunals; and these private tribunals employ assassins as executioners, as was done, for example, by Mahomet before he had established his power officially, and by the Ribbon lodges of Ireland in their long struggle with the landlords. Under such circumstances, the assassin goes free although everybody in the district knows who he is and what he has done. They do not betray him, partly because they justify him exactly as the regular Government justifies its official executioner, and partly because they would themselves be assassinated if they betrayed him: another method learnt from the official government. Given a tribunal, employing a slayer who has no personal quarrel with the slain; and there is clearly no moral difference between official and unofficial killing.

In short, all men are anarchists with regard to laws which are against their consciences, either in the preamble or in the penalty. In London our worst anarchists are the magistrates, because many of them are so old and ignorant that when they are called upon to administer any law that is based on ideas or knowledge

less than half a century old, they disagree with it, and
being mere ordinary homebred private Englishmen without any respect for law in the abstract, naïvely set the
example of violating it. In this instance the man lags
behind the law; but when the law lags behind the man,
he becomes equally an anarchist. When some huge
change in social conditions, such as the industrial revolution of the eighteenth and nineteenth centuries, throws
our legal and industrial institutions out of date, Anarchism becomes almost a religion. The whole force of the
most energetic geniuses of the time in philosophy,
economics, and art, concentrates itself on demonstrations
and reminders that morality and law are only conventions, fallible and continually obsolescing. Tragedies in
which the heroes are bandits, and comedies in which
law-abiding and conventionally moral folk are compelled
to satirize themselves by outraging the conscience of the
spectators every time they do their duty, appear simul-
taneously with economic treatises entitled "What is
Property? Theft!" and with histories of "The Conflict between Religion and Science."

Now this is not a healthy state of things. The ad-
vantages of living in society are proportionate, not to
the freedom of the individual from a code, but to the
complexity and subtlety of the code he is prepared not
only to accept but to uphold as a matter of such vital
importance that a lawbreaker at large is hardly to be
tolerated on any plea. Such an attitude becomes impossible when the only men who can make themselves
heard and remembered throughout the world spend all
their energy in raising our gorge against current law,
current morality, current respectability, and legal
property. The ordinary man, uneducated in social theory even when he is schooled in Latin verse, cannot be
set against all the laws of his country and yet persuaded
to regard law in the abstract as vitally necessary to
society. Once he is brought to repudiate the laws and

institutions he knows, he will repudiate the very conception of law and the very groundwork of institutions, ridiculing human rights, extolling brainless methods as "historical," and tolerating nothing except pure empiricism in conduct, with dynamite as the basis of politics and vivisection as the basis of science. That is hideous; but what is to be done? Here am I, for instance, by class a respectable man, by common sense a hater of waste and disorder, by intellectual constitution legally minded to the verge of pedantry, and by temperament apprehensive and economically disposed to the limit of old-maidishness; yet I am, and have always been, and shall now always be, a revolutionary writer, because our laws make law impossible; our liberties destroy all freedom; our property is organized robbery; our morality is an impudent hypocrisy; our wisdom is administered by inexperienced or malexperienced dupes, our power wielded by cowards and weaklings, and our honor false in all its points. I am an enemy of the existing order for good reasons; but that does not make my attacks any less encouraging or helpful to people who are its enemies for bad reasons. The existing order may shriek that if I tell the truth about it, some foolish person may drive it to become still worse by trying to assassinate it. I cannot help that, even if I could see what worse it could do than it is already doing. And the disadvantage of that worst even from its own point of view is that society, with all its prisons and bayonets and whips and ostracisms and starvations, is powerless in the face of the Anarchist who is prepared to sacrifice his own life in the battle with it. Our natural safety from the cheap and devastating explosives which every Russian student can make, and every Russian grenadier has learnt to handle in Manchuria, lies in the fact that brave and resolute men, when they are rascals, will not risk their skins for the good of humanity, and, when they are sympathetic enough to care for humanity, abhor murder, and never commit it until their consciences are outraged beyond endurance. The remedy is, then, simply not to outrage their consciences.

Do not be afraid that they will not make allowances. All men make very large allowances indeed before they stake their own lives in a war to the death with society. Nobody demands or expects the millennium. But there are two things that must be set right, or we shall perish, like Rome, of soul atrophy disguised as empire.

The first is, that the daily ceremony of dividing the wealth of the country among its inhabitants shall be so conducted that no crumb shall go to any able-bodied adults who are not producing by their personal exertions not only a full equivalent for what they take, but a surplus sufficient to provide for their superannuation and pay back the debt due for their nurture.

The second is that the deliberate infliction of malicious injuries which now goes on under the name of punishment be abandoned; so that the thief, the ruffian, the gambler, and the beggar, may without inhumanity be handed over to the law, and made to understand that a State which is too humane to punish will also be too thrifty to waste the life of honest men in watching or restraining dishonest ones. That is why we do not imprison dogs. We even take our chance of their first bite. But if a dog delights to bark and bite, it goes to the lethal chamber. That seems to me sensible. To allow the dog to expiate his bite by a period of torment, and then let him loose in a much more savage condition (for the chain makes a dog savage) to bite again and expiate again, having meanwhile spent a great deal of human life and happiness in the task of chaining and feeding and tormenting him, seems to me idiotic and superstitious. Yet that is what we do to men who bark and bite and steal. It would be far more sensible to put up with their vices, as we put up with their illnesses, until they give more trouble than they are worth, at which point we should, with many apologies and expressions of sympathy, and some generosity in complying with their last wishes, place them in the lethal chamber and get rid of them. Under no circumstances should they be allowed to expiate their misdeeds by a manufactured penalty, to subscribe to a charity, or to compensate the victims. If there is to be no punishment there can be no forgiveness. We shall never have real moral responsibility until everyone knows that his deeds are irrevocable, and that his life depends on his usefulness. Hitherto, alas! humanity has never dared face these hard facts. We frantically scatter conscience money and invent systems of conscience banking, with expiatory penalties, atonements, redemptions, salvations, hospital subscription lists and what not, to enable us to contract-out of the moral code. Not content with the old scapegoat and sacrificial lamb, we deify human saviors, and pray to miraculous virgin intercessors. We attribute mercy to the inexorable; soothe our consciences after committing murder by throwing ourselves on the bosom of divine love; and shrink even from our own gallows because we are forced to admit that it, at least, is irrevocable—as if one hour of imprisonment were not as irrevocable as any execution!

If a man cannot look evil in the face without illusion, he will never know what it really is, or combat it effectually. The few men who have been able (relatively) to do this have been called cynics, and have sometimes had an abnormal share of evil in themselves, corresponding to the abnormal strength of their minds; but they have never done mischief unless they intended to do it. That is why great scoundrels have been beneficent rulers whilst amiable and privately harmless monarchs have ruined their countries by trusting to the hocus-pocus of innocence and guilt, reward and punishment, virtuous indignation and pardon, instead of standing up to the facts without either malice or mercy. Major Barbara

stands up to Bill Walker in that way, with the result
that the ruffian who cannot get hated, has to hate himself.   To relieve this agony he tries to get punished;
but the Salvationist whom he tries to provoke is as merciless as Barbara, and only prays for him.   Then he
tries to pay, but can get nobody to take his money.   His
doom is the doom of Cain, who, failing to find either a
savior, a policeman, or an almoner to help him to pretend that his brother's blood no longer cried from the
ground, had to live and die a murderer.   Cain took care
not to commit another murder, unlike our railway shareholders (I am one) who kill and maim shunters by hundreds to save the cost of automatic couplings, and make
atonement by annual subscriptions to deserving charities.
Had Cain been allowed to pay off his score, he might
possibly have killed Adam and Eve for the mere sake
of a second luxurious reconciliation with God afterwards.   Bodger, you may depend on it, will go on to the
end of his life poisoning people with bad whisky, because he can always depend on the Salvation Army or
the Church of England to negotiate a redemption for him
in consideration of a trifling percentage of his profits.

There is a third condition too, which must be fulfilled
before the great teachers of the world will cease to scoff
at its religions.   Creeds must become intellectually honest.   At present there is not a single credible established
religion in the world.   That is perhaps the most stu-
pendous fact in the whole world-situation.   This play
of mine, Major Barbara, is, I hope, both true and inspired; but whoever says that it all happened, and that
faith in it and understanding of it consist in believing
that it is a record of an actual occurrence, is, to speak
according to Scripture, a fool and a liar, and is hereby
solemnly denounced and cursed as such by me, the
author, to all posterity.

London, June 1906.

ACT I

It is after dinner on a January night, in the library in Lady Britomart Undershaft's house in Wilton Crescent. A large and comfortable settee is in the middle of the room, upholstered in dark leather. A person sitting on it (it is vacant at present) would have, on his right, Lady Britomart's writing-table, with the lady herself busy at it; a smaller writing-table behind him on his left; the door behind him on Lady Britomart's side; and a window with a window-seat directly on his left. Near the window is an armchair.

Lady Britomart is a woman of fifty or thereabouts, well dressed and yet careless of her dress, well bred and quite reckless of her breeding, well mannered and yet appallingly outspoken and indifferent to the opinion of her interlocutors, amiable and yet peremptory, arbitrary, and high-tempered to the last bearable degree, and withal a very typical managing matron of the upper class, treated as a naughty child until she grew into a scolding mother, and finally settling down with plenty of practical ability and worldly experience, limited in the oddest way with domestic and class limitations, conceiving the universe exactly as if it were·a large house in Wilton Crescent, though handling her corner of it very effectively on that assumption, and being quite enlightened and liberal as to the books in the library, the pictures on the walls, the music in the portfolios, and the articles in the papers.

Her son, Stephen, comes in. He is a gravely correct young man under 25, taking himself very seriously, but

*still in some awe of his mother, from childish habit and
bachelor shyness rather than from any weakness of character.*

STEPHEN. Whats the matter?

LADY BRITOMART. Presently, Stephen.

(*Stephen submissively walks to the settee and sits
down. He takes up The Speaker.*)

LADY BRITOMART. Dont begin to read, Stephen. I
shall require all your attention.

STEPHEN. It was only while I was waiting—

LADY BRITOMART. Dont make excuses, Stephen. (*He
puts down The Speaker.*) Now! (*She finishes her
writing; rises; and comes to the settee.*) I have not
kept you waiting v e r y long, I think.

STEPHEN. Not at all, mother.

LADY BRITOMART. Bring me my cushion. (*He takes
the cushion from the chair at the desk and arranges it
for her as she sits down on the settee.*) Sit down. (*He
sits down and fingers his tie nervously.*) Dont fiddle
with your tie, Stephen: there is nothing the matter
with it.

STEPHEN. I beg your pardon. (*He fiddles with his
watch chain instead.*)

LADY BRITOMART. Now are you attending to me,
Stephen?

STEPHEN. Of course, mother.

LADY BRITOMART. No: it's n o t of course. I want
something much more than your everyday matter-of-
course attention. I am going to speak to you very seriously, Stephen. I wish you would let that chain alone.

STEPHEN (*hastily relinquishing the chain*). Have I
done anything to annoy you, mother? If so, it was quite
unintentional.

LADY BRITOMART (*astonished*). Nonsense! (*With
some remorse.*) My poor boy, did you think I was
angry with you?

STEPHEN. What is it, then, mother? You are making me very uneasy.

LADY BRITOMART (*squaring herself at him rather aggressively*). Stephen: may I ask how soon you intend to realize that you are a grown-up man, and that I am only a woman?

STEPHEN (*amazed*). Only a—

LADY BRITOMART. Dont repeat my words, please: it is a most aggravating habit. You must learn to face life seriously, Stephen. I really cannot bear the whole burden of our family affairs any longer. You must advise me: you must assume the responsibility.

STEPHEN. I!

LADY BRITOMART. Yes, you, of course. You were 24 last June. Youve been at Harrow and Cambridge. Youve been to India and Japan. You must know a lot of things, now; unless you have wasted your time most scandalously. Well, a d v i s e me.

STEPHEN (*much perplexed*). You know I have never interfered in the household—

LADY BRITOMART. No: I should think not. I dont want you to order the dinner.

STEPHEN. I mean in our family affairs.

LADY BRITOMART. Well, you must interfere now; for they are getting quite beyond me.

STEPHEN (*troubled*). I have thought sometimes that perhaps I ought; but really, mother, I know so little about them; and what I do know is so painful—it is so impossible to mention some things to you— (*he stops, ashamed*).

LADY BRITOMART. I suppose you mean your father.

STEPHEN (*almost inaudibly*). Yes.

LADY BRITOMART. My dear: we cant go on all our lives not mentioning him. Of course you were quite right not to open the subject until I asked you to; but you are old enough now to be taken into my confidence, and to help me to deal with him about the girls.

STEPHEN. But the girls are all right. They are engaged.

LADY BRITOMART (*complacently*). Yes: I have made a very good match for Sarah. Charles Lomax will be a millionaire at 35. But that is ten years ahead; and in the meantime his trustees cannot under the terms of his father's will allow him more than £800 a year.

STEPHEN. But the will says also that if he increases his income by his own exertions, they may double the increase.

LADY BRITOMART. Charles Lomax's exertions are much more likely to decrease his income than to increase it. Sarah will have to find at least another £800 a year for the next ten years; and even then they will be as poor as church mice. And what about Barbara? I thought Barbara was going to make the most brilliant career of all of you. And what does she do? Joins the Salvation Army; discharges her maid; lives on a pound a week; and walks in one evening with a professor of Greek whom she has picked up in the street, and who pretends to be a Salvationist, and actually plays the big drum for her in public because he has fallen head over ears in love with her.

STEPHEN. I was certainly rather taken aback when I heard they were engaged. Cusins is a very nice fellow, certainly: nobody would ever guess that he was born in Australia; but—

LADY BRITOMART. Oh, Adolphus Cusins will make a very good husband. After all, nobody can say a word against Greek: it stamps a man at once as an educated gentleman. And my family, thank Heaven, is not a pig-headed Tory one. We are Whigs, and believe in liberty. Let snobbish people say what they please: Barbara shall marry, not the man they like, but the man *I* like.

STEPHEN. Of course I was thinking only of his income. However, he is not likely to be extravagant.

LADY BRITOMART. Dont be too sure of that, Stephen. I know your quiet, simple, refined, poetic people like Adolphus—quite content with the best of everything! They cost more than your extravagant people, who are always as mean as they are second rate. No: Barbara will need at least £2000 a year. You see it means two additional households. Besides, my dear, y o u must marry soon. I dont approve of the present fashion of philandering bachelors and late marriages; and I am trying to arrange something for you.

STEPHEN. It's very good of you, mother; but perhaps I had better arrange that for myself.

LADY BRITOMART. Nonsense! you are much too young to begin matchmaking: you would be taken in by some pretty little nobody. Of course I dont mean that you are not to be consulted: you know that as well as I do. (*Stephen closes his lips and is silent.*) Now dont sulk, Stephen.

STEPHEN. I am not sulking, mother. What has all this got to do with—with—with my father?

LADY BRITOMART. My dear Stephen: where is the money to come from? It is easy enough for you and the other children to live on my income as long as we are in the same house; but I cant keep four families in four separate houses. You know how poor my father is: he has barely seven thousand a year now; and really, if he were not the Earl of Stevenage, he would have to give up society. He can do nothing for us. He says, naturally enough, that it is absurd that he should be asked to provide for the children of a man who is rolling in money. You see, Stephen, your father must be fabulously wealthy, because there is always a war going on somewhere.

STEPHEN. You need not remind me of that, mother. I have hardly ever opened a newspaper in my life without seeing our name in it. The Undershaft torpedo! The Undershaft quick firers! The Undershaft ten inch!

the Undershaft disappearing rampart gun! the Undershaft submarine! and now the Undershaft aerial battleship! At Harrow they called me the Woolwich Infant. At Cambridge it was the same. A little brute at King's who was always trying to get up revivals, spoilt my Bible—your first birthday present to me—by writing under my name, " Son and heir to Undershaft and Lazarus, Death and Destruction Dealers: address, Christendom and Judea." But that was not so bad as the way I was kowtowed to everywhere because my father was making millions by selling cannons.

LADY BRITOMART. It is not only the cannons, but the war loans that Lazarus arranges under cover of giving credit for the cannons. You know, Stephen, it's perfectly scandalous. Those two men, Andrew Undershaft and Lazarus, positively have Europe under their thumbs. That is why your father is able to behave as he does. He is above the law. Do you think Bismarck or Gladstone or Disraeli could have openly defied every social and moral obligation all their lives as your father has? They simply wouldnt have dared. I asked Gladstone to take it up. I asked The Times to take it up. I asked the Lord Chamberlain to take it up. But it was just like asking them to declare war on the Sultan. They w o u l d n t. They said they couldnt touch him. I believe they were afraid.

STEPHEN. What could they do? He does not actually break the law.

LADY BRITOMART. Not break the law! He is always breaking the law. He broke the law when he was born: his parents were not married.

STEPHEN. Mother! Is that true?

LADY BRITOMART. Of course it's true: that was why we separated.

STEPHEN. He married without letting you know this!

LADY BRITOMART (rather taken aback by this inference). Oh no. To do Andrew justice, that was not the sort of thing he did. Besides, you know the Undershaft motto: Unashamed. Everybody knew.

STEPHEN. But you said that was why you separated.

LADY BRITOMART. Yes, because he was not content with being a foundling himself: he wanted to disinherit you for another foundling. That was what I couldnt stand.

STEPHEN (*ashamed*). Do you mean for—for—for—

LADY BRITOMART. Dont stammer, Stephen. Speak distinctly.

STEPHEN. But this so frightful to me, mother. To have to speak to you about such things!

LADY BRITOMART. It's not pleasant for me, either, especially if you are still so childish that you must make it worse by a display of embarrassment. It is only in the middle classes, Stephen, that people get into a state of dumb helpless horror when they find that there are wicked people in the world. In our class, we have to decide what is to be done with wicked people; and nothing should disturb our self-possession. Now ask your question properly.

STEPHEN. Mother: you have no consideration for me. For Heaven's sake either treat me as a child, as you always do, and tell me nothing at all; or tell me everything and let me take it as best I can.

LADY BRITOMART. Treat you as a child! What do you mean? It is most unkind and ungrateful of you to say such a thing. You know I have never treated any of you as children. I have always made you my companions and friends, and allowed you perfect freedom to do and say whatever you liked, so long as you liked what I could approve of.

STEPHEN (*desperately*). I daresay we have been the very imperfect children of a very perfect mother; but I do beg you to let me alone for once, and tell me about this horrible business of my father wanting to set me aside for another son.

LADY BRITOMART (*amazed*). Another son! I never said anything of the kind. I never dreamt of such a thing. This is what comes of interrupting me.

STEPHEN. But you said—

LADY BRITOMART (*cutting him short*). Now be a good boy, Stephen, and listen to me patiently. The Undershafts are descended from a foundling in the parish of St. Andrew Undershaft in the city. That was long ago, in the reign of James the First. Well, this foundling was adopted by an armorer and gun-maker. In the course of time the foundling succeeded to the business; and from some notion of gratitude, or some vow or something, he adopted another foundling, and left the business to him. And that foundling did the same. Ever since that, the cannon business has always been left to an adopted foundling named Andrew Undershaft.

STEPHEN. But did they never marry? Were there no legitimate sons?

LADY BRITOMART. Oh yes: they married just as your father did; and they were rich enough to buy land for their own children and leave them well provided for. But they always adopted and trained some foundling to succeed them in the business; and of course they always quarrelled with their wives furiously over it. Your father was adopted in that way; and he pretends to consider himself bound to keep up the tradition and adopt somebody to leave the business to. Of course I was not going to stand that. There may have been some reason for it when the Undershafts could only marry women in their own class, whose sons were not fit to govern great estates. But there could be no excuse for passing over m y son.

STEPHEN (*dubiously*). I am afraid I should make a poor hand of managing a cannon foundry.

LADY BRITOMART. Nonsense! you could easily get a manager and pay him a salary.

STEPHEN. My father evidently had no great opinion of my capacity.

LADY BRITOMART. Stuff, child! you were only a baby: it had nothing to do with your capacity. Andrew did it on principle, just as he did every perverse and wicked thing on principle. When my father remonstrated, Andrew actually told him to his face that history tells us of only two successful institutions: one the Undershaft firm, and the other the Roman Empire under the Antonines. That was because the Antonine emperors all adopted their successors. Such rubbish! The Stevenages are as good as the Antonines, I hope; and you are a Stevenage. But that was Andrew all over. There you have the man! Always clever and unanswerable when he was defending nonsense and wickedness: always awkward and sullen when he had to behave sensibly and decently!

STEPHEN. Then it was on my account that your home life was broken up, mother. I am sorry.

LADY BRITOMART. Well, dear, there were other differences. I really cannot bear an immoral man. I am not a Pharisee, I hope; and I should not have minded his merely d o i n g wrong things: we are none of us perfect. But your father didnt exactly d o wrong things: he said them and thought them: that was what was so dreadful. He really had a sort of religion of wrongness. Just as one doesnt mind men practising immorality so long as they own that they are in the wrong by preaching morality; so I couldnt forgive Andrew for preaching immorality while he practised morality. You would all have grown up without principles, without any knowledge of right and wrong, if he had been in the house. You know, my dear, your father was a very attractive man in some ways. Children did not dislike him; and he took advantage of it to put the wickedest ideas into their heads, and make them quite unmanageable. I did not dislike him myself:

very far from it; but nothing can bridge over moral disagreement.

STEPHEN. All this simply bewilders me, mother. People may differ about matters of opinion, or even about religion; but how can they differ about right and wrong?   Right is right; and wrong is wrong; and if a man cannot distinguish them properly, he is either a fool or a rascal: thats all.

LADY BRITOMART (*touched*). Thats my own boy (*she pats his cheek*)! Your father never could answer that: he used to laugh and get out of it under cover of some affectionate nonsense. And now that you understand the situation, what do you advise me to do?

STEPHEN. Well, what c a n you do?

LADY BRITOMART. I must get the money somehow.

STEPHEN. We cannot take money from him. I had rather go and live in some cheap place like Bedford Square or even Hampstead than take a farthing of his money.

LADY BRITOMART. But after all, Stephen, our present income comes from Andrew.

STEPHEN (*shocked*). I never knew that.

LADY BRITOMART. Well, you surely didnt suppose your grandfather had anything to give me. The Stevenages could not do everything for you. We gave you social position. Andrew had to contribute s o m e- t h i n g. He had a very good bargain, I think.

STEPHEN (*bitterly*). We are utterly dependent on him and his cannons, then?

LADY BRITOMART. Certainly not: the money is settled. But he provided it. So you see it is not a question of taking money from him or not: it is simply a question of how much. I dont want any more for myself.

STEPHEN. Nor do I.

LADY BRITOMART. But Sarah does; and Barbara does. That is, Charles Lomax and Adolphus Cusins will cost them more. So I must put my pride in my pocket and ask for it, I suppose. That is your advice, Stephen, is it not?

STEPHEN. No.

LADY BRITOMART (*sharply*). Stephen!

STEPHEN. Of course if you are determined—

LADY BRITOMART. I am not determined: I ask your advice; and I am waiting for it. I will not have all the responsibility thrown on my shoulders.

STEPHEN (*obstinately*). I would die sooner than ask him for another penny.

LADY BRITOMART (*resignedly*). You mean that *I* must ask him. Very well, Stephen: it shall be as you wish. You will be glad to know that your grandfather concurs. But he thinks I ought to ask Andrew to come here and see the girls. After all, he must have some natural affection for them.

STEPHEN. Ask him here!!!

LADY BRITOMART. Do n o t repeat my words, Stephen. Where else can I ask him?

STEPHEN. I never expected you to ask him at all.

LADY BRITOMART. Now dont tease, Stephen. Come! you see that it is necessary that he should pay us a visit, dont you?

STEPHEN (*reluctantly*). I suppose so, if the girls cannot do without his money.

LADY BRITOMART. Thank you, Stephen: I knew you would give me the right advice when it was properly explained to you. I have asked your father to come this evening. (*Stephen bounds from his seat.*) Dont jump, Stephen: it fidgets me.

STEPHEN (*in utter consternation*). Do you mean to say that my father is coming here to-night—that he may be here at any moment?

LADY BRITOMART (*looking at her watch*). I said nine. (*He gasps. She rises.*) Ring the bell, please. (*Stephen goes to the smaller writing table; presses a button on it; and sits at it with his elbows on the table and his*

head in his hands, outwitted and overwhelmed.) It is
ten minutes to nine yet; and I have to prepare the girls.
I asked Charles Lomax and Adolphus to dinner on purpose that they might be here. Andrew had better see
them in case he should cherish any delusions as to their
being capable of supporting their wives. (*The butler
enters: Lady Britomart goes behind the settee to speak
to him.*) Morrison: go up to the drawingroom and tell
everybody to come down here at once. (*Morrison withdraws. Lady Britomart turns to Stephen.*) Now remember, Stephen: I shall need all your countenance and
authority. (*He rises and tries to recover some vestige
of these attributes.*) Give me a chair, dear. (*He pushes
a chair forward from the wall to where she stands, near
the smaller writing table. She sits down; and he goes
to the arm-chair, into which he throws himself.*) I dont
know how Barbara will take it. Ever since they made
her a major in the Salvation Army she has developed a
propensity to have her own way and order people about
which quite cows me sometimes. It's not ladylike: I'm
sure I dont know where she picked it up. Anyhow, Barbara shant bully m e; but still it's just as well that
your father should be here before she has time to refuse
to meet him or make a fuss. Dont look nervous, Stephen;
it will only encourage Barbara to make difficulties. *I*
am nervous enough, goodness knows; but I dont shew it.

*Sarah and Barbara come in with their respective young
men, Charles Lomax and Adolphus Cusins. Sarah is
slender, bored, and mundane. Barbara is robuster, jol-
lier, much more energetic. Sarah is fashionably dressed:
Barbara is in Salvation Army uniform. Lomax, a young
man about town, is like many other young men about
town. He is afflicted with a frivolous sense of humor
which plunges him at the most inopportune moments
into paroxysms of imperfectly suppressed laughter.
Cusins is a spectacled student, slight, thin haired, and
sweet voiced, with a more complex form of Lomax's*

complaint. His sense of humor is intellectual and subtle, and is complicated by an appalling temper. The life-long struggle of a benevolent temperament and a high conscience against impulses of inhuman ridicule and fierce impatience has set up a chronic strain which has visibly wrecked his constitution. He is a most implacable, determined, tenacious, intolerant person who by mere force of character presents himself as—and indeed actually is—considerate, gentle, explanatory, even mild and apologetic, capable possibly of murder, but not of cruelty or coarseness. By the operation of some instinct which is not merciful enough to blind him with the illusions of love, he is obstinately bent on marrying Barbara. Lomax likes Sarah and thinks it will be rather a lark to marry her. Consequently he has not attempted to resist Lady Britomart's arrangements to that end.

All four look as if they had been having a good deal of fun in the drawingroom. The girls enter first, leaving the swains outside. Sarah comes to the settee. Barbara comes in after her and stops at the door.

BARBARA. Are Cholly and Dolly to come in?

LADY BRITOMART (*forcibly*). Barbara: I will not have Charles called Cholly: the vulgarity of it positively makes me ill.

BARBARA. It's all right, mother. Cholly is quite correct nowadays. Are they to come in?

LADY BRITOMART. Yes, if they will behave themselves.

BARBARA (*through the door*). Come in, Dolly, and behave yourself.

Barbara comes to her mother's writing table. Cusins enters smiling, and wanders towards Lady Britomart.

SARAH (*calling*). Come in, Cholly. (*Lomax enters, controlling his features very imperfectly, and places himself vaguely between Sarah and Barbara.*)

LADY BRITOMART (*peremptorily*). Sit down, all of you. (*They sit. Cusins crosses to the window and seats*

*himself there. Lomax takes a chair. Barbara sits at
the writing table and Sarah on the settee.*) I dont in
the least know what you are laughing at, Adolphus. I
am surprised at you, though I expected nothing better
from Charles Lomax.

CUSINS (*in a remarkably gentle voice*). Barbara has
been trying to teach me the West Ham Salvation March.

LADY BRITOMART. I see nothing to laugh at in that;
nor shòuld you if you are really converted.

CUSINS (*sweetly*). You were not present. It was
really funny, I believe.

LOMAX. Ripping.

LADY BRITOMART. Be quiet, Charles. Now listen to
me, children. Your father is coming here this evening.
(*General stupefaction.*)

LOMAX (*remonstrating*). Oh I say!

LADY BRITOMART. You are not called on to say anything, Charles.

SARAH. Are you serious, mother?

LADY BRITOMART. Of course I am serious. It is on
your account, Sarah, and also on Charles's. (*Silence.
Charles looks painfully unworthy.*) I hope you are not
going to object, Barbara.

BARBARA. I! why should I? My father has a soul
to be saved like anybody else. Hes quite welcome as
far as I am concerned.

LOMAX (*still remonstrant*). But really, dont you
know! Oh I say!

LADY BRITOMART (*frigidly*). What do you wish to
convey, Charles?

LOMAX. Well, you must admit that this is a bit thick.

LADY BRITOMART (*turning with ominous suavity to
Cusins*). Adolphus: you are a professor of Greek. Can
you translate Charles Lomax's remarks into reputable
English for us?

CUSINS (*cautiously*). If I may say so, Lady Brit, I
think Charles has rather happily expressed what we all

feel. Homer, speaking of Autolycus, uses the same phrase. πυκινὸν δόμον ἐλθεῖν means a bit thick.

LOMAX (*handsomely*). Not that I mind, you know, if Sarah dont.

LADY BRITOMART (*crushingly*). Thank you. Have I y o u r permission, Adolphus, to invite my own husband to my own house?

CUSINS (*gallantly*). You have my unhesitating support in everything you do.

LADY BRITOMART. Sarah: have you nothing to say?

SARAH. Do you mean that he is coming regularly to live here?

LADY BRITOMART. Certainly not. The spare room is ready for him if he likes to stay for a day or two and see a little more of you; but there are limits.

SARAH. Well, he cant eat us, I suppose. *I* dont mind.

LOMAX (*chuckling*). I wonder how the old man will take it.

LADY BRITOMART. Much as the old woman will, no doubt, Charles.

LOMAX (*abashed*). I didnt mean—at least—

LADY BRITOMART. You didnt t h i n k, Charles. You never do; and the result is, you never mean anything. And now please attend to me, children. Your father will be quite a stranger to us.

LOMAX. I suppose he hasnt seen Sarah since she was a little kid.

LADY BRITOMART. Not since she was a little kid, Charles, as you express it with that elegance of diction and refinement of thought that seem never to desert you. Accordingly—er— (*impatiently*) Now I have forgotten what I was going to say. That comes of your provoking me to be sarcastic, Charles. Adolphus: will you kindly tell me where I was.

CUSINS (*sweetly*). You were saying that as Mr. Undershaft has not seen his children since they were babies, he will form his opinion of the way you have

brought them up from their behavior to-night, and that
therefore you wish us all to be particularly careful to
conduct ourselves well, especially Charles.

LOMAX. Look here: Lady Brit didnt say that.

LADY BRITOMART (*vehemently*). I did, Charles.
Adolphus's recollection is perfectly correct. It is most
important that you should be good; and I do beg you
for once not to pair off into opposite corners and giggle
and whisper while I am speaking to your father.

BARBARA. All right, mother. We'll do you credit.

LADY BRITOMART. Remember, Charles, that Sarah
will want to feel proud of you instead of ashamed of
you.

LOMAX. Oh I say! theres nothing to be exactly proud
of, dont you know.

LADY BRITOMART. Well, try and look as if there was.
*Morrison, pale and dismayed, breaks into the room in
unconcealed disorder.*

MORRISON. Might I speak a word to you, my lady?

LADY BRITOMART. Nonsense! Shew him up.

MORRISON. Yes, my lady. (*He goes.*)

LOMAX. Does Morrison know who it is?

LADY BRITOMART. Of course. Morrison has always
been with us.

LOMAX. It must be a regular corker for him, dont
you know.

LADY BRITOMART. Is this a moment to get on my
nerves, Charles, with your outrageous expressions?

LOMAX. But this is something out of the ordinary,
really—

MORRISON (*at the door*). The—er—Mr. Undershaft.
(*He retreats in confusion.*)

*Andrew Undershaft comes in. All rise. Lady Brito-
mart meets him in the middle of the room behind the
settee.*

*Andrew is, on the surface, a stoutish, easygoing elderly
man, with kindly patient manners, and an engaging sim-*

plicity of character. But he has a watchful, deliberate, waiting, listening face, and formidable reserves of power, both bodily and mental, in his capacious chest and long head. His gentleness is partly that of a strong man who has learnt by experience that his natural grip hurts ordinary people unless he handles them very carefully, and partly the mellowness of age and success. He is also a little shy in his present very delicate situation.

LADY BRITOMART. Good evening, Andrew.

UNDERSHAFT. How d'ye do, my dear.

LADY BRITOMART. You look a good deal older.

UNDERSHAFT (*apologetically*). I a m somewhat older. (*With a touch of courtship.*) Time has stood still with you.

LADY BRITOMART (*promptly*). Rubbish! This is your family.

UNDERSHAFT (*surprised*). Is it so large? I am sorry to say my memory is failing very badly in some things. (*He offers his hand with paternal kindness to Lomax.*)

LOMAX (*jerkily shaking his hand*). Ahdedoo.

UNDERSHAFT. I can see you are my eldest. I am very glad to meet you again, my boy.

LOMAX (*remonstrating*). No but look here dont you know— (*Overcome.*) Oh I say!

LADY BRITOMART (*recovering from momentary speechlessness*). Andrew: do you mean to say that you dont remember how many children you have?

UNDERSHAFT. Well, I am afraid I—. They have grown so much—er. Am I making any ridiculous mistake? I may as well confess: I recollect only one son. But so many things have happened since, of course—er—

LADY BRITOMART (*decisively*). Andrew: you are talking nonsense. Of course you have only one son.

UNDERSHAFT. Perhaps you will be good enough to introduce me, my dear.

LADY BRITOMART. That is Charles Lomax, who is engaged to Sarah.

UNDERSHAFT. My dear sir, I beg your pardon.

LOMAX. Notatall. Delighted, I assure you.

LADY BRITOMART. This is Stephen.

UNDERSHAFT (*bowing*). Happy to make your acquaintance, Mr. Stephen. Then (*going to Cusins*) y o u must be my son. (*Taking Cusins' hands in his.*) How are you, my young friend? (*To Lady Britomart.*) He is very like you, my love.

CUSINS. You flatter me, Mr. Undershaft. My name is Cusins: engaged to Barbara. (*Very explicitly.*) That is Major Barbara Undershaft, of the Salvation Army. That is Sarah, your second daughter. This is Stephen Undershaft, your son.

UNDERSHAFT. My dear Stephen, I b e g your pardon.

STEPHEN. Not at all.

UNDERSHAFT. Mr. Cusins: I am much indebted to you for explaining so precisely. (*Turning to Sarah.*) Barbara, my dear—

SARAH (*prompting him*). Sarah.

UNDERSHAFT. Sarah, of course. (*They shake hands. He goes over to Barbara.*) Barbara—I am right this time, I hope.

BARBARA. Quite right. (*They shake hands.*)

LADY BRITOMART (*resuming command*). Sit down, all of you. Sit down, Andrew. (*She comes forward and sits on the settee. Cusins also brings his chair forward on her left. Barbara and Stephen resume their seats. Lomax gives his chair to Sarah and goes for another.*)

UNDERSHAFT. Thank you, my love.

LOMAX (*conversationally, as he brings a chair forward between the writing table and the settee, and offers it to Undershaft*). Takes you some time to find out exactly where you are, dont it?

UNDERSHAFT (*accepting the chair*). That is not what

embarrasses me, Mr. Lomax. My difficulty is that if I play the part of a father, I shall produce the effect of an intrusive stranger; and if I play the part of a discreet stranger, I may appear a callous father.

LADY BRITOMART. There is no need for you to play any part at all, Andrew. You had much better be sincere and natural.

UNDERSHAFT (*submissively*). Yes, my dear: I daresay that will be best. (*Making himself comfortable.*) Well, here I am. Now what can I do for you all?

LADY BRITOMART. You need not do anything, Andrew. You are one of the family. You can sit with us and enjoy yourself.

Lomax's too long suppressed mirth explodes in agonized neighings.

LADY BRITOMART (*outraged*). Charles Lomax: if you can behave yourself, behave yourself. If not, leave the room.

LOMAX. I'm awfully sorry, Lady Brit; but really, you know, upon my soul! (*He sits on the settee between Lady Britomart and Undershaft, quite overcome.*)

BARBARA. Why dont you laugh if you want to, Cholly? It's good for your inside.

LADY BRITOMART. Barbara: you have had the education of a lady. Please let your father see that; and dont talk like a street girl.

UNDERSHAFT. Never mind me, my dear. As you know, I am not a gentleman; and I was never educated.

LOMAX (*encouragingly*). Nobody'd know it, I assure you. You look all right, you know.

CUSINS. Let me advise you to study Greek, Mr. Undershaft. Greek scholars are privileged men. Few of them know Greek; and none of them know anything else; but their position is unchallengeable. Other languages are the qualifications of waiters and commercial travellers: Greek is to a man of position what the hallmark is to silver.

BARBARA. Dolly: dont be insincere. Cholly: fetch your concertina and play something for us.

LOMAX (*doubtfully to Undershaft*). Perhaps that sort of thing isnt in your line, eh?

UNDERSHAFT. I am particularly fond of music.

LOMAX (*delighted*). Are you? Then I'll get it. (*He goes upstairs for the instrument.*)

UNDERSHAFT. Do you play, Barbara?

BARBARA. Only the tambourine. But Cholly's teaching me the concertina.

UNDERSHAFT. Is Cholly also a member of the Salvation Army?

BARBARA. No: he says it's bad form to be a dissenter. But I dont despair of Cholly. I made him come yesterday to a meeting at the dock gates, and took the collection in his hat.

LADY BRITOMART. It is not my doing, Andrew. Barbara is old enough to take her own way. She has no father to advise her.

BARBARA. Oh yes she has. There are no orphans in the Salvation Army.

UNDERSHAFT. Your father there has a great many children and plenty of experience, eh?

BARBARA (*looking at him with quick interest and nodding*). Just so. How did y o u come to understand that? (*Lomax is heard at the door trying the concertina.*)

LADY BRITOMART. Come in, Charles. Play us something at once.

LOMAX. Righto! (*He sits down in his former place, and preludes.*)

UNDERSHAFT. One moment, Mr. Lomax. I am rather interested in the Salvation Army. Its motto might be my own: Blood and Fire.

LOMAX (*shocked*). But not your sort of blood and fire, you know.

UNDERSHAFT. My sort of blood cleanses: my sort of fire purifies.

BARBARA. So do ours. Come down to-morrow to my shelter—the West Ham shelter—and see what we're doing. We're going to march to a great meeting in the Assembly Hall at Mile End. Come and see the shelter and then march with us: it will do you a lot of good. Can you play anything?

UNDERSHAFT. In my youth I earned pennies, and even shillings occasionally, in the streets and in public house parlors by my natural talent for stepdancing. Later on, I became a member of the Undershaft orchestral society, and performed passably on the tenor trombone.

LOMAX (*scandalized*). Oh I say!

BARBARA. Many a sinner has played himself into heaven on the trombone, thanks to the Army.

LOMAX (*to Barbara, still rather shocked*). Yes; but what about the cannon business, dont you know? (*To Undershaft.*) Getting into heaven is not exactly in your line, is it?

LADY BRITOMART. Charles!!!

LOMAX. Well; but it stands to reason, dont it? The cannon business may be necessary and all that: we cant get on without cannons; but it isnt right, you know. On the other hand, there may be a certain amount of tosh about the Salvation Army—I belong to the Established Church myself—but still you cant deny that it's religion; and you cant go against religion, can you? At least unless youre downright immoral, dont you know.

UNDERSHAFT. You hardly appreciate my position, Mr. Lomax—

LOMAX (*hastily*). I'm not saying anything against you personally, you know.

UNDERSHAFT. Quite so, quite so. But consider for a moment. Here I am, a manufacturer of mutilation and murder. I find myself in a specially amiable humor just now because, this morning, down at the foundry, we blew twenty-seven dummy soldiers into fragments with a gun which formerly destroyed only thirteen.

LOMAX (*leniently*). Well, the more destructive war becomes, the sooner it will be abolished, eh?

UNDERSHAFT. Not at all. The more destructive war becomes the more fascinating we find it. No, Mr. Lomax: I am obliged to you for making the usual excuse for my trade; but I am not ashamed of it. I am not one of those men who keep their morals and their business in watertight compartments. All the spare money my trade rivals spend on hospitals, cathedrals and other receptacles for conscience money, I devote to experiments and researches in improved methods of destroying life and property. I have always done so; and I always shall. Therefore your Christmas card moralities of peace on earth and goodwill among men are of no use to me. Your Christianity, which enjoins you to resist not evil, and to turn the other cheek, would make me a bankrupt. M y morality—m y religion—must have a place for cannons and torpedoes in it.

STEPHEN (*coldly—almost sullenly*). You speak as if there were half a dozen moralities and religions to choose from, instead of one true morality and one true religion.

UNDERSHAFT. For me there is only one true morality; but it might not fit you, as you do not manufacture aerial battleships. There is only one true morality for every man; but every man has not the same true morality.

LOMAX (*overtaxed*). Would you mind saying that again? I didnt quite follow it.

CUSINS. It's quite simple. As Euripides says, one man's meat is another man's poison morally as well as physically.

UNDERSHAFT. Precisely.

LOMAX. Oh, t h a t. Yes, yes, yes. True. True.

STEPHEN. In other words, some men are honest and some are scoundrels.

BARBARA. Bosh. There are no scoundrels.

UNDERSHAFT. Indeed? Are there any good men?

BARBARA. No. Not one. There are neither good men nor scoundrels: there are just children of one Father; and the sooner they stop calling one another names the better. You neednt talk to me: I know them. Ive had scores of them through my hands: scoundrels, criminals, infidels, philanthropists, missionaries, county councillors, all sorts. Theyre all just the same sort of sinner; and theres the same salvation ready for them all.

UNDERSHAFT. May I ask have you ever saved a maker of cannons?

BARBARA. No. Will you let me try?

UNDERSHAFT. Well, I will make a bargain with you. If I go to see you to-morrow in your Salvation Shelter, will you come the day after to see me in my cannon works?

BARBARA. Take care. It may end in your giving up the cannons for the sake of the Salvation Army.

UNDERSHAFT. Are you sure it will not end in your giving up the Salvation Army for the sake of the cannons?

BARBARA. I will take my chance of that.

UNDERSHAFT. And I will take my chance of the other. (*They shake hands on it.*) Where is your shelter?

BARBARA. In West Ham. At the sign of the cross. Ask anybody in Canning Town. Where are your works?

UNDERSHAFT. In Perivale St. Andrews. At the sign of the sword. Ask anybody in Europe.

LOMAX. Hadnt I better play something?

BARBARA. Yes. Give us Onward, Christian Soldiers.

LOMAX. Well, thats rather a strong order to begin with, dont you know. Suppose I sing Thou'rt passing hence, my brother. It's much the same tune.

BARBARA. It's too melancholy. You get saved,

Cholly; and youll pass hence, my brother, without making such a fuss about it.

Lady Britomart. Really, Barbara, you go on as if religion were a pleasant subject. Do have some sense of propriety.

Undershaft. I do not find it an unpleasant subject, my dear. It is the only one that capable people really care for.

Lady Britomart (*looking at her watch*). Well, if you are determined to have it, I insist on having it in a proper and respectable way. Charles: ring for prayers. (*General amazement. Stephen rises in dismay.*)

Lomax (*rising*). Oh I say!

Undershaft (*rising*). I am afraid I must be going.

Lady Britomart. You cannot go now, Andrew: it would be most improper. Sit down. What will the servants think?

Undershaft. My dear: I have conscientious scruples. May I suggest a compromise? If Barbara will conduct a little service in the drawingroom, with Mr. Lomax as organist, I will attend it willingly. I will even take part, if a trombone can be procured.

Lady Britomart. Dont mock, Andrew.

Undershaft (*shocked—to Barbara*). You dont think I am mocking, my love, I hope.

Barbara. No, of course not; and it wouldnt matter if you were: half the Army came to their first meeting for a lark. (*Rising.*) Come along. Come, Dolly, Come, Cholly. (*She goes out with Undershaft, who opens the door for her. Cusins rises.*)

Lady Britomart. I will not be disobeyed by everybody. Adolphus: sit down. Charles: you may go. You are not fit for prayers: you cannot keep your countenance.

Lomax. Oh I say! (*He goes out.*)

Lady Britomart (*continuing*). But you, Adolphus,

can behave yourself if you choose to. I insist on your staying.

CUSINS. My dear Lady Brit: there are things in the family prayer book that I couldnt bear to hear you say.

LADY BRITOMART. What things, pray?

CUSINS. Well, you would have to say before all the servants that we have done things we ought not to have done, and left undone things we ought to have done, and that there is no health in us. I cannot bear to hear you doing yourself such an injustice, and Barbara such an injustice. As for myself, I flatly deny it: I have done my best. I shouldnt dare to marry Barbara—I couldnt look you in the face—if it were true. So I must go to the drawingroom.

LADY BRITOMART (*offended*). Well, go. (*He starts for the door.*) And remember this, Adolphus (*he turns to listen*): I have a very strong suspicion that you went to the Salvation Army to worship Barbara and nothing else. And I quite appreciate the very clever way in which you systematically humbug me. I have found you out. Take care Barbara doesnt. Thats all.

CUSINS (*with unruffled sweetness*). Dont tell on me. (*He goes out.*)

LADY BRITOMART. Sarah: if you want to go, go. Anything's better than to sit there as if you wished you were a thousand miles away.

SARAH (*languidly*). Very well, mamma. (*She goes.*)

Lady Britomart, with a sudden flounce, gives way to a little gust of tears.

STEPHEN (*going to her*). Mother: whats the matter?

LADY BRITOMART (*swishing away her tears with her handkerchief*). Nothing. Foolishness. You can go with him, too, if you like, and leave me with the servants.

STEPHEN. Oh, you mustnt think that, mother. I—I dont like him.

LADY BRITOMART. The others do. That is the injustice of a woman's lot. A woman has to bring up her children; and that means to restrain them, to deny them things they want, to set them tasks, to punish them when they do wrong, to do all the unpleasant things. And then the father, who has nothing to do but pet them and spoil them, comes in when all her work is done and steals their affection from her.

STEPHEN. He has not stolen our affection from you. It is only curiosity.

LADY BRITOMART (*violently*). I wont be consoled, Stephen. There is nothing the matter with me. (*She rises and goes towards the door.*)

STEPHEN. Where are you going, mother?

LADY BRITOMART. To the drawingroom, of course. (*She goes out. Onward, Christian Soldiers, on the concertina, with tambourine accompaniment, is heard when the door opens.*) Are you coming, Stephen?

STEPHEN. No. Certainly not. (*She goes. He sits down on the settee, with compressed lips and an expression of strong dislike.*)

END OF ACT I.

ACT II

The yard of the West Ham shelter of the Salvation Army is a cold place on a January morning. The building itself, an old warehouse, is newly whitewashed. Its gabled end projects into the yard in the middle, with a door on the ground floor, and another in the loft above it without any balcony or ladder, but with a pulley rigged over it for hoisting sacks. Those who come from this central gable end into the yard have the gateway leading to the street on their left, with a stone horse-trough just beyond it, and, on the right, a penthouse shielding a table from the weather. There are forms at the table; and on them are seated a man and a woman, both much down on their luck, finishing a meal of bread (one thick slice each, with margarine and golden syrup) and diluted milk.

The man, a workman out of employment, is young, agile, a talker, a poser, sharp enough to be capable of anything in reason except honesty or altruistic considerations of any kind. The woman is a commonplace old bundle of poverty and hard-worn humanity. She looks sixty and probably is forty-five. If they were rich people, gloved and muffed and well wrapped up in furs and overcoats, they would be numbed and miserable; for it is a grindingly cold, raw, January day; and a glance at the background of grimy warehouses and leaden sky visible over the whitewashed walls of the yard would drive any idle rich person straight to the Mediterranean. But these two, being no more troubled with visions of the Mediterranean than of the moon, and being compelled to keep more of their clothes in the pawnshop, and less on their persons, in winter than in summer, are not de-

*pressed by the cold: rather are they stung into vivacity,
to which their meal has just now given an almost jolly
turn. The man takes a pull at his mug, and then gets
up and moves about the yard with his hands deep in his
pockets, occasionally breaking into a stepdance.*

THE WOMAN. Feel better arter your meal, sir?

THE MAN. No. Call that a meal! Good enough for
you, praps; but wot is it to me, an intelligent workin
man.

THE WOMAN. Workin man! Wot are you?

THE MAN. Painter.

THE WOMAN (*sceptically*). Yus, I dessay.

THE MAN. Yus, you dessay! I know. Every loafer
that cant do nothink calls isself a painter. Well, I'm a
real painter: grainer, finisher, thirty-eight bob a week
when I can get it.

THE WOMAN. Then why dont you go and get it?

THE MAN. I'll tell you why. Fust: I'm intelligent
—fffff! it's rotten cold here (*he dances a step or two*)—
yes: intelligent beyond the station o life into which it
has pleased the capitalists to call me; and they dont like
a man that sees through em. Second, an intelligent bein
needs a doo share of appiness; so I drink somethink
cruel when I get the chawnce. Third, I stand by my
class and do as little as I can so's to leave arf the job
for me fellow workers. Fourth, I'm fly enough to know
wots inside the law and wots outside it; and inside it
I do as the capitalists do: pinch wot I can lay me ands
on. In a proper state of society I am sober, industrious
and honest: in Rome, so to speak, I do as the Romans
do. Wots the consequence? When trade is bad—and
it's rotten bad just now—and the employers az to sack
arf their men, they generally start on me.

THE WOMAN. Whats your name?

THE MAN. Price. Bronterre O'Brien Price. Usually called Snobby Price, for short.

THE WOMAN. Snobby's a carpenter, aint it? You said you was a painter.

PRICE. Not that kind of snob, but the genteel sort. I'm too uppish, owing to my intelligence, and my father being a Chartist and a reading, thinking man: a stationer, too. I'm none of your common hewers of wood and drawers of water; and dont you forget it. (*He returns to his seat at the table, and takes up his mug.*) Wots y o u r name?

THE WOMAN. Rummy Mitchens, sir.

PRICE (*quaffing the remains of his milk to her*). Your elth, Miss Mitchens.

RUMMY (*correcting him*). Missis Mitchens.

PRICE. Wot! Oh Rummy, Rummy! Respectable married woman, Rummy, gittin rescued by the Salvation Army by pretendin to be a bad un. Same old game!

RUMMY. What am I to do? I cant starve. Them Salvation lasses is dear good girls; but the better you are, the worse they likes to think you were before they rescued you. Why shouldnt they av a bit o credit, poor loves? theyre worn to rags by their work. And where would they get the money to rescue us if we was to let on we're no worse than other people? You know what ladies and gentlemen are.

PRICE. Thievin swine! Wish I ad their job, Rummy, all the same. Wot does Rummy stand for? Pet name praps?

RUMMY. Short for Romola.

PRICE. For wot!?

RUMMY. Romola. It was out of a new book. Somebody me mother wanted me to grow up like.

PRICE. We're companions in misfortune, Rummy. Both on us got names that nobody cawnt pronounce. Consequently I'm Snobby and youre Rummy because Bill and Sally wasnt good enough for our parents. Such is life!

RUMMY. Who saved you, Mr. Price? Was it Major Barbara?

PRICE. No: I come here on my own. I'm goin to be Bronterre O'Brien Price, the converted painter. I know wot they like. I'll tell em how I blasphemed and gambled and wopped my poor old mother——

RUMMY (*shocked*). Used you to beat your mother?

PRICE. Not likely. She used to beat me. No matter: you come and listen to the converted painter, and youll hear how she was a pious woman that taught me me prayers at er knee, an how I used to come home drunk and drag her out o bed be er snow white airs, an lam into er with the poker.

RUMMY. Thats whats so unfair to us women. Your confessions is just as big lies as ours: you dont tell what you really done no more than us; but you men can tell your lies right out at the meetins and be made much of for it; while the sort o confessions we az to make az to be whispered to one lady at a time. It aint right, spite of all their piety.

PRICE. Right! Do you spose the Army 'd be allowed if it went and did right? Not much. It combs our air and makes us good little blokes to be robbed and put upon. But I'll play the game as good as any of em. I'll see somebody struck by lightnin, or hear a voice sayin " Snobby Price: where will you spend eternity? " I'll ave a time of it, I tell you.

RUMMY. You wont be let drink, though.

PRICE. I'll take it out in gorspellin, then. I dont want to drink if I can get fun enough any other way.

Jenny Hill, a pale, overwrought, pretty Salvation lass of 18, comes in through the yard gate, leading Peter Shirley, a half hardened, half worn-out elderly man, weak with hunger.

JENNY (*supporting him*). Come! pluck up. I'll get you something to eat. Youll be all right then.

PRICE (*rising and hurrying officiously to take the old*

man off Jenny's hands).   Poor old man!   Cheer up, brother: youll find rest and peace and appiness ere. Hurry up with the food, miss: e's fair done.   (*Jenny hurries into the shelter.*)   Ere, buck up, daddy! shes fetchin y'a thick slice o breadn treacle, an a mug o sky-blue.   (*He seats him at the corner of the table.*)

RUMMY (*gaily*).   Keep up your old art!   Never say die!

SHIRLEY.   I'm not an old man.   I'm ony 46.   I'm as good as ever I was.   The grey patch come in my hair before I was thirty.   All it wants is three pennorth o hair dye: am I to be turned on the streets to starve for it?   Holy God!   I've worked ten to twelve hours a day since I was thirteen, and paid my way all through; and now am I to be thrown into the gutter and my job given to a young man that can do it no better than me because Ive black hair that goes white at the first change?

PRICE (*cheerfully*).   No good jawrin about it.   Youre ony a jumped-up, jerked-off, orspittle-turned-out incurable of an ole workin man: who cares about you?   Eh?   Make the thievin swine give you a meal: theyve stole many a one from you.   Get a bit o your own back. (*Jenny returns with the usual meal.*)   There you are, brother.   Awsk a blessin an tuck that into you.

SHIRLEY (*looking at it ravenously but not touching it, and crying like a child*).   I never took anything before.

JENNY (*petting him*).   Come, come! the Lord sends it to you: he wasnt above taking bread from his friends; and why should you be?   Besides, when we find you a job you can pay us for it if you like.

SHIRLEY (*eagerly*).   Yes, yes: thats true.   I can pay you back: its only a loan.   (*Shivering.*)   Oh Lord! oh Lord!   (*He turns to the table and attacks the meal ravenously.*)

JENNY.   Well, Rummy, are you more comfortable now?

Rummy. God bless you, lovey! youve fed my body and saved my soul, havent you? (*Jenny, touched, kisses her.*) Sit down and rest a bit: you must be ready to drop.

Jenny. Ive been going hard since morning. But theres more work than we can do. I mustnt stop.

Rummy. Try a prayer for just two minutes. Youll work all the better after.

Jenny (*her eyes lighting up*). Oh isnt it wonderful how a few minutes prayer revives you! I was quite lightheaded at twelve o'clock, I was so tired; but Major Barbara just sent me to pray for five minutes; and I was able to go on as if I had only just begun. (*To Price.*) Did you have a piece of bread?

Price (*with unction*). Yes, miss; but Ive got the piece that I value more; and thats the peace that passeth hall hannerstennin.

Rummy (*fervently*). Glory Hallelujah!

Bill Walker, a rough customer of about 25, appears at the yard gate and looks malevolently at Jenny.

Jenny. That makes me so happy. When you say that, I feel wicked for loitering here. I must get to work again.

She is hurrying to the shelter, when the new-comer moves quickly up to the door and intercepts her. His manner is so threatening that she retreats as he comes at her truculently, driving her down the yard.

Bill. I know you. Youre the one that took away my girl. Youre the one that set er agen me. Well, I'm goin to av er out. Not that I care a curse for her or you: see? But I'll let er know; and I'll let y o u know. I'm goin to give er a doin thatll teach er to cut away from me. Now in with you and tell er to come out afore I come in and kick er out. Tell er Bill Walker wants er. She'll know what that means; and if she keeps me waitin itll be worse. You stop to jaw back at me; and I'll start on you: d'ye hear? Theres your way. In you go. (*He takes her by the arm and slings*

*her towards the door of the shelter. She falls on her
hand and knee. Rummy helps her up again.*)

PRICE (*rising, and venturing irresolutely towards
Bill*). Easy there, mate. She aint doin you no arm.

BILL. Who are you callin mate? (*Standing over him
threateningly.*) Youre goin to stand up for her, are
you? Put up your ands.

RUMMY (*running indignantly to him to scold him*).
Oh, you great brute— (*He instantly swings his left
hand back against her face. She screams and reels back
to the trough, where she sits down, covering her bruised
face with her hands and rocking herself and moaning
with pain.*)

JENNY (*going to her*). Oh God forgive you! How
could you strike an old woman like that?

BILL (*seizing her by the hair so violently that she also
screams, and tearing her away from the old woman*).
You Gawd forgive me again and I'll Gawd forgive you
one on the jaw thatll stop you prayin for a week.
(*Holding her and turning fiercely on Price.*) Av you
anything to say agen it? Eh?

PRICE (*intimidated*). No, matey: she aint anything
to do with me.

BILL. Good job for you! I'd put two meals into you
and fight you with one finger after, you starved cur.
(*To Jenny.*) Now are you goin to fetch out Mog Habbijam; or am I to knock your face off you and fetch her
myself?

JENNY (*writhing in his grasp*). Oh please someone
go in and tell Major Barbara— (*she screams again as
he wrenches her head down; and Price and Rummy flee
into the shelter*).

BILL. You want to go in and tell your Major of me,
do you?

JENNY. Oh please dont drag my hair. Let me go.

BILL. Do you or dont you? (*She stifles a scream.*)
Yes or no.

JENNY. God give me strength—

BILL (*striking her with his fist in the face*). Go and
shew her that, and tell her if she wants one like it to
come and interfere with me. (*Jenny, crying with pain,
goes into the shed. He goes to the form and addresses
the old man.*) Here: finish your mess; and get out o
my way.

SHIRLEY (*springing up and facing him fiercely, with
the mug in his hand*). You take a liberty with me, and
I'll smash you over the face with the mug and cut your
eye out. Aint you satisfied—young whelps like you—
with takin the bread out o the mouths of your elders
that have brought you up and slaved for you, but you
must come shovin and cheekin and bullyin in here, where
the bread o charity is sickenin in our stummicks?

BILL (*contemptuously, but backing a little*). Wot
good are you, you old palsy mug? Wot good are you?

SHIRLEY. As good as you and better. I'll do a day's
work agen you or any fat young soaker of your age.
Go and take my job at Horrockses, where I worked for
ten year. They want young men there: they cant afford
to keep men over forty-five. Theyre very sorry—give
you a character and happy to help you to get anything
suited to your years—sure a steady man wont be long
out of a job. Well, let em try y o u. Theyll find the
differ. What do y o u know? Not as much as how to
beeyave yourself—layin your dirty fist across the mouth
of a respectable woman!

BILL. Dont provoke me to lay it acrost yours: d'ye
hear?

SHIRLEY (*with blighting contempt*). Yes: you like
an old man to hit, dont you, when youve finished with
the women. I aint seen you hit a young one yet.

BILL (*stung*). You lie, you old soupkitchener, you.
There was a young man here. Did I offer to hit him
or did I not?

SHIRLEY. Was he starvin or was he not? Was he

a man or only a crosseyed thief an a loafer? Would you hit my son-in-law's brother?

BILL. Who's he?

SHIRLEY. Todger Fairmile o Balls Pond. Him that won £20 off the Japanese wrastler at the music hall by standin out 17 minutes 4 seconds agen him.

BILL (*sullenly*). I'm no music hall wrastler. Can he box?

SHIRLEY. Yes: an you cant.

BILL. Wot! I cant, cant I? Wots that you say (*threatening him*)?

SHIRLEY (*not budging an inch*). Will you box Todger Fairmile if I put him on to you? Say the word.

BILL (*subsiding with a slouch*). I'll stand up to any man alive, if he was ten Todger Fairmiles. But I dont set up to be a perfessional.

SHIRLEY (*looking down on him with unfathomable disdain*). You box! Slap an old woman with the back o your hand! You hadnt even the sense to hit her where a magistrate couldnt see the mark of it, you silly young lump of conceit and ignorance. Hit a girl in the jaw and ony make her cry! If Todger Fairmile'd done it, she wouldnt a got up inside o ten minutes, no more than you would if he got on to you. Yah! I'd set about you myself if I had a week's feedin in me instead o two months starvation. (*He returns to the table to finish his meal.*)

BILL (*following him and stooping over him to drive the taunt in*). You lie! you have the bread and treacle in you that you come here to beg.

SHIRLEY (*bursting into tears*). Oh God! it's true: I'm only an old pauper on the scrap heap. (*Furiously.*) But youll come to it yourself; and then youll know. Youll come to it sooner than a teetotaller like me, fillin yourself with gin at this hour o the mornin!

BILL. I'm no gin drinker, you old liar; but when I want to give my girl a bloomin good idin I like to av a bit o devil in me: see? An here I am, talkin to a rotten old blighter like you sted o givin her wot for. (*Working himself into a rage.*) I'm goin in there to fetch her out. (*He makes vengefully for the shelter door.*)

SHIRLEY. Youre goin to the station on a stretcher, more likely; and theyll take the gin and the devil out of you there when they get you inside. You mind what youre about: the major here is the Earl o Stevenage's granddaughter.

BILL (*checked*). Garn!

SHIRLEY. Youll see.

BILL (*his resolution oozing*). Well, I aint done nothin to er.

SHIRLEY. Spose she said you did! who'd believe you?

BILL (*very uneasy, skulking back to the corner of the penthouse*). Gawd! theres no jastice in this country. To think wot them people can do! I'm as good as er.

SHIRLEY. Tell her so. Its just what a fool like you would do.

Barbara, brisk and businesslike, comes from the shelter with a note book, and addresses herself to Shirley. Bill, cowed, sits down in the corner on a form, and turns his back on them.

BARBARA. Good morning.

SHIRLEY (*standing up and taking off his hat*). Good morning, miss.

BARBARA. Sit down: make yourself at home. (*He hesitates; but she puts a friendly hand on his shoulder and makes him obey.*) Now then! since youve made friends with us, we want to know all about you. Names and addresses and trades.

SHIRLEY. Peter Shirley. Fitter. Chucked out two months ago because I was too old.

BARBARA (*not at all surprised*). Youd pass still. Why didnt you dye your hair?

SHIRLEY. I did. Me age come out at a coroner's inquest on me daughter.

BARBARA. Steady?

SHIRLEY. Teetotaller. Never out of a job before. Good worker. And sent to the knackers like an old horse!

BARBARA. No matter: if you did your part God will do his.

SHIRLEY (*suddenly stubborn*). My religion's no concern of anybody but myself.

BARBARA (*guessing*). *I* know. Secularist?

SHIRLEY (*hotly*). Did I offer to deny it?

BARBARA. Why should you? My own father's a Secularist, I think. Our Father—yours and mine—fulfils himself in many ways; and I daresay he knew what he was about when he made a Secularist of you. So buck up, Peter! we can always find a job for a steady man like you. (*Shirley, disarmed, touches his hat. She turns from him to Bill.*) Whats y o u r name?

BILL (*insolently*). Wots that to you?

BARBARA (*calmly making a note*). Afraid to give his name. Any trade?

BILL. Who's afraid to give his name? (*Doggedly, with a sense of heroically defying the House of Lords in the person of Lord Stevenage.*) If you want to bring a charge agen me, bring it. (*She waits, unruffled.*) My name's Bill Walker.

BARBARA (*as if the name were familiar: trying to remember how*). Bill Walker? (*Recollecting.*) Oh, I know: youre the man that Jenny Hill was praying for inside just now. (*She enters his name in her note book.*)

BILL. Who's Jenny Hill? And what call has she to pray for me?

BARBARA. I dont know. Perhaps it was you that cut her lip.

BILL (*defiantly*). Yes, it w a s me that cut her lip. I aint afraid o y o u.

BARBARA. How could you be, since youre not afraid of God? Youre a brave man, Mr. Walker. It takes some pluck to do o u r work here; but none of us dare lift our hand against a girl like that, for fear of her father in heaven.

BILL (*sullenly*). I want none o your cantin jaw. I suppose you think I come here to beg from you, like this damaged lot here. Not me. I dont want your bread and scrape and catlap. I dont believe in your Gawd, no more than you do yourself.

BARBARA (*sunnily apologetic and ladylike, as on a new footing with him*). Oh, I beg your pardon for putting your name down, Mr. Walker. I didnt understand. I'll strike it out.

BILL (*taking this as a slight, and deeply wounded by it*). Eah! you let my name alone. Aint it good enough to be in your book?

BARBARA (*considering*). Well, you see, theres no use putting down your name unless I can do something for you, is there? Whats your trade?

BILL (*still smarting*). Thats no concern o yours.

BARBARA. Just so. (*Very businesslike.*) I'll put you down as (*writing*) the man who—struck—poor little Jenny Hill—in the mouth.

BILL (*rising threateningly*). See here. Ive ad enough o this.

BARBARA (*quite sunny and fearless*). What did you come to us for?

BILL. I come for my girl, see? I come to take her out o this and to break er jawr for her.

BARBARA (*complacently*). You see I was right about your trade. (*Bill, on the point of retorting furiously, finds himself, to his great shame and terror, in danger of crying instead. He sits down again suddenly.*) Whats her name?

BILL (*dogged*). Er name's Mog Abbijam: thats wot her name is.

BARBARA. Oh, she's gone to Canning Town, to our barracks there.

BILL (*fortified by his resentment of Mog's perfidy*). Is she? (*Vindictively.*) Then I'm goin to Kennintahn arter her. (*He crosses to the gate; hesitates; finally comes back at Barbara.*) Are you lyin to me to get shut o me?

BARBARA. I dont want to get shut of you. I want to keep you here and save your soul. Youd better stay: youre going to have a bad time today, Bill.

BILL. Who's goin to give it to me? You, praps.

BARBARA. Someone you dont believe in. But youll be glad afterwards.

BILL (*slinking off*). I'll go to Kennintahn to be out o the reach o your tongue. (*Suddenly turning on her with intense malice.*) And if I dont find Mog there, I'll come back and do two years for you, selp me Gawd if I don't!

BARBARA (*a shade kindlier, if possible*). It's no use, Bill. Shes got another bloke.

BILL. Wot!

BARBARA. One of her own converts. He fell in love with her when he saw her with her soul saved, and her face clean, and her hair washed.

BILL (*surprised*). Wottud she wash it for, the carroty slut? It's red.

BARBARA. It's quite lovely now, because she wears a new look in her eyes with it. It's a pity youre too late. The new bloke has put your nose out of joint, Bill.

BILL. I'll put his nose out o joint for him. Not that I care a curse for her, mind that. But I'll teach her to drop me as if I was dirt. And I'll teach him to meddle with my judy. Wots iz bleedin name?

BARBARA. Sergeant Todger Fairmile.

SHIRLEY (*rising with grim joy*). I'll go with him, miss. I want to see them two meet. I'll take him to the infirmary when it's over.

BILL (*to Shirley, with undissembled misgiving*). Is that im you was speakin on?

SHIRLEY. Thats him.

BILL. Im that wrastled in the music all?

SHIRLEY. The competitions at the National Sportin Club was worth nigh a hundred a year to him. Hes gev em up now for religion; so hes a bit fresh for want of the exercise he was accustomed to. Hell be glad to see you. Come along.

BILL. Wots is weight?

SHIRLEY. Thirteen four. (*Bill's last hope expires.*)

BARBARA. Go and talk to him, Bill. He'll convert you.

SHIRLEY. He'll convert your head into a mashed potato.

BILL (*sullenly*). I aint afraid of him. I aint afraid of ennybody. But he can lick me. Shes done me. (*He sits down moodily on the edge of the horse trough.*)

SHIRLEY. You aint goin. I thought not. (*He resumes his seat.*)

BARBARA (*calling*). Jenny!

JENNY (*appearing at the shelter door with a plaster on the corner of her mouth*). Yes, Major.

BARBARA. Send Rummy Mitchens out to clear away here.

JENNY. I think shes afraid.

BARBARA (*her resemblance to her mother flashing out for a moment*). Nonsense! she must do as shes told.

JENNY (*calling into the shelter*). Rummy: the Major says you must come.

Jenny comes to Barbara, purposely keeping on the side next Bill, lest he should suppose that she shrank from him or bore malice.

BARBARA. Poor little Jenny! Are you tired? (*Looking at the wounded cheek.*) Does it hurt?

JENNY. No: it's all right now. It was nothing.

BARBARA (*critically*). It was as hard as he could hit, I expect. Poor Bill! You dont feel angry with him, do you?

JENNY. Oh no, no, no: indeed I dont, Major, bless his poor heart! (*Barbara kisses her; and she runs away merrily into the shelter. Bill writhes with an agonizing return of his new and alarming symptoms, but says nothing. Rummy Mitchens comes from the shelter.*)

BARBARA (*going to meet Rummy*). Now Rummy, bustle. Take in those mugs and plates to be washed; and throw the crumbs about for the birds.

Rummy takes the three plates and mugs; but Shirley takes back his mug from her, as there is still some milk left in it.

RUMMY. There aint any crumbs. This aint a time to waste good bread on birds.

PRICE (*appearing at the shelter door*). Gentleman come to see the shelter, Major. Says hes your father.

BARBARA. All right. Coming. (*Snobby goes back into the shelter, followed by Barbara.*)

RUMMY (*stealing across to Bill and addressing him in a subdued voice, but with intense conviction*). I'd av the lor of you, you flat eared pignosed potwalloper, if she'd let me. Youre no gentleman, to hit a lady in the face. (*Bill, with greater things moving in him, takes no notice.*)

SHIRLEY (*following her*). Here! in with you and dont get yourself into more trouble by talking.

RUMMY (*with hauteur*). I aint ad the pleasure o being hintroduced to you, as I can remember. (*She goes into the shelter with the plates.*)

SHIRLEY. Thats the—

BILL (*savagely*). Dont you talk to me, d'ye hear. You lea me alone, or I'll do you a mischief. I'm not dirt under y o u r feet, anyway.

SHIRLEY (*calmly*). Dont you be afeerd. You aint such prime company that you need expect to be sought after. (*He is about to go into the shelter when Barbara comes out, with Undershaft on her right.*)

BARBARA. Oh there you are, Mr. Shirley! (*Between

them.) This is my father: I told you he was a Secularist, didnt I? Perhaps youll be able to comfort one
another.

UNDERSHAFT (*startled*). A Secularist! Not the
least in the world: on the contrary, a confirmed mystic.

BARBARA. Sorry, I'm sure. By the way, papa, what
i s your religion—in case I have to introduce you again?

UNDERSHAFT. My religion? Well, my dear, I am a
Millionaire. That is my religion.

BARBARA. Then I'm afraid you and Mr. Shirley wont
be able to comfort one another after all. Youre not a
Millionaire, are you, Peter?

SHIRLEY. No; and proud of it.

UNDERSHAFT (*gravely*). Poverty, my friend, is not
a thing to be proud of.

SHIRLEY (*angrily*). Who made your millions for
you? Me and my like. Whats kep us poor? Keepin
you rich. I wouldnt have your conscience, not for all
your income.

UNDERSHAFT. I wouldnt have your income, not for
all your conscience, Mr. Shirley. (*He goes to the penthouse and sits down on a form.*)

BARBARA (*stopping Shirley adroitly as he is about to
retort*). You wouldnt think he was my father, would
you, Peter? Will you go into the shelter and lend the
lasses a hand for a while: we're worked off our feet.

SHIRLEY (*bitterly*). Yes: I'm in their debt for a
meal, aint I?

BARBARA. Oh, not because youre in their debt; but
for love of them, Peter, for love of them. (*He cannot
understand, and is rather scandalized.*) There! dont
stare at me. In with you; and give that conscience of
yours a holiday (*bustling him into the shelter*).

SHIRLEY (*as he goes in*). Ah! it's a pity you never
was trained to use your reason, miss. Youd have been
a very taking lecturer on Secularism.

Barbara turns to her father.

Undershaft. Never mind me, my dear. Go about your work; and let me watch it for a while.

Barbara. All right.

Undershaft. For instance, whats the matter with that out-patient over there?

Barbara (*looking at Bill, whose attitude has never changed, and whose expression of brooding wrath has deepened*). Oh, we shall cure him in no time. Just watch. (*She goes over to Bill and waits. He glances up at her and casts his eyes down again, uneasy, but grimmer than ever.*) It w o u l d be nice to just stamp on Mog Habbijam's face, wouldnt it, Bill?

Bill (*starting up from the trough in consternation*). It's a lie: I never said so. (*She shakes her head.*) Who told you wot was in my mind?

Barbara. Only your new friend.

Bill. Wot new friend?

Barbara. The devil, Bill. When he gets round people they get miserable, just like you.

Bill (*with a heartbreaking attempt at devil-may-care cheerfulness*). I aint miserable. (*He sits down again, and stretches his legs in an attempt to seem indifferent.*)

Barbara. Well, if youre happy, why dont you look happy, as we do?

Bill (*his legs curling back in spite of him*). I'm appy enough, I tell you. Why dont you lea me alown? Wot av I done to y o u? I aint smashed y o u r face, av I?

Barbara (*softly: wooing his soul*). It's not me thats getting at you, Bill.

Bill. Who else is it?

Barbara. Somebody that doesnt intend you to smash women's faces, I suppose. Somebody or something that wants to make a man of you.

Bill (*blustering*). Make a man o m e! Aint I a man? eh? aint I a man? Who sez I'm not a man?

Barbara. Theres a man in you somewhere, I suppose. But why did he let you hit poor little Jenny Hill? That wasnt very manly of him, was it?

BILL (*tormented*). Av done with it, I tell you. Chack it. I'm sick of your Jenny Ill and er silly little face.

BARBARA. Then why do you keep thinking about it? Why does it keep coming up against you in your mind? Youre not getting converted, are you?

BILL (*with conviction*). Not ME. Not likely. Not arf.

BARBARA. Thats right, Bill. Hold out against it. Put out your strength. Dont lets get you cheap. Todger Fairmile said he wrestled for three nights against his Salvation harder than he ever wrestled with the Jap at the music hall. He gave in to the Jap when his arm was going to break. But he didnt give in to his salvation until his heart was going to break. Perhaps youll escape that. You havnt any heart, have you?

BILL. Wot d'ye mean? Wy aint I got a art the same as ennybody else?

BARBARA. A man with a heart wouldnt have bashed poor little Jenny's face, would he?

BILL (*almost crying*). Ow, w i l l you lea me alown? Av I ever offered to meddle with y o u, that you come naggin and provowkin me lawk this? (*He writhes convulsively from his eyes to his toes.*)

BARBARA (*with a steady soothing hand on his arm and a gentle voice that never lets him go*). It's your soul thats hurting you, Bill, and not me. Weve been through it all ourselves. Come with us, Bill. (*He looks wildly round*). To brave manhood on earth and eternal glory in heaven. (*He is on the point of breaking down.*) Come. (*A drum is heard in the shelter; and Bill, with a gasp, escapes from the spell as Barbara turns quickly. Adolphus enters from the shelter with a big drum.*) Oh! there you are, Dolly. Let me introduce a new friend of mine, Mr. Bill Walker. This is my bloke, Bill: Mr. Cusins. (*Cusins salutes with his drumstick.*)

BILL. Goin to marry im?

BARBARA. Yes.

BILL (*fervently*). Gord elp im! Gawd elp im!

BARBARA. Why? Do you think he wont be happy with me?

BILL. Ive only ad to stand it for a mornin: e'll av to stand it for a lifetime.

CUSINS. That is a frightful reflection, Mr. Walker. But I cant tear myself away from her.

BILL. Well, I can. (*To Barbara.*) Eah! do you know where I'm going to, and wot I'm goin to do?

BARBARA. Yes: youre going to heaven; and youre coming back here before the week's out to tell me so.

BILL. You lie. I'm goin to Kennintahn, to spit in Todger Fairmile's eye. I bashed Jenny Ill's face; and now I'll get me own face bashed and come back and shew it to er. E'll it me ardern I it e r. Thatll make us square. (*To Adolphus.*) Is that fair or is it not? Youre a genlmn: you oughter know.

BARBARA. Two black eyes wont make one white one, Bill.

BILL. I didnt ast y o u. Cawnt you never keep your mahth shut? I ast the genlmn.

CUSINS (*reflectively*). Yes: I think youre right, Mr. Walker. Yes: I should do it. Its curious: its exactly what an ancient Greek would have done.

BARBARA. But what good will it do?

CUSINS. Well, it will give Mr. Fairmile some exercise; and it will satisfy Mr. Walker's soul.

BILL. Rot! there aint no sach a thing as a soul. Ah kin you tell wether Ive a soul or not? You never seen it.

BARBARA. Ive seen it hurting you when you went against it.

BILL (*with compressed aggravation*). If you was my girl and took the word out o me mahth lawk thet, I'd give you suthink youd feel urtin, so I would. (*To Adolphus.*) You take my tip, mate. Stop er jawr; or

youll die afore your time. (*With intense expression.*)
Wore aht: thets wot youll be: wore aht. (*He goes away
through the gate.*)

CUSINS (*looking after him*). I wonder!

BARBARA. Dolly! (*indignant, in her mother's manner.*)

CUSINS. Yes, my dear, it's very wearing to be in
love with you. If it lasts, I quite think I shall die
young.

BARBARA. Should you mind?

CUSINS. Not at all. (*He is suddenly softened, and
kisses her over the drum, evidently not for the first time,
as people cannot kiss over a big drum without practice.
Undershaft coughs.*)

BARBARA. It's all right, papa, weve not forgotten
you. Dolly: explain the place to papa: I havnt time.
(*She goes busily into the shelter.*)

*Undershaft and Adolphus now have the yard to them-
selves. Undershaft, seated on a form, and still keenly
attentive, looks hard at Adolphus. Adolphus looks hard
at him.*

UNDERSHAFT. I fancy you guess something of what
is in my mind, Mr. Cusins. (*Cusins flourishes his drumsticks as if in the act of beating a lively rataplan, but
makes no sound.*) Exactly so. But suppose Barbara
finds you out!

CUSINS. You know, I do not admit that I am imposing on Barbara. I am quite genuinely interested in
the views of the Salvation Army. The fact is, I am a
sort of collector of religions; and the curious thing is
that I find I can believe them all. By the way, have
you any religion?

UNDERSHAFT. Yes.

CUSINS. Anything out of the common?

UNDERSHAFT. Only that there are two things necessary to Salvation.

CUSINS (*disappointed, but polite*). Ah, the Church

Catechism.   Charles Lomax also belongs to the Established Church.

UNDERSHAFT.   The two things are—

CUSINS.   Baptism and—

UNDERSHAFT.   No.   Money and gunpowder.

CUSINS (*surprised, but interested*).   That is the general opinion of our governing classes.   The novelty is in hearing any man confess it.

UNDERSHAFT.   Just so.

CUSINS.   Excuse me: is there any place in your religion for honor, justice, truth, love, mercy and so forth?

UNDERSHAFT.   Yes: they are the graces and luxuries of a rich, strong, and safe life.

CUSINS.   Suppose one is forced to choose between them and money or gunpowder?

UNDERSHAFT.   Choose money a n d gunpowder; for without enough of both you cannot afford the others.

CUSINS.   That is your religion?

UNDERSHAFT.   Yes.

The cadence of this reply makes a full close in the conversation.   Cusins twists his face dubiously and contemplates Undershaft.   Undershaft contemplates him.

CUSINS.   Barbara wont stand that.   You will have to choose between your religion and Barbara.

UNDERSHAFT.   So will you, my friend.   She will find out that that drum of yours is hollow.

CUSINS.   Father Undershaft: you are mistaken: I am a sincere Salvationist.   You do not understand the Salvation Army.   It is the army of joy, of love, of courage: it has banished the fear and remorse and despair of the old hell-ridden evangelical sects: it marches to fight the devil with trumpet and drum, with music and dancing, with banner and palm, as becomes a sally from heaven by its happy garrison.   It picks the waster out of the public house and makes a man of him: it finds a worm wriggling in a back kitchen, and lo! a woman! Men and women of rank too, sons and daughters of the

Highest. It takes the poor professor of Greek, the most artificial and self-suppressed of human creatures, from his meal of roots, and lets loose the rhapsodist in him; reveals the true worship of Dionysos to him; sends him down the public street drumming dithyrambs (*he plays a thundering flourish on the drum*).

UNDERSHAFT. You will alarm the shelter.

CUSINS. Oh, they are accustomed to these sudden ecstasies of piety. However, if the drum worries you— (*he pockets the drumsticks; unhooks the drum; and stands it on the ground opposite the gateway*).

UNDERSHAFT. Thank you.

CUSINS. You remember what Euripides says about your money and gunpowder?

UNDERSHAFT. No.

CUSINS (*declaiming*).

> One and another
> In money and guns may outpass his brother;
> And men in their millions float and flow
> And seethe with a million hopes as leaven;
> And they win their will; or they miss their will;
> And their hopes are dead or are pined for still;
> > But whoe'er can know
> > As the long days go
> That to live is happy, has found h i s heaven.

My translation: what do you think of it?

UNDERSHAFT. I think, my friend, that if you wish to know, as the long days go, that to live is happy, you must first acquire money enough for a decent life, and power enough to be your own master.

CUSINS. You are damnably discouraging. (*He resumes his declamation.*)

> Is it so hard a thing to see
> That the spirit of God—whate'er it be—
> The Law that abides and changes not, ages long,
> The Eternal and Nature-born: these things be strong?

What else is Wisdom? What of Man's endeavor,
Or God's high grace so lovely and so great?
To stand from fear set free? to breathe and wait?
To hold a hand uplifted over Fate?
And shall not Barbara be loved for ever?

UNDERSHAFT. Euripides mentions Barbara, does he?

CUSINS. It is a fair translation. The word means Loveliness.

UNDERSHAFT. May I ask—as Barbara's father—how much a year she is to be loved for ever on?

CUSINS. As Barbara's father, that is more your affair than mine. I can feed her by teaching Greek: that is about all.

UNDERSHAFT. Do you consider it a good match for her?

CUSINS (*with polite obstinacy*). Mr. Undershaft: I am in many ways a weak, timid, ineffectual person; and my health is far from satisfactory. But whenever I feel that I must have anything, I get it, sooner or later. I feel that way about Barbara. I dont like marriage: I feel intensely afraid of it; and I dont know what I shall do with Barbara or what she will do with me. But I feel that I and nobody else must marry her. Please regard that as settled.—Not that I wish to be arbitrary; but why should I waste your time in discussing what is inevitable?

UNDERSHAFT. You mean that you will stick at nothing: not even the conversion of the Salvation Army to the worship of Dionysos.

CUSINS. The business of the Salvation Army is to save, not to wrangle about the name of the pathfinder. Dionysos or another: what does it matter?

UNDERSHAFT (*rising and approaching him*). Professor Cusins: you are a young man after my own heart.

CUSINS. Mr. Undershaft: you are, as far as I am

able to gather, a most infernal old rascal; but you appeal very strongly to my sense of ironic humor.

Undershaft mutely offers his hand. They shake.

UNDERSHAFT (*suddenly concentrating himself*). And now to business.

CUSINS. Pardon me. We were discussing religion. Why go back to such an uninteresting and unimportant subject as business?

UNDERSHAFT. Religion is our business at present, because it is through religion alone that we can win Barbara.

CUSINS. Have you, too, fallen in love with Barbara?

UNDERSHAFT. Yes, with a father's love.

CUSINS. A father's love for a grown-up daughter is the most dangerous of all infatuations. I apologize for mentioning my own pale, coy, mistrustful fancy in the same breath with it.

UNDERSHAFT. Keep to the point. We have to win her; and we are neither of us Methodists.

CUSINS. That doesnt matter. The power Barbara wields here—the power that wields Barbara herself—is not Calvinism, not Presbyterianism, not Methodism—

UNDERSHAFT. Not Greek Paganism either, eh?

CUSINS. I admit that. Barbara is quite original in her religion.

UNDERSHAFT (*triumphantly*). Aha! Barbara Undershaft would be. Her inspiration comes from within herself.

CUSINS. How do you suppose it got there?

UNDERSHAFT (*in towering excitement*). It is the Undershaft inheritance. I shall hand on my torch to my daughter. She shall make my converts and preach my gospel—

CUSINS. What! Money and gunpowder!

UNDERSHAFT. Yes, money and gunpowder; freedom and power; command of life and command of death.

Cusins (*urbanely: trying to bring him down to earth*). This is extremely interesting, Mr. Undershaft. Of course you know that you are mad.

Undershaft (*with redoubled force*). And you?

Cusins. Oh, mad as a hatter. You are welcome to my secret since I have discovered yours. But I am astonished. Can a madman make cannons?

Undershaft. Would anyone else than a madman make them? And now (*with surging energy*) question for question. Can a sane man translate Euripides?

Cusins. No.

Undershaft (*seizing him by the shoulder*). Can a sane woman make a man of a waster or a woman of a worm?

Cusins (*reeling before the storm*). Father Colossus —Mammoth Millionaire—

Undershaft (*pressing him*). Are there two mad people or three in this Salvation shelter to-day?

Cusins. You mean Barbara is as mad as we are!

Undershaft (*pushing him lightly off and resuming his equanimity suddenly and completely*). Pooh, Professor! let us call things by their proper names. I am a millionaire; you are a poet; Barbara is a savior of souls. What have we three to do with the common mob of slaves and idolaters? (*He sits down again with a shrug of contempt for the mob.*)

Cusins. Take care! Barbara is in love with the common people. So am I. Have you never felt the romance of that love?

Undershaft (*cold and sardonic*). Have you ever been in love with Poverty, like St. Francis? Have you ever been in love with Dirt, like St. Simeon? Have you ever been in love with disease and suffering, like our nurses and philanthropists? Such passions are not virtues, but the most unnatural of all the vices. This love of the common people may please an earl's granddaughter and a university professor; but I have been a

common man and a poor man; and it has no romance for
me. Leave it to the poor to pretend that poverty is a
blessing: leave it to the coward to make a religion of
his cowardice by preaching humility: we know better
than that. We three must stand together above the
common people: how else can we help their children to
climb up beside us? Barbara must belong to us, not
to the Salvation Army.

CUSINS. Well, I can only say that if you think you
will get her away from the Salvation Army by talking
to her as you have been talking to me, you dont know
Barbara.

UNDERSHAFT. My friend: I never ask for what I
can buy.

CUSINS (*in a white fury*). Do I understand you to
imply that you can buy Barbara?

UNDERSHAFT. No; but I can buy the Salvation Army.

CUSINS. Quite impossible.

UNDERSHAFT. You shall see. All religious organizations exist by selling themselves to the rich.

CUSINS. Not the Army. That is the Church of the
poor.

UNDERSHAFT. All the more reason for buying it.

CUSINS. I dont think you quite know what the Army
does for the poor.

UNDERSHAFT. Oh yes I do. It draws their teeth:
that is enough for me—as a man of business—

CUSINS. Nonsense. It makes them sober—

UNDERSHAFT. I prefer sober workmen. The profits
are larger.

CUSINS. —honest—

UNDERSHAFT. Honest workmen are the most eco-
nomical.

CUSINS. —attached to their homes—

UNDERSHAFT. So much the better: they will put up
with anything sooner than change their shop.

CUSINS. —happy—

UNDERSHAFT. An invaluable safeguard against revolution.

CUSINS. —unselfish—

UNDERSHAFT. Indifferent to their own interests, which suits me exactly.

CUSINS. —with their thoughts on heavenly things—

UNDERSHAFT (*rising*). And not on Trade Unionism nor Socialism. Excellent.

CUSINS (*revolted*). You really are an infernal old rascal.

UNDERSHAFT (*indicating Peter Shirley, who has just come from the shelter and strolled dejectedly down the yard between them*). And this is an honest man!

SHIRLEY. Yes; and what av I got by it? (*he passes on bitterly and sits on the form, in the corner of the penthouse*).

Snobby Price, beaming sanctimoniously, and Jenny Hill, with a tambourine full of coppers, come from the shelter and go to the drum, on which Jenny begins to count the money.

UNDERSHAFT (*replying to Shirley*). Oh, your employers must have got a good deal by it from first to last. (*He sits on the table, with one foot on the side form. Cusins, overwhelmed, sits down on the same form nearer the shelter. Barbara comes from the shelter to the middle of the yard. She is excited and a little overwrought.*)

BARBARA. Weve just had a splendid experience meeting at the other gate in Cripps's lane. Ive hardly ever seen them so much moved as they were by your confession, Mr. Price.

PRICE. I could almost be glad of my past wickedness if I could believe that it would elp to keep hathers stright.

BARBARA. So it will, Snobby. How much, Jenny?

JENNY. Four and tenpence, Major.

BARBARA. Oh Snobby, if you had given your poor

mother just one more kick, we should have got the whole
five shillings!

PRICE. If she heard you say that, miss, she'd be sorry
I didnt. But I'm glad. Oh what a joy it will be to
her when she hears I'm saved!

UNDERSHAFT. Shall I contribute the odd twopence,
Barbara? The millionaire's mite, eh? (*He takes a
couple of pennies from his pocket.*)

BARBARA. How did you make that twopence?

UNDERSHAFT. As usual. By selling cannons, torpedoes, submarines, and my new patent Grand Duke
hand grenade.

BARBARA. Put it back in your pocket. You cant buy
your Salvation here for twopence: you must work it out.

UNDERSHAFT. Is twopence not enough? I can afford
a little more, if you press me.

BARBARA. Two million millions would not be enough.
There is bad blood on your hands; and nothing but good
blood can cleanse them. Money is no use. Take it
away. (*She turns to Cusins.*) Dolly: you must write
another letter for me to the papers. (*He makes a wry
face.*) Yes: I know you dont like it; but it must be
done. The starvation this winter is beating us: everybody is unemployed. The General says we must close
this shelter if we cant get more money. I force the
collections at the meetings until I am ashamed: dont I,
Snobby?

PRICE. It's a fair treat to see you work it, Miss. The
way you got them up from three-and-six to four-and-ten
with that hymn, penny by penny and verse by verse,
was a caution. Not a Cheap Jack on Mile End Waste
could touch you at it.

BARBARA. Yes; but I wish we could do without it. I
am getting at last to think more of the collection than
of the people's souls. And what are those hatfuls of
pence and halfpence? We want thousands! tens of
thousands! hundreds of thousands! I want to convert

people, not to be always begging for the Army in a way I'd die sooner than beg for myself.

UNDERSHAFT (*in profound irony*). Genuine unselfishness is capable of anything, my dear.

BARBARA (*unsuspectingly, as she turns away to take the money from the drum and put it in a cash bag she carries*). Yes, isnt it? (*Undershaft looks sardonically at Cusins.*)

CUSINS (*aside to Undershaft*). Mephistopheles! Machiavelli!

BARBARA (*tears coming into her eyes as she ties the bag and pockets it*). How are we to feed them? I cant talk religion to a man with bodily hunger in his eyes. (*Almost breaking down.*) It's frightful.

JENNY (*running to her*). Major, dear—

BARBARA (*rebounding*). No, dont comfort me. It will be all right. We shall get the money.

UNDERSHAFT. How?

JENNY. By praying for it, of course. Mrs. Baines says she prayed for it last night; and she has never prayed for it in vain: never once. (*She goes to the gate and looks out into the street.*)

BARBARA (*who has dried her eyes and regained her composure*). By the way, dad, Mrs. Baines has come to march with us to our big meeting this afternoon; and she is very anxious to meet you, for some reason or other. Perhaps she'll convert you.

UNDERSHAFT. I shall be delighted, my dear.

JENNY (*at the gate: excitedly*). Major! Major! heres that man back again.

BARBARA. What man?

JENNY. The man that hit me. Oh, I hope hes coming back to join us.

Bill Walker, with frost on his jacket, comes through the gate, his hands deep in his pockets and his chin sunk between his shoulders, like a cleaned-out gambler. He halts between Barbara and the drum.

BARBARA. Hullo, Bill! Back already!

BILL (*nagging at her*). Bin talkin ever sence, av you?

BARBARA. Pretty nearly. Well, has Todger paid you out for poor Jenny's jaw?

BILL. No he aint.

BARBARA. I thought your jacket looked a bit snowy.

BILL. So it is snowy. You want to know where the snow come from, dont you?

BARBARA. Yes.

BILL. Well, it come from off the ground in Parkinses Corner in Kennintahn. It got rubbed off be my shoulders: see?

BARBARA. Pity you didnt rub some off with your knees, Bill! That would have done you a lot of good.

BILL (*with sour mirthless humor*). I was saving another man's knees at the time. E was kneelin on my ed, so e was.

JENNY. Who was kneeling on your head?

BILL. Todger was. E was prayin for me: prayin comfortable with me as a carpet. So was Mog. So was the ole bloomin meetin. Mog she sez "O Lord break is stubborn spirit; but dont urt is dear art." That was wot she said. "Dont urt is dear art"! An er bloke—thirteen stun four!—kneelin wiv all is weight on me. Funny, aint it?

JENNY. Oh no. We're so sorry, Mr. Walker.

BARBARA (*enjoying it frankly*). Nonsense! of course it's funny. Served you right, Bill! You must have done something to him first.

BILL (*doggedly*). I did wot I said I'd do. I spit in is eye. E looks up at the sky and sez, "O that I should be fahnd worthy to be spit upon for the gospel's sake!" e sez; an Mog sez "Glory Allelloolier!"; and then e called me Brother, an dahned me as if I was a kid and e was me mother washin me a Setterda nawt. I adnt just no show wiv im at all. Arf the street prayed; an the tother arf larfed fit to split theirselves. (*To Barbara.*) There! are you settisfawd nah?

BARBARA (*her eyes dancing*). Wish I'd been there, Bill.

BILL. Yes: youd a got in a hextra bit o talk on me, wouldnt you?

JENNY. I'm so sorry, Mr. Walker.

BILL (*fiercely*). Dont you go bein sorry for me: youve no call. Listen ere. I broke your jawr.

JENNY. No, it didnt hurt me: indeed it didnt, except for a moment. It was only that I was frightened.

BILL. I dont want to be forgive be you, or be ennybody. Wot I did I'll pay for. I tried to get me own jawr broke to settisfaw you—

JENNY (*distressed*). Oh no—

BILL (*impatiently*). Tell y'I did: cawnt you listen to wots bein told you? All I got be it was bein made a sight of in the public street for me pains. Well, if I cawnt settisfaw you one way, I can another. Listen ere! I ad two quid saved agen the frost; an Ive a pahnd of it left. A mate o mine last week ad words with the judy e's goin to marry. E give er wot-for; an e's bin fined fifteen bob. E ad a right to it er because they was goin to be marrid; but I adnt no right to it you; so put anather fawv bob on an call it a pahnd's worth. (*He produces a sovereign.*) Eres the money. Take it; and lets av no more o your forgivin an prayin and your Major jawrin me. Let wot I done be done and paid for; and lct there be a end of it.

JENNY. Oh, I couldnt take it, Mr. Walker. But if you would give a shilling or two to poor Rummy Mitchens! you really did hurt her; and shes old.

BILL (*contemptuously*). Not likely. I'd give her anather as soon as look at er. Let her av the lawr o me as she threatened! S h e aint forgiven me: not mach. Wot I done to er is not on me mawnd—wot she (*indicating Barbara*) might call on me conscience—no more than stickin a pig. It's this Christian game o yours that I wont av played agen me: this bloomin forgivin an naggin an jawrin that makes a man that sore that iz lawf's a burdn to im. I wont av it, I tell you; so take your money and stop throwin your silly bashed face hup agen me.

JENNY. Major: may I take a little of it for the Army?

BARBARA. No: the Army is not to be bought. We want your soul, Bill; and we'll take nothing less.

BILL (*bitterly*). I know. It aint enough. Me an me few shillins is not good enough for you. Youre a earl's grendorter, you are. Nothin less than a underd pahnd for you.

UNDERSHAFT. Come, Barbara! you could do a great deal of good with a hundred pounds. If you will set this gentleman's mind at ease by taking his pound, I will give the other ninety-nine. (*Bill, astounded by such opulence, instinctively touches his cap.*)

BARBARA. Oh, youre too extravagant, papa. Bill offers twenty pieces of silver. All you need offer is the other ten. That will make the standard price to buy anybody who's for sale. I'm not; and the Army's not. (*To Bill.*) Youll never have another quiet moment, Bill, until you come round to us. You cant stand out against your salvation.

BILL (*sullenly*). I cawnt stend aht agen music-all wrastlers and artful tongued women. Ive offered to pay. I can do no more. Take it or leave it. There it is. (*He throws the sovereign on the drum, and sits down on the horse-trough. The coin fascinates Snobby Price, who takes an early opportunity of dropping his cap on it.*)

Mrs. Baines comes from the shelter. She is dressed as a Salvation Army Commissioner. She is an earnest looking woman of about 40, with a caressing, urgent voice, and an appealing manner.

BARBARA. This is my father, Mrs. Baines. (*Undershaft comes from the table, taking his hat off with marked civility.*) Try what you can do with him. He wont listen to me, because he remembers what a fool I was when I was a baby. (*She leaves them together and chats with Jenny.*)

MRS. BAINES. Have you been shewn over the shelter, Mr. Undershaft? You know the work we're doing, of course.

UNDERSHAFT (*very civilly*). The whole nation knows it, Mrs. Baines.

MRS. BAINES. No, sir: the whole nation does not know it, or we should not be crippled as we are for want of money to carry our work through the length and breadth of the land. Let me tell you that there would have been rioting this winter in London but for us.

UNDERSHAFT. You really think so?

MRS. BAINES. I know it. I remember 1886, when you rich gentlemen hardened your hearts against the cry of the poor. They broke the windows of your clubs in Pall Mall.

UNDERSHAFT (*gleaming with approval of their method*). And the Mansion House Fund went up next day from thirty thousand pounds to seventy-nine thousand! I remember quite well.

MRS. BAINES. Well, wont you help me to get at the people? They wont break windows then. Come here, Price. Let me shew you to this gentleman (*Price comes to be inspected*). Do you remember the window breaking?

PRICE. My ole father thought it was the revolution, maam.

MRS. BAINES. Would you break windows now?

PRICE. Oh no maam. The windows of eaven av bin opened to me. I know now that the rich man is a sinner like myself.

RUMMY (*appearing above at the loft door*). Snobby Price!

SNOBBY. Wot is it?

RUMMY. Your mother's askin for you at the other gate in Crippses Lane. She's heard about your confession (*Price turns pale*).

MRS. BAINES. Go, Mr. Price; and pray with her.

JENNY. You can go through the shelter, Snobby.

PRICE (*to Mrs. Baines*). I couldnt face her now, maam, with all the weight of my sins fresh on me. Tell her she'll find her son at ome, waitin for her in prayer. (*He skulks off through the gate, incidentally stealing the sovereign on his way out by picking up his cap from the drum.*)

MRS. BAINES (*with swimming eyes*). You see how we take the anger and the bitterness against you out of their hearts, Mr. Undershaft.

UNDERSHAFT. It is certainly most convenient and gratifying to all large employers of labor, Mrs. Baines.

MRS. BAINES. Barbara: Jenny: I have good news: most wonderful news. (*Jenny runs to her.*) My prayers have been answered. I told you they would, Jenny, didn't I?

JENNY. Yes, yes.

BARBARA (*moving nearer to the drum*). Have we got money enough to keep the shelter open?

MRS. BAINES. I hope we shall have enough to keep all the shelters open. Lord Saxmundham has promised us five thousand pounds—

BARBARA. Hooray!

JENNY. Glory!

MRS. BAINES. —if—

BARBARA. "If!" If what?

MRS. BAINES. —if five other gentlemen will give a thousand each to make it up to ten thousand.

BARBARA. Who is Lord Saxmundham? I never heard of him.

UNDERSHAFT (*who has pricked up his ears at the peer's name, and is now watching Barbara curiously*).

A new creation, my dear. You have heard of Sir Horace Bodger?

BARBARA. Bodger! Do you mean the distiller? Bodger's whisky!

UNDERSHAFT. That is the man. He is one of the greatest of our public benefactors. He restored the cathedral at Hakington. They made him a baronet for that. He gave half a million to the funds of his party: they made him a baron for that.

SHIRLEY. What will they give him for the five thousand?

UNDERSHAFT. There is nothing left to give him. So the five thousand, I should think, is to save his soul.

MRS. BAINES. Heaven grant it may! Oh Mr. Undershaft, you have some very rich friends. Cant you help us towards the other five thousand? We are going to hold a great meeting this afternoon at the Assembly Hall in the Mile End Road. If I could only announce that one gentleman had come forward to support Lord Saxmundham, others would follow. Dont you know somebody? couldnt you? wouldnt you? (*her eyes fill with tears*) oh, think of those poor people, Mr. Undershaft: think of how much it means to them, and how little to a great man like you.

UNDERSHAFT (*sardonically gallant*). Mrs. Baines: you are irresistible. I cant disappoint you; and I cant deny myself the satisfaction of making Bodger pay up. You shall have your five thousand pounds.

MRS. BAINES. Thank God!

UNDERSHAFT. You dont thank m e?

MRS. BAINES. Oh sir, dont try to be cynical: dont be ashamed of being a good man. The Lord will bless you abundantly; and our prayers will be like a strong fortification round you all the days of your life. (*With a touch of caution.*) You will let me have the cheque to shew at the meeting, wont you? Jenny: go in and fetch a pen and ink. (*Jenny runs to the shelter door.*)

UNDERSHAFT. Do not disturb Miss Hill: I have a fountain pen. (*Jenny halts. He sits at the table and writes the cheque. Cusins rises to make more room for him. They all watch him silently.*)

BILL (*cynically, aside to Barbara, his voice and accent horribly debased*). Wot prawce Selvytion nah?

BARBARA. Stop. (*Undershaft stops writing: they all turn to her in surprise.*) Mrs. Baines: are you really going to take this money?

MRS. BAINES (*astonished*). Why not, dear?

BARBARA. Why not! Do you know what my father is? Have you forgotten that Lord Saxmundham is Bodger the whisky man? Do you remember how we implored the County Council to stop him from writing Bodger's Whisky in letters of fire against the sky; so that the poor drink-ruined creatures on the embankment could not wake up from their snatches of sleep without being reminded of their deadly thirst by that wicked sky sign? Do you know that the worst thing I have had to fight here is not the devil, but Bodger, Bodger, Bodger, with his whisky, his distilleries, and his tied houses? Are you going to make our shelter another tied house for him, and ask me to keep it?

BILL. Rotten drunken whisky it is too.

MRS. BAINES. Dear Barbara: Lord Saxmundham has a soul to be saved like any of us. If heaven has found the way to make a good use of his money, are we to set ourselves up against the answer to our prayers?

BARBARA. I know he has a soul to be saved. Let him come down here; and I'll do my best to help him to his salvation. But he wants to send his cheque down to buy us, and go on being as wicked as ever.

UNDERSHAFT (*with a reasonableness which Cusins alone perceives to be ironical*). My dear Barbara: alcohol is a very necessary article. It heals the sick—

BARBARA. It does nothing of the sort.

UNDERSHAFT. Well, it assists the doctor: that is perhaps a less questionable way of putting it. It makes life bearable to millions of people who could not endure their existence if they were quite sober. It enables Parliament to do things at eleven at night that no sane person would do at eleven in the morning. Is it Bodger's fault that this inestimable gift is deplorably abused by less than one per cent of the poor? (*He turns again to the table; signs the cheque; and crosses it.*)

Mrs. Baines. Barbara: will there be less drinking or more if all those poor souls we are saving come tomorrow and find the doors of our shelters shut in their faces? Lord Saxmundham gives us the money to stop drinking—to take his own business from him.

Cusins (*impishly*). Pure self-sacrifice on Bodger's part, clearly! Bless dear Bodger! (*Barbara almost breaks down as Adolphus, too, fails her.*)

Undershaft (*tearing out the cheque and pocketing the book as he rises and goes past Cusins to Mrs. Baines*). I also, Mrs. Baines, may claim a little disinterestedness. Think of my business! think of the widows and orphans! the men and lads torn to pieces with shrapnel and poisoned with lyddite (*Mrs. Baines shrinks; but he goes on remorsely*)! the oceans of blood, not one drop of which is shed in a really just cause! the ravaged crops! the peaceful peasants forced, women and men, to till their fields under the fire of opposing armies on pain of starvation! the bad blood of the fierce little cowards at home who egg on others to fight for the gratification of their national vanity! All this makes money for me: I am never richer, never busier than when the papers are full of it. Well, it is your work to preach peace on earth and goodwill to men. (*Mrs. Baines's face lights up again.*) Every convert you make is a vote against war. (*Her lips move in prayer.*) Yet I give you this money to help you to hasten my own commercial ruin. (*He gives her the cheque.*)

Cusins (*mounting the form in an ecstasy of mischief*).

The millennium will be inaugurated by the unselfishness of Undershaft and Bodger. Oh be joyful! (*He takes the drumsticks from his pockets and flourishes them.*)

MRS. BAINES (*taking the cheque*). The longer I live the more proof I see that there is an Infinite Goodness that turns everything to the work of salvation sooner or later. Who would have thought that any good could have come out of war and drink? And yet their profits are brought today to the feet of salvation to do its blessed work. (*She is affected to tears.*)

JENNY (*running to Mrs. Baines and throwing her arms round her*). Oh dear! how blessed, how glorious it all is!

CUSINS (*in a convulsion of irony*). Let us seize this unspeakable moment. Let us march to the great meeting at once. Excuse me just an instant. (*He rushes into the shelter. Jenny takes her tambourine from the drum head.*)

MRS. BAINES. Mr. Undershaft: have you ever seen a thousand people fall on their knees with one impulse and pray? Come with us to the meeting. Barbara shall tell them that the Army is saved, and saved through you.

CUSINS (*returning impetuously from the shelter with a flag and a trombone, and coming between Mrs. Baines and Undershaft*). You shall carry the flag down the first street, Mrs. Baines (*he gives her the flag*). Mr. Undershaft is a gifted trombonist: he shall intone an Olympian diapason to the West Ham Salvation March. (*Aside to Undershaft, as he forces the trombone on him.*) Blow, Machiavelli, blow.

UNDERSHAFT (*aside to him, as he takes the trombone*). The trumpet in Zion! (*Cusins rushes to the drum, which he takes up and puts on. Undershaft continues, aloud*) I will do my best. I could vamp a bass if I knew the tune.

CUSINS. It is a wedding chorus from one of Donizetti's operas; but we have converted it. We convert everything to good here, including Bodger. You remember the chorus. "For thee immense rejoicing— immenso giubilo—immenso giubilo." (*With drum obbligato.*) Rum tum ti tum tum, tum tum ti ta—

BARBARA. Dolly: you are breaking my heart.

CUSINS. What is a broken heart more or less here? Dionysos Undershaft has descended. I am possessed.

MRS. BAINES. Come, Barbara: I must have my dear Major to carry the flag with me.

JENNY. Yes, yes, Major darling.

CUSINS (*snatches the tambourine out of Jenny's hand and mutely offers it to Barbara*).

BARBARA (*coming forward a little as she puts the offer behind her with a shudder, whilst Cusins recklessly tosses the tambourine back to Jenny and goes to the gate*). I cant come.

JENNY. Not come!

MRS. BAINES (*with tears in her eyes*). Barbara: do you think I am wrong to take the money?

BARBARA (*impulsively going to her and kissing her*). No, no: God help you, dear, you must: you are saving the Army. Go; and may you have a great meeting!

JENNY. But arnt you coming?

BARBARA. No. (*She begins taking off the silver S brooch from her collar.*)

MRS. BAINES. Barbara: what are you doing?

JENNY. Why are you taking your badge off? You cant be going to leave us, Major.

BARBARA (*quietly*). Father: come here.

UNDERSHAFT (*coming to her*). My dear! (*Seeing that she is going to pin the badge on his collar, he retreats to the penthouse in some alarm.*)

BARBARA (*following him*). Dont be frightened. (*She pins the badge on and steps back towards the table, shewing him to the others.*) There! It's not much for £5000, is it?

MRS. BAINES. Barbara: if you wont come and pray
w i t h us, promise me you will pray f o r us.

BARBARA. I cant pray now. Perhaps I shall never
pray again.

MRS. BAINES. Barbara!

JENNY. Major!

BARBARA (*almost delirious*). I cant bear any more.
Quick march!

CUSINS (*calling to the procession in the street outside*). Off we go. Play up, there! I m m e n s o g i u-
b i l o. (*He gives the time with his drum; and the
band strikes up the march, which rapidly becomes more
distant as the procession moves briskly away.*)

MRS. BAINES. I must go, dear. Youre overworked:
you will be all right tomorrow. We'll never lose you.
Now Jenny: step out with the old flag. Blood and Fire!
(*She marches out through the gate with her flag.*)

JENNY. Glory Hallelujah! (*flourishing her tambourine and marching*).

UNDERSHAFT (*to Cusins, as he marches out past him
easing the slide of his trombone*). " My ducats and my
daughter "!

CUSINS (*following him out*). Money and gunpowder!

BARBARA. Drunkenness and Murder! My God:
why hast thou forsaken me?

*She sinks on the form with her face buried in her
hands. The march passes away into silence. Bill Walker
steals across to her.*

BILL (*taunting*). Wot prawce Selvytion nah?

SHIRLEY. Dont you hit her when shes down.

BILL. She it me wen aw wiz dahn. Waw shouldnt I
git a bit o me own back?

BARBARA (*raising her head*). I didnt take y o u r
money, Bill. (*She crosses the yard to the gate and
turns her back on the two men to hide her face from
them.*)

BILL (*sneering after her*). Naow, it warnt enough

for you.   (*Turning to the drum, he misses the money.*)
Ellow! If you aint took it summun else az. Weres it
gorn? Blame me if Jenny Ill didnt take it arter all!

RUMMY (*screaming at him from the loft*). You lie,
you dirty blackguard! Snobby Price pinched it off the
drum wen e took ap iz cap. I was ap ere all the time
an see im do it.

BILL.   Wot! Stowl maw money! Waw didnt you
call thief on him, you silly old mucker you?

RUMMY.   To serve you aht for ittin me acrost the fice.
It's cost y'pahnd, that az. (*Raising a pæan of squalid
triumph.*) I done you. I'm even with you. Ive ad it
aht o y— (*Bill snatches up Shirley's mug and hurls
it at her.   She slams the loft door and vanishes.   The
mug smashes against the door and falls in fragments.*)

BILL (*beginning to chuckle*).   Tell us, ole man, wot
o'clock this mornin was it wen im as they call Snobby
Prawce was sived?

BARBARA (*turning to him more composedly, and with
unspoiled sweetness*).   About half past twelve, Bill.
And he pinched your pound at a quarter to two. *I* know.
Well, you cant afford to lose it. I'll send it to you.

BILL (*his voice and accent suddenly improving*).   Not
if I was to starve for it.   *I* aint to be bought.

SHIRLEY.   Aint you? Youd sell yourself to the devil
for a pint o beer; ony there aint no devil to make the
offer.

BILL (*unshamed*).   So I would, mate, and often av,
cheerful. But s h e cawnt buy me. (*Approaching Barbara.*) You wanted my soul, did you? Well, you aint
got it.

BARBARA.   I nearly got it, Bill. But weve sold it back
to you for ten thousand pounds.

SHIRLEY.   And dear at the money!

BARBARA.   No, Peter: it was worth more than money.

BILL (*salvationproof*).   It's no good: you cawnt get
rahnd me nah. I dont blieve in it; and Ive seen today

that I was right. (*Going.*)   So long, old soupkitchener!
Ta, ta, Major Earl's Grendorter! (*Turning at the gate.*)
Wot prawce Selvytion nah?   Snobby Prawce! Ha! ha!

BARBARA (*offering her hand*). Goodbye, Bill.

BILL (*taken aback, half plucks his cap off; then shoves
it on again defiantly*). Git aht. (*Barbara drops her
hand, discouraged. He has a twinge of remorse.*) But
thets aw rawt, you knaow. Nathink pasnl. Naow
mellice. So long, Judy. (*He goes.*)

BARBARA. No malice. So long, Bill.

SHIRLEY (*shaking his head*). You make too much of
him, Miss, in your innocence.

BARBARA (*going to him*). Peter: I'm like you now.
Cleaned out, and lost my job.

SHIRLEY. Youve youth an hope. Thats two better
than me.

BARBARA. I'll get you a job, Peter. Thats hope for
you: the youth will have to be enough for me. (*She
counts her money.*)   I have just enough left for two
teas at Lockharts, a Rowton doss for you, and my tram
and bus home. (*He frowns and rises with offended
pride. She takes his arm.*) Dont be proud, Peter: it's
sharing between friends. And promise me youll talk to
me and not let me cry. (*She draws him towards the
gate.*)

SHIRLEY. Well, I'm not accustomed to talk to the
like of you—

BARBARA (*urgently*). Yes, yes: you must talk to me.
Tell me about Tom Paine's books and Bradlaugh's
lectures. Come along.

SHIRLEY. Ah, if you would only read Tom Paine in
the proper spirit, Miss! (*They go out through the gate
together.*)

END OF ACT II.

ACT III

Next day after lunch Lady Britomart is writing in the library in Wilton Crescent. Sarah is reading in the armchair near the window. Barbara, in ordinary dress, pale and brooding, is on the settee. Charles Lomax enters. Coming forward between the settee and the writing table, he starts on seeing Barbara fashionably attired and in low spirits.

LOMAX. Youve left off your uniform!

Barbara says nothing; but an expression of pain passes over her face.

LADY BRITOMART (*warning him in low tones to be careful*). Charles!

LOMAX (*much concerned, sitting down sympathetically on the settee beside Barbara*). I'm awfully sorry, Barbara. You know I helped you all I could with the concertina and so forth. (*Momentously.*) Still, I have never shut my eyes to the fact that there is a certain amount of tosh about the Salvation Army. Now the claims of the Church of England—

LADY BRITOMART. Thats enough, Charles. Speak of something suited to your mental capacity.

LOMAX. But surely the Church of England is suited to all our capacities.

BARBARA (*pressing his hand*). Thank you for your sympathy, Cholly. Now go and spoon with Sarah.

LOMAX (*rising and going to Sarah*). How is my ownest today?

SARAH. I wish you wouldnt tell Cholly to do things, Barbara. He always comes straight and does them. Cholly: we're going to the works at Perivale St. Andrews this afternoon.

LOMAX.   What works?

SARAH.   The cannon works.

LOMAX.   What! Your governor's shop!

SARAH.   Yes.

LOMAX.   Oh I say!

Cusins enters in poor condition. He also starts visibly when he sees Barbara without her uniform.

BARBARA.   I expected you this morning, Dolly. Didnt you guess that?

CUSINS (*sitting down beside her*).   I'm sorry. I have only just breakfasted.

SARAH.   But weve just finished lunch.

BARBARA.   Have you had one of your bad nights?

CUSINS.   No: I had rather a good night: in fact, one of the most remarkable nights I have ever passed.

BARBARA.   The meeting?

CUSINS.   No: after the meeting.

LADY BRITOMART.   You should have gone to bed after the meeting. What were you doing?

CUSINS.   Drinking.

LADY BRITOMART.   ⎫ ⎧ Adolphus!
SARAH.   ⎪ ⎪ Dolly!
BARBARA.   ⎬ ⎨ Dolly!
LOMAX.   ⎭ ⎩ Oh I say!

LADY BRITOMART.   What were you drinking, may I ask?

CUSINS.   A most devilish kind of Spanish burgundy, warranted free from added alcohol: a Temperance burgundy in fact. Its richness in natural alcohol made any addition superfluous.

BARBARA.   Are you joking, Dolly?

CUSINS (*patiently*).   No. I have been making a night of it with the nominal head of this household: that is all.

LADY BRITOMART.   Andrew made you drunk!

CUSINS.   No: he only provided the wine. I think it was Dionysos who made me drunk. (*To Barbara.*) I told you I was possessed.

LADY BRITOMART. Youre not sober yet. Go home to bed at once.

CUSINS. I have never before ventured to reproach you, Lady Brit; but how could you marry the Prince of Darkness?

LADY BRITOMART. It was much more excusable to marry him than to get drunk with him. That is a new accomplishment of Andrew's, by the way. He usent to drink.

CUSINS. He doesnt now. He only sat there and completed the wreck of my moral basis, the rout of my convictions, the purchase of my soul. He cares for you, Barbara. That is what makes him so dangerous to me.

BARBARA. That has nothing to do with it, Dolly. There are larger loves and diviner dreams than the fireside ones. You know that, dont you?

CUSINS. Yes: that is our understanding. I know it. I hold to it. Unless he can win me on that holier ground he may amuse me for a while; but he can get no deeper hold, strong as he is.

BARBARA. Keep to that; and the end will be right. Now tell me what happened at the meeting?

CUSINS. It was an amazing meeting. Mrs. Baines almost died of emotion. Jenny Hill went stark mad with hysteria. The Prince of Darkness played his trombone like a madman: its brazen roarings were like the laughter of the damned. 117 conversions took place then and there. They prayed with the most touching sincerity and gratitude for Bodger, and for the anonymous donor of the £5000. Your father would not let his name be given.

LOMAX. That was rather fine of the old man, you know. Most chaps would have wanted the advertisement.

CUSINS. He said all the charitable institutions would be down on him like kites on a battle field if he gave his name.

LADY BRITOMART. Thats Andrew all over. He never

does a proper thing without giving an improper reason for it.

CUSINS. He convinced me that I have all my life been doing improper things for proper reasons.

LADY BRITOMART. Adolphus: now that Barbara has left the Salvation Army, you had better leave it too. I will not have you playing that drum in the streets.

CUSINS. Your orders are already obeyed, Lady Brit.

BARBARA. Dolly: were you ever really in earnest about it? Would you have joined if you had never seen me?

CUSINS (*disingenuously*). Well—er—well, possibly, as a collector of religions—

LOMAX (*cunningly*). Not as a drummer, though, you know. You are a very clearheaded brainy chap, Cholly; and it must have been apparent to you that there is a certain amount of tosh about—

LADY BRITOMART. Charles: if you must drivel, drivel like a grown-up man and not like a schoolboy.

LOMAX (*out of countenance*). Well, drivel is drivel, dont you know, whatever a man's age.

LADY BRITOMART. In good society in England, Charles, men drivel at all ages by repeating silly formulas with an air of wisdom. Schoolboys make their own formulas out of slang, like you. When they reach your age, and get political private secretaryships and things of that sort, they drop slang and get their formulas out of The Spectator or The Times. You had better confine yourself to The Times. You will find that there is a certain amount of tosh about The Times; but at least its language is reputable.

LOMAX (*overwhelmed*). You are so awfully strong-minded, Lady Brit—

LADY BRITOMART. Rubbish! (*Morrison comes in.*) What is it?

MORRISON. If you please, my lady, Mr. Undershaft has just drove up to the door.

LADY BRITOMART. Well, let him in. (*Morrison hesitates.*) Whats the matter with you?

MORRISON. Shall I announce him, my lady; or is he at home here, so to speak, my lady?

LADY BRITOMART. Announce him.

MORRISON. Thank you, my lady. You wont mind my asking, I hope. The occasion is in a manner of speaking new to me.

LADY BRITOMART. Quite right. Go and let him in.

MORRISON. Thank you, my lady. (*He withdraws.*)

LADY BRITOMART. Children: go and get ready. (*Sarah and Barbara go upstairs for their out-of-door wraps.*) Charles: go and tell Stephen to come down here in five minutes: you will find him in the drawing room. (*Charles goes.*) Adolphus: tell them to send round the carriage in about fifteen minutes. (*Adolphus goes.*)

MORRISON (*at the door*). Mr. Undershaft.

Undershaft comes in. Morrison goes out.

UNDERSHAFT. Alone! How fortunate!

LADY BRITOMART (*rising*). Dont be sentimental, Andrew. Sit down. (*She sits on the settee: he sits beside her, on her left. She comes to the point before he has time to breathe.*) Sarah must have £800 a year until Charles Lomax comes into his property. Barbara will need more, and need it permanently, because Adolphus hasnt any property.

UNDERSHAFT (*resignedly*). Yes, my dear: I will see to it. Anything else? for yourself, for instance?

LADY BRITOMART. I want to talk to you about Stephen.

UNDERSHAFT (*rather wearily*). Dont, my dear. Stephen doesnt interest me.

LADY BRITOMART. He does interest me. He is our son.

UNDERSHAFT. Do you really think so? He has induced us to bring him into the world; but he chose his parents very incongruously, I think. I see nothing of myself in him, and less of you.

LADY BRITOMART. Andrew: Stephen is an excellent son, and a most steady, capable, highminded young man. You are simply trying to find an excuse for disinheriting him.

UNDERSHAFT. My dear Biddy: the Undershaft tradition disinherits him. It would be dishonest of me to leave the cannon foundry to my son.

LADY BRITOMART. It would be most unnatural and improper of you to leave it anyone else, Andrew. Do you suppose this wicked and immoral tradition can be kept up for ever? Do you pretend that Stephen could not carry on the foundry just as well as all the other sons of the big business houses?

UNDERSHAFT. Yes: he could learn the office routine without understanding the business, like all the other sons; and the firm would go on by its own momentum until the real Undershaft—probably an Italian or a German—would invent a new method and cut him out.

LADY BRITOMART. There is nothing that any Italian or German could do that Stephen could not do. And Stephen at least has breeding.

UNDERSHAFT. The son of a foundling! nonsense!

LADY BRITOMART. My son, Andrew! And even you may have good blood in your veins for all you know.

UNDERSHAFT. True. Probably I have. That is another argument in favor of a foundling.

LADY BRITOMART. Andrew: dont be aggravating. And dont be wicked. At present you are both.

UNDERSHAFT. This conversation is part of the Undershaft tradition, Biddy. Every Undershaft's wife has treated him to it ever since the house was founded. It is mere waste of breath. If the tradition be ever broken it will be for an abler man than Stephen.

LADY BRITOMART (*pouting*). Then go away.

UNDERSHAFT (*deprecatory*). Go away!

LADY BRITOMART. Yes: go away. If you will do nothing for Stephen, you are not wanted here. Go to your foundling, whoever he is; and look after h i m.

UNDERSHAFT. The fact is, Biddy—

LADY BRITOMART. Dont call me Biddy. I dont call you Andy.

UNDERSHAFT. I will not call my wife Britomart: it is not good sense. Seriously, my love, the Undershaft tradition has landed me in a difficulty. I am getting on in years; and my partner Lazarus has at last made a stand and insisted that the succession must be settled one way or the other; and of course he is quite right. You see, I havnt found a fit successor yet.

LADY BRITOMART (*obstinately*). There is Stephen.

UNDERSHAFT. Thats just it: all the foundlings I can find are exactly like Stephen.

LADY BRITOMART. Andrew!!

UNDERSHAFT. I want a man with no relations and no schooling: that is, a man who would be out of the running altogether if he were not a strong man. And I cant find him. Every blessed foundling nowadays is snapped up in his infancy by Barnardo homes, or School Board officers, or Boards of Guardians; and if he shews the least ability, he is fastened on by schoolmasters; trained to win scholarships like a racehorse; crammed with secondhand ideas; drilled and disciplined in docility and what they call good taste; and lamed for life so that he is fit for nothing but teaching. If you want to keep the foundry in the family, you had better find an eligible foundling and marry him to Barbara.

LADY BRITOMART. Ah! Barbara! Your pet! You would sacrifice Stephen to Barbara.

UNDERSHAFT. Cheerfully. And you, my dear, would boil Barbara to make soup for Stephen.

LADY BRITOMART. Andrew: this is not a question of our likings and dislikings: it is a question of duty. It is your duty to make Stephen your successor.

UNDERSHAFT. Just as much as it is your duty to submit to your husband. Come, Biddy! these tricks of the governing class are of no use with me. I am one of the governing class myself; and it is waste of time giving tracts to a missionary. I have the power in this matter; and I am not to be humbugged into using it for your purposes.

LADY BRITOMART. Andrew: you can talk my head off; but you cant change wrong into right. And your tie is all on one side. Put it straight.

UNDERSHAFT (*disconcerted*). It wont stay unless it's pinned— (*he fumbles at it with childish grimaces*).

Stephen comes in.

STEPHEN (*at the door*). I beg your pardon (*about to retire*).

LADY BRITOMART. No: come in, Stephen. (*Stephen comes forward to his mother's writing table.*)

UNDERSHAFT (*not very cordially*). Good afternoon.

STEPHEN (*coldly*). Good afternoon.

UNDERSHAFT (*to Lady Britomart*). He knows all about the tradition, I suppose?

LADY BRITOMART. Yes. (*To Stephen.*) It is what I told you last night, Stephen.

UNDERSHAFT (*sulkily*). I understand you want to come into the cannon business.

STEPHEN. *I* go into trade! Certainly not.

UNDERSHAFT (*opening his eyes, greatly eased in mind and manner*). Oh! in that case—!

LADY BRITOMART. Cannons are not trade, Stephen. They are enterprise.

STEPHEN. I have no intention of becoming a man of business in any sense. I have no capacity for business and no taste for it. I intend to devote myself to politics.

UNDERSHAFT (*rising*). My dear boy: this is an immense relief to me. And I trust it may prove an equally good thing for the country. I was afraid you would consider yourself disparaged and slighted. *(He moves towards Stephen as if to shake hands with him.)*

LADY BRITOMART *(rising and interposing)*. Stephen: I cannot allow you to throw away an enormous property like this.

STEPHEN *(stiffly)*. Mother: there must be an end of treating me as a child, if you please. *(Lady Britomart recoils, deeply wounded by his tone.)* Until last night I did not take your attitude seriously, because I did not think you meant it seriously. But I find now that you left me in the dark as to matters which you should have explained to me years ago. I am extremely hurt and offended. Any further discussion of my intentions had better take place with my father, as between one man and another.

LADY BRITOMART. Stephen! *(She sits down again; and her eyes fill with tears.)*

UNDERSHAFT *(with grave compassion)*. You see, my dear, it is only the big men who can be treated as children.

STEPHEN. I am sorry, mother, that you have forced me—

UNDERSHAFT *(stopping him)*. Yes, yes, yes, yes: thats all right, Stephen. She wont interfere with you any more: your independence is achieved: you have won your latchkey. Dont rub it in; and above all, dont apologize. *(He resumes his seat.)* Now what about your future, as between one man and another—I beg your pardon, Biddy: as between two men and a woman.

LADY BRITOMART *(who has pulled herself together strongly)*. I quite understand, Stephen. By all means go your own way if you feel strong enough. *(Stephen sits down magisterially in the chair at the writing table with an air of affirming his majority.)*

UNDERSHAFT. It is settled that you do not ask for the succession to the cannon business.

STEPHEN. I hope it is settled that I repudiate the cannon business.

UNDERSHAFT. Come, come! dont be so devilishly sulky: it's boyish. Freedom should be generous. Besides, I owe you a fair start in life in exchange for disinheriting you. You cant become prime minister all at once. Havnt you a turn for something? What about literature, art and so forth?

STEPHEN. I have nothing of the artist about me, either in faculty or character, thank Heaven!

UNDERSHAFT. A philosopher, perhaps? Eh?

STEPHEN. I make no such ridiculous pretension.

UNDERSHAFT. Just so. Well, there is the army, the navy, the Church, the Bar. The Bar requires some ability. What about the Bar?

STEPHEN. I have not studied law. And I am afraid I have not the necessary push—I believe that is the name barristers give to their vulgarity—for success in pleading.

UNDERSHAFT. Rather a difficult case, Stephen. Hardly anything left but the stage, is there? (*Stephen makes an impatient movement.*) Well, come! is there a n y t h i n g you know or care for?

STEPHEN (*rising and looking at him steadily*). I know the difference between right and wrong.

UNDERSHAFT (*hugely tickled*). You dont say so! What! no capacity for business, no knowledge of law, no sympathy with art, no pretension to philosophy; only a simple knowledge of the secret that has puzzled all the philosophers, baffled all the lawyers, muddled all the men of business, and ruined most of the artists: the secret of right and wrong. Why, man, youre a genius, a master of masters, a god! At twenty-four, too!

STEPHEN (*keeping his temper with difficulty*). You are pleased to be facetious. I pretend to nothing more than any honorable English gentleman claims as his birthright (*he sits down angrily*).

UNDERSHAFT. Oh, thats everybody's birthright. Look at poor little Jenny Hill, the Salvation lassie! she would think you were laughing at her if you asked her to stand up in the street and teach grammar or geography or mathematics or even drawingroom dancing; but it never occurs to her to doubt that she can teach morals and religion. You are all alike, you respectable people. You cant tell me the bursting strain of a ten-inch gun, which is a very simple matter; but you all think you can tell me the bursting strain of a man under temptation. You darent handle high explosives; but youre all ready to handle honesty and truth and justice and the whole duty of man, and kill one another at that game. What a country! what a world!

LADY BRITOMART (*uneasily*). What do you think he had better do, Andrew?

UNDERSHAFT. Oh, just what he wants to do. He knows nothing; and he thinks he knows everything. That points clearly to a political career. Get him a private secretaryship to someone who can get him an Under Secretaryship; and then leave him alone. He will find his natural and proper place in the end on the Treasury bench.

STEPHEN (*springing up again*). I am sorry, sir, that you force me to forget the respect due to you as my father. I am an Englishman; and I will not hear the Government of my country insulted. (*He thrusts his hands in his pockets, and walks angrily across to the window.*)

UNDERSHAFT (*with a touch of brutality*). The government of your country! *I* am the government of your country: I, and Lazarus. Do you suppose that you and half a dozen amateurs like you, sitting in a row in that foolish gabble shop, can govern Undershaft and Lazarus? No, my friend: you will do what pays u s. You will make war when it suits us, and keep peace when it doesnt. You will find out that trade requires certain measures when we have decided on those measures. When I want anything to keep my dividends up, you will discover that my want is a national need. When other people want something to keep my dividends down, you will call out the police and military. And in return you shall have the support and applause of my newspapers, and the delight of imagining that you are a great statesman. Government of your country! Be off with you, my boy, and play with your caucuses and leading articles and historic parties and great leaders and burning questions and the rest of your toys. *I* am going back to my counting house to pay the piper and call the tune.

STEPHEN (*actually smiling, and putting his hand on his father's shoulder with indulgent patronage*). Really, my dear father, it is impossible to be angry with you. You don't know how absurd all this sounds to m e. You are very properly proud of having been industrious enough to make money; and it is greatly to your credit that you have made so much of it. But it has kept you in circles where you are valued for your money and deferred to for it, instead of in the doubtless very old-fashioned and behind-the-times public school and university where I formed my habits of mind. It is natural for you to think that money governs England; but you must allow me to think I know better.

UNDERSHAFT. And what d o e s govern England, pray?

STEPHEN. Character, father, character.

UNDERSHAFT. Whose character? Yours or mine?

STEPHEN. Neither yours nor mine, father, but the best elements in the English national character.

UNDERSHAFT. Stephen: Ive found your profession for you. Youre a born journalist. I'll start you with a high-toned weekly review. There!

Stephen goes to the smaller writing table and busies himself with his letters.

*Sarah, Barbara, Lomax, and Cusins come in ready for
walking. Barbara crosses the room to the window and
looks out. Cusins drifts amiably to the armchair, and
Lomax remains near the door, whilst Sarah comes to her
mother.*

SARAH.   Go and get ready, mamma: the carriage is
waiting. (*Lady Britomart leaves the room.*)

UNDERSHAFT (*to Sarah*). Good day, my dear. Good
afternoon, Mr. Lomax.

LOMAX (*vaguely*). Ahdedoo.

UNDERSHAFT (*to Cusins*). Quite well after last night,
Euripides, eh?

CUSINS.   As well as can be expected.

UNDERSHAFT.   Thats right. (*To Barbara.*) So you
are coming to see my death and devastation factory,
Barbara?

BARBARA (*at the window*).   You came yesterday to
see my salvation factory. I promised you a return visit.

LOMAX (*coming forward between Sarah and Undershaft*). Youll find it awfully interesting. Ive been
through the Woolwich Arsenal; and it gives you a ripping feeling of security, you know, to think of the lot
of beggars we could kill if it came to fighting. (*To
Undershaft, with sudden solemnity.*) Still, it must be
rather an awful reflection for you, from the religious
point of view as it were. Youre getting on, you know,
and all that.

SARAH.   You dont mind Cholly's imbecility, papa, do
you?

LOMAX (*much taken aback*). Oh I say!

UNDERSHAFT.   Mr. Lomax looks at the matter in a
very proper spirit, my dear.

LOMAX.   Just so. Thats all I meant, I assure you.

SARAH.   Are you coming, Stephen?

STEPHEN.   Well, I am rather busy—er— (*Magnani-
mously.*) Oh well, yes: I'll come. That is, if there is
room for me.

UNDERSHAFT. I can take two with me in a little motor I am experimenting with for field use. You wont mind its being rather unfashionable. It's not painted yet; but it's bullet proof.

LOMAX (*appalled at the prospect of confronting Wilton Crescent in an unpainted motor*). Oh I s a y!

SARAH. The carriage for me, thank you. Barbara doesnt mind what shes seen in.

LOMAX. I say, Dolly old chap: do you really mind the car being a guy? Because of course if you do I'll go in it. Still—

CUSINS. I prefer it.

LOMAX. Thanks awfully, old man. Come, Sarah. (*He hurries out to secure his seat in the carriage. Sarah follows him.*)

CUSINS (*moodily walking across to Lady Britomart's writing table*). Why are we two coming to this Works Department of Hell? that is what I ask myself.

BARBARA. I have always thought of it as a sort of pit where lost creatures with blackened faces stirred up smoky fires and were driven and tormented by my father? Is it like that, dad?

UNDERSHAFT (*scandalized*). My dear! It is a spotlessly clean and beautiful hillside town.

CUSINS. With a Methodist chapel? Oh d o say theres a Methodist chapel.

UNDERSHAFT. There are two: a Primitive one and a sophisticated one. There is even an Ethical Society; but it is not much patronized, as my men are all strongly religious. In the High Explosives Sheds they object to the presence of Agnostics as unsafe.

CUSINS. And yet they dont object to you!

BARBARA. Do they obey all your orders?

UNDERSHAFT. I never give them any orders. When I speak to one of them it is " Well, Jones, is the baby doing well? and has Mrs. Jones made a good recovery? " " Nicely, thank you, sir." And thats all.

Cusins. But Jones has to be kept in order. How do you maintain discipline among your men?

Undershaft. I dont. They do. You see, the one thing Jones wont stand is any rebellion from the man under him, or any assertion of social equality between the wife of the man with 4 shillings a week less than himself, and Mrs. Jones! Of course they all rebel against me, theoretically. Practically, every man of them keeps the man just below him in his place. I never meddle with them. I never bully them. I dont even bully Lazarus. I say that certain things are to be done; but I dont order anybody to do them. I dont say, mind you, that there is no ordering about and snubbing and even bullying. The men snub the boys and order them about; the carmen snub the sweepers; the artisans snub the unskilled laborers; the foremen drive and bully both the laborers and artisans; the assistant engineers find fault with the foremen; the chief engineers drop on the assistants; the departmental managers worry the chiefs; and the clerks have tall hats and hymnbooks and keep up the social tone by refusing to associate on equal terms with anybody. The result is a colossal profit, which comes to me.

Cusins (*revolted*). You really are a—well, what I was saying yesterday.

Barbara. What was he saying yesterday?

Undershaft. Never mind, my dear. He thinks I have made you unhappy. Have I?

Barbara. Do you think I can be happy in this vulgar silly dress? I! who have worn the uniform. Do you understand what you have done to me? Yesterday I had a man's soul in my hand. I set him in the way of life with his face to salvation. But when we took your money he turned back to drunkenness and derision. (*With intense conviction.*) I will never forgive you that. If I had a child, and you destroyed its body with your explosives—if you murdered Dolly with your horrible guns—I could forgive you if my forgiveness would open the gates of heaven to you. But to take a human soul from me, and turn it into the soul of a wolf! that is worse than any murder.

Undershaft. Does my daughter despair so easily? Can you strike a man to the heart and leave no mark on him?

Barbara (*her face lighting up*). Oh, you are right: he can never be lost now: where was my faith?

Cusins. Oh, clever clever devil!

Barbara. You may be a devil; but God speaks through you sometimes. (*She takes her father's hands and kisses them.*) You have given me back my happiness: I feel it deep down now, though my spirit is troubled.

Undershaft. You have learnt something. That always feels at first as if you had lost something.

Barbara. Well, take me to the factory of death, and let me learn something more. There must be some truth or other behind all this frightful irony. Come, Dolly. (*She goes out.*)

Cusins. My guardian angel! (*To Undershaft.*) Avaunt! (*He follows Barbara.*)

Stephen (*quietly, at the writing table*). You must not mind Cusins, father. He is a very amiable good fellow; but he is a Greek scholar and naturally a little eccentric.

Undershaft. Ah, quite so. Thank you, Stephen. Thank you. (*He goes out.*)

Stephen smiles patronizingly; buttons his coat responsibly; and crosses the room to the door. Lady Britomart, dressed for out-of-doors, opens it before he reaches it. She looks round for the others; looks at Stephen; and turns to go without a word.

Stephen (*embarrassed*). Mother—

Lady Britomart. Dont be apologetic, Stephen. And dont forget that you have outgrown your mother. (*She goes out.*)

Perivale St. Andrews lies between two Middlesex hills, half climbing the northern one. It is an almost smokeless town of white walls, roofs of narrow green slates or red tiles, tall trees, domes, campaniles, and slender chimney shafts, beautifully situated and beautiful in itself. The best view of it is obtained from the crest of a slope about half a mile to the east, where the high explosives are dealt with. The foundry lies hidden in the depths between, the tops of its chimneys sprouting like huge skittles into the middle distance. Across the crest runs a platform of concrete, with a parapet which suggests a fortification, because there is a huge cannon of the obsolete Woolwich Infant pattern peering across it at the town. The cannon is mounted on an experimental gun carriage: possibly the original model of the Undershaft disappearing rampart gun alluded to by Stephen. The parapet has a high step inside which serves as a seat.

Barbara is leaning over the parapet, looking towards the town. On her right is the cannon; on her left the end of a shed raised on piles, with a ladder of three or four steps up to the door, which opens outwards and has a little wooden landing at the threshold, with a fire bucket in the corner of the landing. The parapet stops short of the shed, leaving a gap which is the beginning of the path down the hill through the foundry to the town. Behind the cannon is a trolley carrying a huge conical bombshell, with a red band painted on it. Further from the parapet, on the same side, is a deck chair, near the door of an office, which, like the sheds, is of the lightest possible construction.

Cusins arrives by the path from the town.

BARBARA. Well?

CUSINS. Not a ray of hope. Everything perfect, wonderful, real. It only needs a cathedral to be a heavenly city instead of a hellish one.

BARBARA. Have you found out whether they have done anything for old Peter Shirley.

CUSINS. They have found him a job as gatekeeper and timekeeper. He's frightfully miserable. He calls the timekeeping brainwork, and says he isnt used to it; and his gate lodge is so splendid that hes ashamed to use the rooms, and skulks in the scullery.

BARBARA. Poor Peter!

Stephen arrives from the town. He carries a field-glass.

STEPHEN (*enthusiastically*). Have you two seen the place? Why did you leave us?

CUSINS. I wanted to see everything I was not intended to see; and Barbara wanted to make the men talk.

STEPHEN. Have you found anything discreditable?

CUSINS. No. They call him Dandy Andy and are proud of his being a cunning old rascal; but it's all horribly, frightfully, immorally, unanswerably perfect.

Sarah arrives.

SARAH. Heavens! what a place! (*She crosses to the trolley.*) Did you see the nursing home!? (*She sits down on the shell.*)

STEPHEN. Did you see the libraries and schools!?

SARAH. Did you see the ball room and the banqueting chamber in the Town Hall!?

STEPHEN. Have you gone into the insurance fund, the pension fund, the building society, the various applications of co-operation!?

Undershaft comes from the office, with a sheaf of telegrams in his hands.

UNDERSHAFT. Well, have you seen everything? I'm sorry I was called away. (*Indicating the telegrams.*) News from Manchuria.

STEPHEN. Good news, I hope.

UNDERSHAFT. Very.

STEPHEN. Another Japanese victory?

UNDERSHAFT. Oh, I dont know. Which side wins does not concern us here. No: the good news is that the aerial battleship is a tremendous success. At the first

trial it has wiped out a fort with three hundred soldiers
in it.

CUSINS (*from the platform*). Dummy soldiers?

UNDERSHAFT. No: the real thing. (*Cusins and Barbara exchange glances. Then Cusins sits on the step and buries his face in his hands. Barbara gravely lays her hand on his shoulder, and he looks up at her in a sort of whimsical desperation.*) Well, Stephen, what do you think of the place?

STEPHEN. Oh, magnificent. A perfect triumph of organization. Frankly, my dear father, I have been a fool: I had no idea of what it all meant—of the wonderful forethought, the power of organization, the administrative capacity, the financial genius, the colossal capital it represents. I have been repeating to myself as I came through your streets " Peace hath her victories no less renowned than War." I have only one misgiving about it all.

UNDERSHAFT. Out with it.

STEPHEN. Well, I cannot help thinking that all this provision for every want of your workmen may sap their independence and weaken their sense of responsibility. And greatly as we enjoyed our tea at that splendid restaurant—how they gave us all that luxury and cake and jam and cream for threepence I really cannot imagine!—still you must remember that restaurants break up home life. Look at the continent, for instance! Are you sure so much pampering is really good for the men's characters?

UNDERSHAFT. Well you see, my dear boy, when you are organizing civilization you have to make up your mind whether trouble and anxiety are good things or not. If you decide that they are, then, I take it, you simply dont organize civilization; and there you are, with trouble and anxiety enough to make us all angels! But if you decide the other way, you may as well go through with it. However, Stephen, our characters are safe here. A sufficient dose of anxiety is always provided by the fact that we may be blown to smithereens at any moment.

SARAH. By the way, papa, where do you make the explosives?

UNDERSHAFT. In separate little sheds, like that one. When one of them blows up, it costs very little; and only the people quite close to it are killed.

Stephen, who is quite close to it, looks at it rather scaredly, and moves away quickly to the cannon. At the same moment the door of the shed is thrown abruptly open; and a foreman in overalls and list slippers comes out on the little landing and holds the door open for Lomax, who appears in the doorway.

LOMAX (*with studied coolness*). My good fellow: you neednt get into a state of nerves. Nothing's going to happen to you; and I suppose it wouldnt be the end of the world if anything did. A little bit of British pluck is what y o u want, old chap. (*He descends and strolls across to Sarah.*)

UNDERSHAFT (*to the foreman*). Anything wrong, Bilton?

BILTON (*with ironic calm*). Gentleman walked into the high explosives shed and lit a cigaret, sir: thats all.

UNDERSHAFT. Ah, quite so. (*To Lomax.*) Do you happen to remember what you did with the match?

LOMAX. Oh come! I'm not a fool. I took jolly good care to blow it out before I chucked it away.

BILTON. The top of it was red hot inside, sir.

LOMAX. Well, suppose it was! I didnt chuck it into any of y o u r messes.

UNDERSHAFT. Think no more of it, Mr. Lomax. By the way, would you mind lending me your matches?

LOMAX (*offering his box*). Certainly.

UNDERSHAFT. Thanks. (*He pockets the matches.*)

LOMAX (*lecturing to the company generally*). You know, these high explosives dont go off like gunpowder,

except when theyre in a gun. When theyre spread
loose, you can put a match to them without the least
risk: they just burn quietly like a bit of paper. (*Warming to the scientific interest of the subject.*) Did you
know that, Undershaft? Have you ever tried?

UNDERSHAFT. Not on a large scale, Mr. Lomax. Bilton will give you a sample of gun cotton when you are
leaving if you ask him. You can experiment with it at
home. (*Bilton looks puzzled.*)

SARAH. Bilton will do nothing of the sort, papa. I
suppose it's your business to blow up the Russians and
Japs; but you might really stop short of blowing up
poor Cholly. (*Bilton gives it up and retires into the
shed.*)

LOMAX. My ownest, there is no danger. (*He sits
beside her on the shell.*)

Lady Britomart arrives from the town with a bouquet.

LADY BRITOMART (*coming impetuously between Undershaft and the deck chair*). Andrew: you shouldnt
have let me see this place.

UNDERSHAFT. Why, my dear?

LADY BRITOMART. Never mind why: you shouldnt
have: thats all. To think of all that (*indicating the
town*) being yours! and that you have kept it to yourself
all these years!

UNDERSHAFT. It does not belong to me. I belong to
it. It is the Undershaft inheritance.

LADY BRITOMART. It is not. Your ridiculous cannons
and that noisy banging foundry may be the Undershaft
inheritance; but all that plate and linen, all that furniture and those houses and orchards and gardens belong
to us. They belong to m e: they are not a man's business. I wont give them up. You must be out of your
senses to throw them all away; and if you persist in
such folly, I will call in a doctor.

UNDERSHAFT (*stooping to smell the bouquet*). Where
did you get the flowers, my dear?

LADY BRITOMART. Your men presented them to me in your William Morris Labor Church.

CUSINS (*springing up*). Oh! It needed only that. A Labor Church!

LADY BRITOMART. Yes, with Morris's words in mosaic letters ten feet high round the dome. No MAN IS GOOD ENOUGH TO BE ANOTHER MAN'S MASTER. The cynicism of it!

UNDERSHAFT. It shocked the men at first, I am afraid. But now they take no more notice of it than of the ten commandments in church.

LADY BRITOMART. Andrew: you are trying to put me off the subject of the inheritance by profane jokes. Well, you shant. I dont ask it any longer for Stephen: he has inherited far too much of your perversity to be fit for it. But Barbara has rights as well as Stephen. Why should not Adolphus succeed to the inheritance? I could manage the town for him; and he can look after the cannons, if they are really necessary.

UNDERSHAFT. I should ask nothing better if Adolphus were a foundling. He is exactly the sort of new blood that is wanted in English business. But hes not a foundling; and theres an end of it.

CUSINS (*diplomatically*). Not quite. (*They all turn and stare at him. He comes from the platform past the shed to Undershaft.*) I think— Mind! I am not committing myself in any way as to my future course—but I t h i n k the foundling difficulty can be got over.

UNDERSHAFT. What do you mean?

CUSINS. Well, I have something to say which is in the nature of a confession.

SARAH.
LADY BRITOMART. } Confession!
BARBARA.
STEPHEN.

LOMAX. Oh I say!

CUSINS. Yes, a confession. Listen, all. Until I met

Barbara I thought myself in the main an honorable, truthful man, because I wanted the approval of my conscience more than I wanted anything else. But the moment I saw Barbara, I wanted her far more than the approval of my conscience.

LADY BRITOMART. Adolphus!

CUSINS. It is true. You accused me yourself, Lady Brit, of joining the Army to worship Barbara; and so I did. She bought my soul like a flower at a street corner; but she bought it for herself.

UNDERSHAFT. What! Not for Dionysos or another?

CUSINS. Dionysos and all the others are in herself. I adored what was divine in her, and was therefore a true worshipper. But I was romantic about her too. I thought she was a woman of the people, and that a marriage with a professor of Greek would be far beyond the wildest social ambitions of her rank.

LADY BRITOMART. Adolphus!!

LOMAX. Oh I s a y !!!

CUSINS. When I learnt the horrible truth—

LADY BRITOMART. What do you mean by the horrible truth, pray?

CUSINS. That she was enormously rich; that her grandfather was an earl; that her father was the Prince of Darkness—

UNDERSHAFT. Chut!

CUSINS. —and that I was only an adventurer trying to catch a rich wife, then I stooped to deceive her about my birth.

BARBARA. Dolly!

LADY BRITOMART. Your birth! Now Adolphus, dont dare to make up a wicked story for the sake of these wretched cannons. Remember: I have seen photographs of your parents; and the Agent General for South Western Australia knows them personally and has assured me that they are most respectable married people.

CUSINS. So they are in Australia; but here they are

outcasts. Their marriage is legal in Australia, but not in England. My mother is my father's deceased wife's sister; and in this island I am consequently a foundling. (*Sensation.*) Is the subterfuge good enough, Machiavelli?

UNDERSHAFT (*thoughtfully*). Biddy: this may be a way out of the difficulty.

LADY BRITOMART. Stuff! A man cant make cannons any the better for being his own cousin instead of his proper self (*she sits down in the deck chair with a bounce that expresses her downright contempt for their casuistry*).

UNDERSHAFT (*to Cusins*). You are an educated man. That is against the tradition.

CUSINS. Once in ten thousand times it happens that the schoolboy is a born master of what they try to teach him. Greek has not destroyed my mind: it has nourished it. Besides, I did not learn it at an English public school.

UNDERSHAFT. Hm! Well, I cannot afford to be too particular: you have cornered the foundling market. Let it pass. You are eligible, Euripides: you are eligible.

BARBARA (*coming from the platform and interposing between Cusins and Undershaft*). Dolly: yesterday morning, when Stephen told us all about the tradition, you became very silent; and you have been strange and excited ever since. Were you thinking of your birth then?

CUSINS. When the finger of Destiny suddenly points at a man in the middle of his breakfast, it makes him thoughtful. (*Barbara turns away sadly and stands near her mother, listening perturbedly.*)

UNDERSHAFT. Aha! You have had your eye on the business, my young friend, have you?

CUSINS. Take care! There is an abyss of moral horror between me and your accursed aerial battleships.

UNDERSHAFT. Never mind the abyss for the present. Let us settle the practical details and leave your final decision open. You know that you will have to change your name. Do you object to that?

CUSINS. Would any man named Adolphus—any man called Dolly!—object to be called something else?

UNDERSHAFT. Good. Now, as to money! I propose to treat you handsomely from the beginning. You shall start at a thousand a year.

CUSINS (*with sudden heat, his spectacles twinkling with mischief*). A thousand! You dare offer a miserable thousand to the son-in-law of a millionaire! No, by Heavens, Machiavelli! you shall not cheat m e. You cannot do without me; and I can do without you. I must have two thousand five hundred a year for two years. At the end of that time, if I am·a failure, I go. But if I am a success, and stay on, you must give me the other five thousand.

UNDERSHAFT. What other five thousand?

CUSINS. To make the two years up to five thousand a year. The two thousand five hundred is only half pay in case I should turn out a failure. The third year I must have ten per cent on the profits.

UNDERSHAFT (*taken aback*). Ten per cent! Why, man, do you know what my profits are?

CUSINS. Enormous, I hope: otherwise I shall require twentyfive per cent.

UNDERSHAFT. But, Mr. Cusins, this is a serious matter of business. You are not bringing any capital into the concern.

CUSINS. What! no capital! Is my mastery of Greek no capital? Is my access to the subtlest thought, the loftiest poetry yet attained by humanity, no capital? My character! my intellect! my life! my career! what Barbara calls my soul! are these no capital? Say another word; and I double my salary.

UNDERSHAFT. Be reasonable—

Cusins (*peremptorily*). Mr. Undershaft: you have my terms. Take them or leave them.

Undershaft (*recovering himself*). Very well. I note your terms; and I offer you half.

Cusins (*disgusted*). Half!

Undershaft (*firmly*). Half.

Cusins. You call yourself a gentleman; and you offer me half!!

Undershaft. I do not call myself a gentleman; but I offer you half.

Cusins. This to your future partner! your successor! your son-in-law!

Barbara. You are selling your own soul, Dolly, not mine. Leave me out of the bargain, please.

Undershaft. Come! I will go a step further for Barbara's sake. I will give you three fifths; but that is my last word.

Cusins. Done!

Lomax. Done in the eye. Why, *I* only get eight hundred, you know.

Cusins. By the way, Mac, I am a classical scholar, not an arithmetical one. Is three fifths more than half or less?

Undershaft. More, of course.

Cusins. I would have taken two hundred and fifty. How you can succeed in business when you are willing to pay all that money to a University don who is obviously not worth a junior clerk's wages!—well! What will Lazarus say?

Undershaft. Lazarus is a gentle romantic Jew who cares for nothing but string quartets and stalls at fashionable theatres. He will get the credit of your rapacity in money matters, as he has hitherto had the credit of mine. You are a shark of the first order, Euripides. So much the better for the firm!

Barbara. Is the bargain closed, Dolly? Does your soul belong to him now?

CUSINS. No: the price is settled: that is all. The real tug of war is still to come. What about the moral question?

LADY BRITOMART. There is no moral question in the matter at all, Adolphus. You must simply sell cannons and weapons to people whose cause is right and just, and refuse them to foreigners and criminals.

UNDERSHAFT (*determinedly*). No: none of that. You must keep the true faith of an Armorer, or you dont come in here.

CUSINS. What on earth is the true faith of an Armorer?

UNDERSHAFT. To give arms to all men who offer an honest price for them, without respect of persons or principles: to aristocrat and republican, to Nihilist and Tsar, to Capitalist and Socialist, to Protestant and Catholic, to burglar and policeman, to black man white man and yellow man, to all sorts and conditions, all nationalities, all faiths, all follies, all causes and all crimes. The first Undershaft wrote up in his shop IF GOD GAVE THE HAND, LET NOT MAN WITHHOLD THE SWORD. The second wrote up ALL HAVE THE RIGHT TO FIGHT: NONE HAVE THE RIGHT TO JUDGE. The third wrote up TO MAN THE WEAPON: TO HEAVEN THE VICTORY. The fourth had no literary turn; so he did not write up anything; but he sold cannons to Napoleon under the nose of George the Third. The fifth wrote up PEACE SHALL NOT PREVAIL SAVE WITH A SWORD IN HER HAND. The sixth, my master, was the best of all. He wrote up NOTHING IS EVER DONE IN THIS WORLD UNTIL MEN ARE PREPARED TO KILL ONE ANOTHER IF IT IS NOT DONE. After that, there was nothing left for the seventh to say. So he wrote up, simply, UNASHAMED.

CUSINS. My good Machiavelli, I shall certainly write something up on the wall; only, as I shall write it in Greek, you wont be able to read it. But as to your Armorer's faith, if I take my neck out of the noose of my own morality I am not going to put it into the noose of yours. I shall sell cannons to whom I please and refuse them to whom I please. So there!

UNDERSHAFT. From the moment when you become Andrew Undershaft, you will never do as you please again. Dont come here lusting for power, young man.

CUSINS. If power were my aim I should not come here for it. Y o u have no power.

UNDERSHAFT. None of my own, certainly.

CUSINS. I have more power than you, more will. You do not drive this place: it drives you. And what drives the place?

UNDERSHAFT (*enigmatically*). A will of which I am a part.

BARBARA (*startled*). Father! Do you know what you are saying; or are you laying a snare for my soul?

CUSINS. Dont listen to his metaphysics, Barbara. The place is driven by the most rascally part of society, the money hunters, the pleasure hunters, the military promotion hunters; and he is their slave.

UNDERSHAFT. Not necessarily. Remember the Armorer's Faith. I will take an order from a good man as cheerfully as from a bad one. If you good people prefer preaching and shirking to buying my weapons and fighting the rascals, dont blame me. I can make cannons: I cannot make courage and conviction. Bah! You tire me, Euripides, with your morality mongering. Ask Barbara: s h e understands. (*He suddenly takes Barbara's hands, and looks powerfully into her eyes.*) Tell him, my love, what power really means.

BARBARA (*hypnotized*). Before I joined the Salvation Army, I was in my own power; and the consequence was that I never knew what to do with myself. When I joined it, I had not time enough for all the things I had to do.

UNDERSHAFT (*approvingly*). Just so. And why was that, do you suppose?

BARBARA. Yesterday I should have said, because I was in the power of God. (*She resumes her self-possession, withdrawing her hands from his with a power equal to his own.*) But you came and shewed me that I was in the power of Bodger and Undershaft. Today I feel—oh! how can I put into words? Sarah: do you remember the earthquake at Cannes, when we were little children?—how little the surprise of the first shock mattered compared to the dread and horror of waiting for the second? That is how I feel in this place today. I stood on the rock I thought eternal; and without a word of warning it reeled and crumbled under me. I was safe with an infinite wisdom watching me, an army marching to Salvation with me; and in a moment, at a stroke of your pen in a cheque book, I stood alone; and the heavens were empty. That was the first shock of the earthquake: I am waiting for the second.

UNDERSHAFT. Come, come, my daughter! dont make too much of your little tinpot tragedy. What do we do here when we spend years of work and thought and thousands of pounds of solid cash on a new gun or an aerial battleship that turns out just a hairsbreadth wrong after all? Scrap it. Scrap it without wasting another hour or another pound on it. Well, you have made for yourself something that you call a morality or a religion or what not. It doesnt fit the facts. Well, scrap it. Scrap it and get one that does fit. That is what is wrong with the world at present. It scraps its obsolete steam engines and dynamos; but it wont scrap its old prejudices and its old moralities and its old religions and its old political constitutions. Whats the result? In machinery it does very well; but in morals and religion and politics it is working at a loss that brings it nearer bankruptcy every year. Dont persist in that folly. If your old religion broke down yesterday, get a newer and a better one for tomorrow.

BARBARA. Oh how gladly I would take a better one

to my soul! But you offer me a worse one. (*Turning on him with sudden vehemence.*) Justify yourself: shew me some light through the darkness of this dreadful place, with its beautifully clean workshops, and respectable workmen, and model homes.

UNDERSHAFT. Cleanliness and respectability do not need justification, Barbara: they justify themselves. I see no darkness here, no dreadfulness. In your Salvation shelter I saw poverty, misery, cold and hunger. You gave them bread and treacle and dreams of heaven. I give from thirty shillings a week to twelve thousand a year. They find their own dreams; but I look after the drainage.

BARBARA. And their souls?

UNDERSHAFT. I save their souls just as I saved yours.

BARBARA (*revolted*). Y o u saved my soul! What do you mean?

UNDERSHAFT. I fed you and clothed you and housed you. I took care that you should have money enough to live handsomely—more than enough; so that you could be wasteful, careless, generous. That saved your soul from the seven deadly sins.

BARBARA (*bewildered*). The seven deadly sins!

UNDERSHAFT. Yes, the deadly seven. (*Counting on his fingers.*) Food, clothing, firing, rent, taxes, respectability and children. Nothing can lift those seven millstones from Man's neck but money; and the spirit cannot soar until the millstones are lifted. I lifted them from your spirit. I enabled Barbara to become Major Barbara; and I saved her from the crime of poverty.

CUSINS. Do you call poverty a crime?

UNDERSHAFT. The worst of crimes. All the other crimes are virtues beside it: all the other dishonors are chivalry itself by comparison. Poverty blights whole cities; spreads horrible pestilences; strikes dead the very souls of all who come within sight, sound or smell of it. What y o u call crime is nothing: a murder here and a theft there, a blow now and a curse then: what do they matter? they are only the accidents and illnesses of life: there are not fifty genuine professional criminals in London. But there are millions of poor people, abject people, dirty people, ill fed, ill clothed people. They poison us morally and physically: they kill the happiness of society: they force us to do away with our own liberties and to organize unnatural cruelties for fear they should rise against us and drag us down into their abyss. Only fools fear crime: we all fear poverty. Pah! (*turning on Barbara*) you talk of your half-saved ruffian in West Ham: you accuse me of dragging his soul back to perdition. Well, bring him to me here; and I will drag his soul back again to salvation for you. Not by words and dreams; but by thirtyeight shillings a week, a sound house in a handsome street, and a permanent job. In three weeks he will have a fancy waistcoat; in three months a tall hat and a chapel sitting; before the end of the year he will shake hands with a duchess at a Primrose League meeting, and join the Conservative Party.

BARBARA. And will he be the better for that?

UNDERSHAFT. You know he will. Dont be a hypocrite, Barbara. He will be better fed, better housed, better clothed, better behaved; and his children will be pounds heavier and bigger. That will be better than an American cloth mattress in a shelter, chopping firewood, eating bread and treacle, and being forced to kneel down from time to time to thank heaven for it: knee drill, I think you call it. It is cheap work converting starving men with a Bible in one hand and a slice of bread in the other. I will undertake to convert West Ham to Mahometanism on the same terms. Try your hand on m y men: their souls are hungry because their bodies are full.

BARBARA. And leave the east end to starve?

UNDERSHAFT (*his energetic tone dropping into one of*

bitter and brooding remembrance). *I* was an east ender. I moralized and starved until one day I swore that I would be a full-fed free man at all costs—that nothing should stop me except a bullet, neither reason nor morals nor the lives of other men. I said " Thou shalt starve ere I starve "; and with that word I became free and great. I was a dangerous man until I had my will: now I am a useful, beneficent, kindly person. That is the history of most self-made millionaires, I fancy. When it is the history of every Englishman we shall have an England worth living in.

LADY BRITOMART. Stop making speeches, Andrew. This is not the place for them.

UNDERSHAFT (*punctured*). My dear: I have no other means of conveying my ideas.

LADY BRITOMART. Your ideas are nonsense. You got on because you were selfish and unscrupulous.

UNDERSHAFT. Not at all. I had the strongest scruples about poverty and starvation. Your moralists are quite unscrupulous about both: they make virtues of them. I had rather be a thief than a pauper. I had rather be a murderer than a slave. I dont want to be either; but if you force the alternative on me, then, by Heaven, I'll choose the braver and more moral one. I hate poverty and slavery worse than any other crimes whatsoever. And let me tell you this. Poverty and slavery have stood up for centuries to your sermons and leading articles: they will not stand up to my machine guns. Dont preach at them: dont reason with them. Kill them.

BARBARA. Killing. Is that your remedy for everything?

UNDERSHAFT. It is the final test of conviction, the only lever strong enough to overturn a social system, the only way of saying Must. Let six hundred and seventy fools loose in the street; and three policemen can scatter them. But huddle them together in a certain house in Westminster; and let them go through certain ceremonies and call themselves certain names until at last they get the courage to kill; and your six hundred and seventy fools become a government. Your pious mob fills up ballot papers and imagines it is governing its masters; but the ballot paper that really governs is the paper that has a bullet wrapped up in it.

CUSINS. That is perhaps why, like most intelligent people, I never vote.

UNDERSHAFT. Vote! Bah! When you vote, you only change the names of the cabinet. When you shoot, you pull down governments, inaugurate new epochs, abolish old orders and set up new. Is that historically true, Mr. Learned Man, or is it not?

CUSINS. It is historically true. I loathe having to admit it. I repudiate your sentiments. I abhor your nature. I defy you in every possible way. Still, it is true. But it ought not to be true.

UNDERSHAFT. Ought, ought, ought, ought, ought! Are you going to spend your life saying ought, like the rest of our moralists? Turn your oughts into shalls, man. Come and make explosives with me. Whatever can blow men up can blow society up. The history of the world is the history of those who had courage enough to embrace this truth. Have you the courage to embrace it, Barbara?

LADY BRITOMART. Barbara, I positively forbid you to listen to your father's abominable wickedness. And you, Adolphus, ought to know better than to go about saying that wrong things are true. What does it matter whether they are true if they are wrong?

UNDERSHAFT. What does it matter whether they are wrong if they are true?

LADY BRITOMART (*rising*). Children: come home instantly. Andrew: I am exceedingly sorry I allowed you to call on us. You are wickeder than ever. Come at once.

BARBARA (*shaking her head*). It's no use running away from wicked people, mamma.

LADY BRITOMART. It is every use. It shews your disapprobation of them.

BARBARA. It does not save them.

LADY BRITOMART. I can see that you are going to disobey me. Sarah: are you coming home or are you not?

SARAH. I daresay it's very wicked of papa to make cannons; but I dont think I shall cut him on that account.

LOMAX (*pouring oil on the troubled waters*). The fact is, you know, there is a certain amount of tosh about this notion of wickedness. It doesnt work. You must look at facts. Not that I would say a word in favor of anything wrong; but then, you see, all sorts of chaps are always doing all sorts of things; and we have to fit them in somehow, dont you know. What I mean is that you cant go cutting everybody; and thats about what it comes to. (*Their rapt attention to his eloquence makes him nervous.*) Perhaps I dont make myself clear.

LADY BRITOMART. You are lucidity itself, Charles. Because Andrew is successful and has plenty of money to give to Sarah, you will flatter him and encourage him in his wickedness.

LOMAX (*unruffled*). Well, where the carcase is, there will the eagles be gathered, dont you know. (*To Undershaft.*) Eh? What?

UNDERSHAFT. Precisely. By the way, m a y I call you Charles?

LOMAX. Delighted. Cholly is the usual ticket.

UNDERSHAFT (*to Lady Britomart*). Biddy—

LADY BRITOMART (*violently*). Dont dare call me Biddy. Charles Lomax: you are a fool. Adolphus Cusins: you are a Jesuit. Stephen: you are a prig. Barbara: you are a lunatic. Andrew: you are a vulgar tradesman. Now you all know my opinion; and m y conscience is clear, at all events (*she sits down again with a vehemence that almost wrecks the chair*).

UNDERSHAFT. My dear: you are the incarnation of morality. (*She snorts.*) Your conscience is clear and your duty done when you have called everybody names. Come, Euripides! it is getting late; and we all want to get home. Make up your mind.

CUSINS. Understand this, you old demon—

LADY BRITOMART. Adolphus!

UNDERSHAFT. Let him alone, Biddy. Proceed, Euripides.

CUSINS. You have me in a horrible dilemma. I want Barbara.

UNDERSHAFT. Like all young men, you greatly exaggerate the difference between one young woman and another.

BARBARA. Quite true, Dolly.

CUSINS. I also want to avoid being a rascal.

UNDERSHAFT (*with biting contempt*). You lust for personal righteousness, for self-approval, for what you call a good conscience, for what Barbara calls salvation, for what I call patronizing people who are not so lucky as yourself.

CUSINS. I do not: all the poet in me recoils from being a good man. But there are things in me that I must reckon with: pity—

UNDERSHAFT. Pity! The scavenger of misery.

CUSINS. Well, love.

UNDERSHAFT. I know. You love the needy and the outcast: you love the oppressed races, the negro, the Indian ryot, the Pole, the Irishman. Do you love the Japanese? Do you love the Germans? Do you love the English?

CUSINS. No. Every true Englishman detests the English. We are the wickedest nation on earth; and our success is a moral horror.

UNDERSHAFT. That is what comes of your gospel of love, is it?

CUSINS. May I not love even my father-in-law?

UNDERSHAFT. Who wants your love, man? By what right do you take the liberty of offering it to me? I will have your due heed and respect, or I will kill you. But your love. Damn your impertinence!

CUSINS (*grinning*). I may not be able to control my affections, Mac.

UNDERSHAFT. You are fencing, Euripides. You are weakening: your grip is slipping. Come! try your last weapon. Pity and love have broken in your hand: forgiveness is still left.

CUSINS. No: forgiveness is a beggar's refuge. I am with you there: we must pay our debts.

UNDERSHAFT. Well said. Come! you will suit me. Remember the words of Plato.

CUSINS (*starting*). Plato! Y o u dare quote Plato to m e !

UNDERSHAFT. Plato says, my friend, that society cannot be saved until either the Professors of Greek take to making gunpowder, or else the makers of gunpowder become Professors of Greek.

CUSINS. Oh, tempter, cunning tempter!

UNDERSHAFT. Come! choose, man, choose.

CUSINS. But perhaps Barbara will not marry me if I make the wrong choice.

BARBARA. Perhaps not.

CUSINS (*desperately perplexed*). You hear!

BARBARA. Father: do you love nobody?

UNDERSHAFT. I love my best friend.

LADY BRITOMART. And who is that, pray?

UNDERSHAFT. My bravest enemy. That is the man who keeps me up to the mark.

CUSINS. You know, the creature is really a sort of poet in his way. Suppose he is a great man, after all!

UNDERSHAFT. Suppose you stop talking and make up your mind, my young friend.

CUSINS. But you are driving me against my nature. I hate war.

UNDERSHAFT. Hatred is the coward's revenge for being intimidated. Dare you make war on war? Here are the means: my friend Mr. Lomax is sitting on them.

LOMAX (*springing up*). Oh I say! You dont mean that this thing is loaded, do you? My ownest: come off it.

SARAH (*sitting placidly on the shell*). If I am to be blown up, the more thoroughly it is done the better. Dont fuss, Cholly.

LOMAX (*to Undershaft, strongly remonstrant*). Your own daughter, you know.

UNDERSHAFT. So I see. (*To Cusins.*) Well, my friend, may we expect you here at six tomorrow morning?

CUSINS (*firmly*). Not on any account. I will see the whole establishment blown up with its own dynamite before I will get up at five. My hours are healthy, rational hours: eleven to five.

UNDERSHAFT. Come when you please: before a week you will come at six and stay until I turn you out for the sake of your health. (*Calling.*) Bilton! (*He turns to Lady Britomart, who rises.*) My dear: let us leave these two young people to themselves for a moment. (*Bilton comes from the shed.*) I am going to take you through the gun cotton shed.

BILTON (*barring the way*). You cant take anything explosive in here, sir.

LADY BRITOMART. What do you mean? Are you alluding to me?

BILTON (*unmoved*). No, maam. Mr. Undershaft has the other gentleman's matches in his pocket.

LADY BRITOMART (*abruptly*). Oh! I beg your pardon. (*She goes into the shed.*)

UNDERSHAFT. Quite right, Bilton, quite right: here you are. (*He gives Bilton the box of matches.*) Come, Stephen. Come, Charles. Bring Sarah. (*He passes into the shed.*)

Bilton opens the box and deliberately drops the matches into the fire-bucket.

LOMAX. Oh I say! (*Bilton stolidly hands him the empty box.*) Infernal nonsense! Pure scientific ignorance! (*He goes in.*)

SARAH. Am I all right, Bilton?

BILTON. Youll have to put on list slippers, miss: thats all. Weve got em inside. (*She goes in.*)

STEPHEN (*very seriously to Cusins*). Dolly, old fellow, think. Think before you decide. Do you feel that you are a sufficiently practical man? It is a huge undertaking, an enormous responsibility. All this mass of business will be Greek to you.

CUSINS. Oh, I think it will be much less difficult than Greek.

STEPHEN. Well, I just want to say this before I leave you to yourselves. Dont let anything I have said about right and wrong prejudice you against this great chance in life. I have satisfied myself that the business is one of the highest character and a credit to our country. (*Emotionally.*) I am very proud of my father. I— (*Unable to proceed, he presses Cusins' hand and goes hastily into the shed, followed by Bilton.*)

Barbara and Cusins, left alone together, look at one another silently.

CUSINS. Barbara: I am going to accept this offer.

BARBARA. I thought you would.

CUSINS. You understand, dont you, that I had to decide without consulting you. If I had thrown the burden of the choice on you, you would sooner or later have despised me for it.

BARBARA. Yes: I did not want you to sell your soul for me any more than for this inheritance.

CUSINS. It is not the sale of my soul that troubles me: I have sold it too often to care about that. I have sold it for a professorship. I have sold it for an income. I have sold it to escape being imprisoned for refusing to pay taxes for hangmen's ropes and unjust wars and things that I abhor. What is all human conduct but the daily and hourly sale of our souls for trifles? What I am now selling it for is neither money nor position nor comfort, but for reality and for power.

BARBARA. You know that you will have no power, and that he has none.

CUSINS. I know. It is not for myself alone. I want to make power for the world.

BARBARA. I want to make power for the world too; but it must be spiritual power.

CUSINS. I think all power is spiritual: these cannons will not go off by themselves. I have tried to make spiritual power by teaching Greek. But the world can never be really touched by a dead language and a dead civilization. The people must have power; and the people cannot have Greek. Now the power that is made here can be wielded by all men.

BARBARA. Power to burn women's houses down and kill their sons and tear their husbands to pieces.

CUSINS. You cannot have power for good without having power for evil too. Even mother's milk nourishes murderers as well as heroes. This power which only tears men's bodies to pieces has never been so horribly abused as the intellectual power, the imaginative power, the poetic, religious power than can enslave men's souls. As a teacher of Greek I gave the intellectual man weapons against the common man. I now want to give the common man weapons against the intellectual man. I love the common people. I want to arm them against the lawyer, the doctor, the priest, the literary man, the professor, the artist, and the politician, who, once in authority, are the most dangerous, disastrous, and tyrannical of all the fools, rascals, and impostors. I want a democratic power strong enough to force the intellectual oligarchy to use its genius for the general good or else perish.

BARBARA. Is there no higher power than that (*pointing to the shell*)?

CUSINS. Yes: but that power can destroy the higher powers just as a tiger can destroy a man: therefore man must master that power first. I admitted this when the Turks and Greeks were last at war. My best pupil went out to fight for Hellas. My parting gift to him was not a copy of Plato's Republic, but a revolver and a hundred Undershaft cartridges. The blood of every Turk he shot—if he shot any—is on my head as well as on Undershaft's. That act committed me to this place for ever. Your father's challenge has beaten me. Dare I make war on war? I dare. I must. I will. And now, is it all over between us?

BARBARA (*touched by his evident dread of her answer*). Silly baby Dolly! How could it be?

CUSINS (*overjoyed*). Then you—you—you— Oh for my drum! (*He flourishes imaginary drumsticks.*)

BARBARA (*angered by his levity*). Take care, Dolly, take care. Oh, if only I could get away from you and from father and from it all! if I could have the wings of a dove and fly away to heaven!

CUSINS. And leave m e!

BARBARA. Yes, you, and all the other naughty mischievous children of men. But I cant. I was happy in the Salvation Army for a moment. I escaped from the world into a paradise of enthusiasm and prayer and soul saving; but the moment our money ran short, it all came back to Bodger: it was he who saved our people: he, and the Prince of Darkness, my papa. Undershaft and Bodger: their hands stretch everywhere: when we feed a starving fellow creature, it is with their bread, because there is no other bread; when we tend the sick, it is in the hospitals they endow; if we turn from the churches they build, we must kneel on the stones of the streets they pave. As long as that lasts, there is no getting away from them. Turning our backs

on Bodger and Undershaft is turning our backs on
life.

CUSINS. I thought you were determined to turn your
back on the wicked side of life.

BARBARA. There is no wicked side: life is all one.
And I never wanted to shirk my share in whatever evil
must be endured, whether it be sin or suffering. I wish
I could cure you of middle-class ideas, Dolly.

CUSINS (*gasping*). Middle cl—! A snub! A social
snub to m e! from the daughter of a foundling!

BARBARA. That is why I have no class, Dolly: I come
straight out of the heart of the whole people. If I were
middle-class I should turn my back on my father's business; and we should both live in an artistic drawingroom, with you reading the reviews in one corner, and
I in the other at the piano, playing Schumann: both very
superior persons, and neither of us a bit of use. Sooner
than that, I would sweep out the guncotton shed, or be
one of Bodger's barmaids. Do you know what would
have happened if you had refused papa's offer?

CUSINS. I wonder!

BARBARA. I should have given you up and married
the man who accepted it. After all, my dear old mother
has more sense than any of you. I felt like her when I
saw this place—felt that I must have it—that never,
never, never could I let it go; only she thought it was
the houses and the kitchen ranges and the linen and
china, when it was really all the human souls to be
saved: not weak souls in starved bodies, crying with
gratitude for a scrap of bread and treacle, but fullfed,
quarrelsome, snobbish, uppish creatures, all standing on
their little rights and dignities, and thinking that my
father ought to be greatly obliged to them for making
so much money for him—and so he ought. That is
where salvation is really wanted. My father shall never
throw it in my teeth again that my converts were bribed
with bread. (*She is transfigured.*) I have got rid of

the bribe of bread. I have got rid of the bribe of heaven. Let God's work be done for its own sake: the work he had to create us to do because it cannot be done except by living men and women. When I die, let him be in my debt, not I in his; and let me forgive him as becomes a woman of my rank.

CUSINS. Then the way of life lies through the factory of death?

BARBARA. Yes, through the raising of hell to heaven and of man to God, through the unveiling of an eternal light in the Valley of The Shadow. (*Seizing him with both hands.*) Oh, did you think my courage would never come back? did you believe that I was a deserter? that I, who have stood in the streets, and taken my people to my heart, and talked of the holiest and greatest things with them, could ever turn back and chatter foolishly to fashionable people about nothing in a drawingroom? Never, never, never, never: Major Barbara will die with the colors. Oh! and I have my dear little Dolly boy still; and he has found me my place and my work. Glory Hallelujah! (*She kisses him.*)

CUSINS. My dearest: consider my delicate health. I cannot stand as much happiness as you can.

BARBARA. Yes: it is not easy work being in love with me, is it? But it's good for you. (*She runs to the shed, and calls, childlike*) Mamma! Mamma! (*Bilton comes out of the shed, followed by Undershaft.*) I want Mamma.

UNDERSHAFT. She is taking off her list slippers, dear. (*He passes on to Cusins.*) Well? What does she say?

CUSINS. She has gone right up into the skies.

LADY BRITOMART (*coming from the shed and stopping on the steps, obstructing Sarah, who follows with Lomax. Barbara clutches like a baby at her mother's skirt.*) Barbara: when will you learn to be independent and to act and think for yourself? I know as well as possible what that cry of " Mamma, Mamma," means. Always running to me!

SARAH (*touching Lady Britomart's ribs with her finger tips and imitating a bicycle horn*). Pip! pip!

LADY BRITOMART (*highly indignant*). How dare you say Pip! pip! to me, Sarah? You are both very naughty children. What do you want, Barbara?

BARBARA. I want a house in the village to live in with Dolly. (*Dragging at the skirt.*) Come and tell me which one to take.

UNDERSHAFT (*to Cusins*). Six o'clock tomorrow morning, my young friend.

THE END

31